THE 100 BEST COMPANIES TO SELL FOR

THE 100
BEST COMPANIES
TO SELL FOR

MICHAEL DAVID HARKAVY
and
THE PHILIP LIEF GROUP

WILEY

John Wiley & Sons

New York   Chichester   Brisbane   Toronto   Singapore

Library of Congress Cataloging in Publication Data:
Harkavy, Michael David.
    The 100 best companies to sell for / by Michael David Harkavy and
    the Philip Lief Group.
        p.   cm.
      Bibliography: p.
      ISBN 0-471-61288-X
      1. Selling—Vocational guidance.   2. Sales personnel—United
States.   3. Business enterprises—United States—Directories.
4. Corporations—United States—Directories.   I. Philip Lief Group.
II. Title.   III. Title: One hundred best companies to sell for.
HF5438.25.H3725 1989
331.2'0973—dc19   88-30589
                                                                        CIP

Printed in the United States of America
10 9 8 7 6 5 4 3 2 1

LIST OF COMPANIES
PROFILED

CONTENTS

FOOD, FOODSERVICES, and TOBACCO   **164**

INDUSTRIAL and AGRICULTURAL EQUIPMENT   **192**

INSURANCE   **209**

PAPER and ALLIED PRODUCTS   **231**

PHARMACEUTICALS and HEALTH CARE   **251**

PHOTOGRAPHIC and SCIENTIFIC EQUIPMENT   278

PUBLISHING and PRINTING   290

RECREATION, LEISURE, and SPORTING GOODS   304

RUBBER PRODUCTS   315

TEXTILES   323

INTRODUCTION

A sure way to start an argument is to propose a list of the "best" of anything. Regardless of how carefully, exhaustively, or scientifically you compiled the list, some will find fault with it: "How *could* you have included A!" or "How *could* you have left out B!" This book is no exception. To forestall such questions, which have no positive role to play here, it is best to explain why our list was compiled in the first place.

THE PURPOSE OF THIS BOOK

Presumably, you are either interested in pursuing a career in selling or you are already working as a sales rep and want to survey the entire field to see what other opportunities it offers. To help in your endeavors, we identified 18 leading industries in our economy and then surveyed all the companies most prominent in each industry. Finally, after long evaluation, we picked what we felt were the best and most representative of the companies and the most promising and stable of the industries, and we compiled the information presented here. The result is a panoramic yet incisive survey of the position of the field sales rep in American industry, as exemplified by 100 of the major corporations in the country.

This book is designed more to illustrate than to tabulate. Its chief concern is not to assign rankings to various companies (although we have included the 1987 Fortune 500 and some other rankings), but rather to give its readers an idea of the range of industries and companies that make up our economy and of the different kinds of selling they employ. From this array, readers can choose those areas that most interest them personally and professionally and concentrate their career search there.

Keep in mind that there are hundreds and hundreds of other companies—large and small—that are as excellent to sell for as the ones treated here. No one expects the book to settle your career choice for you—although it might. It is really meant to tell you where to look, what to look for, and what kinds of working conditions, markets, selling responsibilities, and compensation you may expect to find in the various companies we have chosen as representative of the different industries. This is not to slight the companies profiled here; selling for any one of them would be a career boost for any rep. You shouldn't, however, confine your research just to what's covered here. Remember, this book is a great place to *begin* a search for an exciting and successful career in selling.

How Do You Fit into Selling?

Many of you already know the answer to that question. You have tried selling, like it, and now you want to continue doing it—only better, with a higher success rate and a fatter paycheck. Others of you may be looking at this book to find the answer. You want to learn what reps do and what they make, and you want to see how you might fit into the picture, if at all. Those of you who are unsure about your commitment to selling should examine the following general characteristic attitudes of salespeople toward three crucial topics and compare your reactions to those given here. Admittedly, there are many kinds of selling, demanding many kinds of skills and backgrounds. Even so, most reps, regardless of their field, share a common sensibility and a common experience with respect to the following topics.

Money. Salespeople like money, and, for the most part, they earn a fair amount of it. Sales generate a company's—any company's—revenues, and companies tend to reward good sales handsomely; generally, even the average wages of sales trainees are good as compared with other nontechnical administrative jobs. Even more telling is the fact that the money sales reps earn is openly and directly related to their activities. Selling is about numbers—making the numbers, meeting the quotas, hitting the targets, achieving the divisional and company goals, all given in unmistakable big round numbers. Salespeople are not at all intimidated at being evaluated on the basis of cold, hard numbers—if a favorable evaluation is rewarded by cold, hard cash.

Work Habits. Many business people work hard and many work smart, but few work as alone as reps do. Although some companies form their sales forces into teams, the more common approach is for a solitary rep to be on the road calling on accounts in a specific territory. Reps make their own schedules, manage their own territories, and service their own customers. They may, and often do, have support teams of technicians, service personnel, and the like, but basically sales reps are on their own. They work out of a permanent office at home and a portable office—maybe no more than customer folders and work forms—in their cars on the road. Except for those in telemarketing, reps generally do not work at the home office. They need, therefore, to be self-disciplined, self-starting, and self-reliant. Most important of all perhaps, sales reps must be able to face down rejection (it takes about five calls to bag one sale) and face up to competition. Hemingway's phrase "grace under pressure" is a neat description of your average rep's daily routine.

Social Skills. The days of the glad-handing, back-slapping, fast-talking drummer are long gone. Today's professional salespeople are business-oriented, product-knowledgeable consultants. They are problem solvers for their customers. They must be able to talk to a company's top executives, its line managers, and its lower echelon operators. They must have excellent communications skills; selling *is* about communications. They must be able to talk *and* to listen, and, most importantly, they must be able to *write*—letters, memos, reports, and instructions—all in clear, concise language. Successful reps also look successful; in this case, the image proclaims the real thing. Finally, good reps know that customer satisfaction is money in the bank. Virtually every rep faces competition. Establishing customer rapport and providing customer service are the successful rep's edge. One-shot deals don't make a career, and good reps are in for the long haul.

What Can Selling Do for You?

Selling offers some very attractive career opportunities. The Dartnell Institute of Financial Research in Chicago recently released a study that presents some fascinating facts about today's field sales reps. The information came from a survey covering 122,000 salespeople at more than 300 companies representing 36 industrial classifications. Some of the resulting national averages are particularly interesting. For instance, the average age for sales reps is 36; 82% are male, 18% female, and 81% have at least some college, if not a degree. The average sales trainee makes $23,000 a year; "semi-experienced" reps (those with less than three years of experience) average about $31,000; and senior reps (those with three or more years of experience) should be earning an average of $40,000.

For this, the reps work hard. They average 5.5 sales calls a day and take an average of 5 calls to make one deal. Typically, they spend 45 hours a week on selling activities and another 15 on nonselling activities (paperwork, traveling, and so on). Just over half use their own cars for traveling (with reimbursement from the company); the rest use company or leased cars. They each average an annual sales volume of more than $1.5 million, and, at the time of the study, they averaged just over seven years on the job.

Averages, of course, don't tell particulars. You have about a 50-50 chance of doing better than this—or of doing worse. In any case, there's no guarantee that a field selling job, even if it is satisfactory in the beginning, will remain so throughout your career. Your priorities may change and so may your lifestyle. Even so, sales experience often provides a good entrée into business with, generally, considerable opportunity to move into other areas as your career progresses.

Today's sales reps must know as much about their customers' businesses as they do about their own. This gives them expertise in the industry they serve and makes them valuable in areas other than direct selling, for instance, in marketing or maybe even product development. Because they must organize themselves, reps often develop good management skills and may prove excellent material for line managers and divisional heads. People who started in sales fill many of the senior executive spots in today's corporations. In addition, when times are tough and companies cut back, those in sales are often the last to go; management thinks long and hard before it bites into its revenue producers.

HOW CAN YOU USE THE INFORMATION HERE?

The company profiles are arranged by industry, so you can get a picture of what sales reps in a given industry earn and do. The industries chosen are mostly in the manufacturing area, and they provide a wide array of products, ranging from raw materials (forest products, fabrics, chemicals, and foods) to high-tech finished goods and services (electronics, computers, and information processing systems). Depending on your education, interests, and background, you can choose one or more related industries (for example, apparel or textiles) to get an all-around idea of the job opportunities offered.

You may also want to look at the most promising, emerging industries. You will note that pharmaceutical companies are very well represented in the text, and this is deliberate because all facets of the health-care industries seem to be on a strong growth curve. Demographics, such as the aging population of the U.S., indicate continued strength in the prescription drug and over-the-counter markets. Also well covered is the computer/office equipment market, where the glamour, high-tech, research-driven companies are clustered.

The flip side of these big glossy industries is that they are fiercely competitive. There are big bucks here, but a lot of people around the world are chasing them. Reps in these industries need high levels of education (college and more) with technical backgrounds (pharmacy, nursing, engineering, electronics, computer science, chemistry, and so on). Candidates for sales jobs in these fields must be in the upper ranks of their graduating classes and demonstrate that they are doers and achievers.

On the other hand, many of the industries covered here do not require exceptionally high levels of education. They do all require commitment and training, but the emphasis is on innate poise and learned skills. For instance, selling in the automotive aftermarket (tires, accessories, and the like) or in the consumer retail market (food, soaps, and cosmetics) requires more drive and savvy than academic degrees. Still, as you've seen, over 80% of the reps working today have had at least some college. Lack of formal education after high school is not fatal, but it is no big help either. In any case, this book presents a wide range of options with respect to job qualifications. You should honestly evaluate your own situation and interests and then match them with suitable industries and companies. A major point of this book is the incredible range of talents and backgrounds that the selling profession needs, utilizes, and rewards.

Each company profile begins with a purely subjective Corporate Culture Index that gives a quick assessment (based on a scale of 1 to 10) of how the company stacks up in several crucial areas—for example, training, support, and benefits. An address and phone number are given for each company so you can get in touch with any that you find especially interesting. Then follows a very brief overview of what that company does and which markets it serves. Where possible, the structure of the company is outlined, and some of its basic market strategies and goals are spelled out. (None of this involves proprietary material, of course; it all stems from public information and on-the-record interviews.) Next is an account of the actual selling operations of the company (qualifications for new hires,

training programs, territory makeup, types of accounts, reps' responsibilities, and so on). This is followed by the company's compensation policies
and a listing of the company's employee benefits. The reader should keep
in mind that information on compensation is based on averages and provides general indications that are not hard-and-fast. Moreover, company
policies differ with regard to salaries, bonuses, incentives, and commissions, and to how these relate to the reps' overall compensation. For the
most part, vacation time amounts to three weeks after five years' employment with a firm. The profile concludes with a short statement recapping
some of the opportunities and challenges the company offers its reps.

The profiles have captured the companies at a particular moment,
and nothing in business remains the same for long. Companies change
and so do markets. Competition changes them; government regulations
change them; customer demands change them. Although the information
here is the latest available and very useful, you should reserve judgment
on any company that interests you until you have made personal contact
and learned about it firsthand. What you can take from this book are some
good ideas on where to look for jobs that are suitable for you. You'll be
able to check out some ideas you may have had for a long time, and you'll
probably be exposed to companies or industries that you may never have
thought of as potential employers. Try them all; it's your future, and now's
the time to begin making the most of it.

Acknowledgments

This book is the product of the labors of many talented people. The outstanding writing skills of Harry L. Wagner, who remained always a delight
to work with, helped to meet a difficult publishing deadline. To Stephen
Fenichell and Yehudah Mirsky we are also very grateful.

Nancy Kalish of The Philip Lief Group supervised the editing process
with the research assistance of Ruth Tenenbaum and Tom Wittenberg of
Harkavy Information Service.

We thank these fact-gathering professionals for their efficient, well-
orchestrated drive to see this book become a fact itself!

Michael David Harkavy
Philip Lief

APPAREL

The saying goes that clothes make the man. They also make for lots of sales. Everybody, young and old, big and small, wears clothes. Talk about market potential!

The apparel market looks promising for the 1990s. The fastest growing age group in the United States, ages thirty-five to fifty-four, is also the age group that consumes the most and has the most to spend on a new suit or an extra pair of slacks. Also, as more and more women enter the work force, they will create new demand for specialized women's workwear. And with more and more people headed for the gym and the jogging path, the demand for sportswear is greater then ever before.

That doesn't mean, however, that apparel salespeople don't have to hustle. As a matter of fact, in the next few years they will have to hustle like never before. Perhaps the biggest challenge facing the American apparel industry is a new, highly competitive international market. The clothing manufacturers of the Far East, who pay their workers very low wages, pose an especially stiff challenge to American companies. America still exports more apparel than it imports, but not by much.

Companies have responded to these challenges in a number of ways. On the political side, the United States government has negotiated trade agreements with China, Hong Kong, Japan, Taiwan, and South Korea that will keep their clothing manufacturers from flooding our markets without putting them out of business. They have also worked to improve factory technologies in what has traditionally been a very labor-intensive industry

(85% of the apparel work force is in manufacture, whereas the figure for most industries is only 75%). They have also developed new "quick response" communications technologies that can provide up-to-date marketing information and help companies keep pace with constantly changing fashions. The "quick response" technologies let apparel manufacturers benefit from a major advantage that they have over foreign competition— their customers are just next door.

In recent years, manufacturers have concentrated on best-selling name brand products like Yves Saint Laurent, Anne Klein, and Perry Ellis. These product lines are especially profitable because they include not just clothing, but accessories like ties and belts, which always sell, even in hard times. As the chairman of Manhattan Industries recently put it, "A man won't pay $500 for a suit, but he will pay $30 for a dress shirt or $15 for a bright pair of suspenders to spruce up his wardrobe."

The apparel industry faces many challenges. In the end, though, it still comes down to salesmanship, keeping your ear to the ground, keeping track of fashion, letting designers and manufacturers know what people want, and convincing retailers that you have what they need.

TRADE ASSOCIATIONS

American Apparel Manufacturers Association 703/524-1864
Federation of Apparel Manufacturers 212/594-0810
Men's Fashion Association of America 212/683-5665

PERIODICALS

Daily News Record
Gentlemen's Quarterly/GQ
Harper's Bazaar
Vogue
WWD (Women's Wear Daily)

HARTMARX CORPORATION

VITAL STATISTICS

Entry Level Salary for Sales: **$65,000–$70,000**
Senior Level Salary for Sales: **$65,000–$70,000**

Benefits

medical/dental: **Yes**	child care: **No**
life insurance: **Yes**	retirement plan: **Yes**
disability: **Yes**	savings investment plan: **Yes**
travel allowance: **N/A**	tuition assistance: **Yes**
company car: **No**	relocation assistance: **Yes**
profit sharing plan: **No**	memberships: **No**
stock purchase plan: **Yes**	

Corporate Culture Index (1 = lowest, 10 = highest)

training:	**9**	security:	**10**
support:	**9**	mobility:	**9**
benefits:	**8**	intangibles:	**9**

Address: 101 North Wacker Drive, Chicago, IL 60606
Contact: National Sales Manager; telephone 312/372-6300 ext. 4278

Hartmarx Corporation ranks 307th on the Fortune 500 list. In 1987 it had sales of more than $1 billion, up 2% from 1986. Profits for the year, at $41 million, were up a whopping 67% over 1986.

Hartmarx Corporation designs, manufactures, and markets fine men's and women's apparel nationwide and, through licensing agreements, in 12 foreign countries as well. About 20% of Hartmarx's manufactured products are sold to affiliated stores, with the remaining 80% sold to other retailers for resale to consumers. The company's operations are divided into four segments: the Men's Apparel Group; Country Miss (women's apparel); Hartmarx Specialty Stores, Inc.; and International. We will concentrate on the first three segments here.

The Men's Apparel Group markets 24 brands of men's clothing and experienced remarkable growth in the 1980s, increasing sales 87% during that time. Two new businesses were added in 1987, the Traditional Apparel Group and Henry Grethel Apparel. By introducing a new softly constructed "natural shoulder" line of elegant suits and an expanded Grethel designer furnishings and sportswear line, these operations have been positioned to appeal to the under-35, more contemporary customer, an important area for growth that was largely untapped by the company's various manufacturing divisions. Especially promising are plans to offer a total Henry Grethel collection with a specific design concept that appeals to the younger, more contemporary customer. The Men's Apparel Group also markets such noted brands as: Hart Schaffner and Marx, Austin Reed, Christian Dior, Jack Nicklaus, Hickey-Freeman, Jaymar-Ruby, Pierre Cardin, and Racquet Club. Hartmarx suit brands range in price from $150 to $200 (Johnny Carson) to $600 plus (Hickey-Freeman).

Country Miss, the company's major women's apparel manufacturer, increased its sales in its own line of Old Mill stores, offsetting a decline in its retail sales due to private label competition. Country Miss markets coordinated sportswear and related separates under the Country Suburbans, Weathervane, and Handmacher labels. It also markets Handmacher women's suits, Color Me Beautiful sportswear, Lady Sansabelt slacks and skirts, and Jaymar-Ruby shorts. Management sees future growth in Country Miss, which is opening about ten stores annually, and in the possibility of designing Henry Grethel women's apparel for a number of areas.

Hartmarx Specialty Stores, Inc. (HSSI) showed a real increase in earnings in 1987 after suffering a loss in 1986. Fall 1987 was the first full season in which all the buying was the responsibility of a centralized merchandising organization. Fashion-conscious customers responded to the exciting new selections, and sales were up in the second half, despite a turndown after the stock market crash of that year because of concerns about the economy. Aggressive expansion (a dozen new HSSI stores opening by the end of 1988) together with a remodeling and repositioning of the company's Kuppenheimer stores and continuing expansion of Country Miss's Old Mill chain make Hartmarx a leader in apparel retailing.

Hartmarx carefully screens and then carefully trains its new sales reps. (New hires are interviewed by *all* key executives.) The company looks for college graduates with some experience in retail selling—preferably in the apparel field. Generally, the company hires from the competition, and it does expect prior sales experience. This requirement is reflected in the training program, which is confined to on-the-job training, learning Hartmarx's products and procedures—not retail apparel selling. New reps (not, strictly speaking, trainees) are rotated through various departments—manufacturing, distribution, customer service, retail—and they also work in tandem with other sales reps and sales managers. New reps are also assigned staff jobs before they are given a sales territory. The whole program lasts for a year, taking place primarily at the company's Chicago headquarters. Only a rep who is deemed fully seasoned is assigned a territory.

Hartmarx has a very stable sales force; few reps leave and openings become available mostly through retirements.

Reps at Hartmarx do not get a company car nor a travel allowance; they pay their own expenses and manage their territories as a small business within the larger business of the company. This is an important consideration since the territories are generally large (four states is a typical size) and reps can expect to spend about 40% of their time on overnights. They work alone, calling on retailers such as department stores and men's and women's specialty stores. The Hartmarx line is sold to "better," more upscale outlets. Reps must be thoroughly familiar with men's and women's fashions, what's in, what's out, and what fabrics, colors, and styles will sell.

Hartmarx reps earn an average of $65,000 to $70,000 and up, but reps must pay their own expenses on the road. Earnings also include a commission on sales and incentives when certain quotas are met. Other benefits include: medical, dental, and life insurance (amount of life insurance equals income); disability and retirement plans; a stock purchase plan, a 401K plan, a savings plan, tuition assistance (available after six months), and paid relocation expenses. There is also a clear career ladder at Hartmarx from sales rep to staff positions in brand management or marketing to sales manager and vice president. Hartmarx believes in promotion from within—and practices it. Additional support includes first-rate ad and promotional materials and administrative/clerical assistance where possible.

The atmosphere at Hartmarx is warm, with employees sharing a sense of pride, spirit, and dedication to quality. The industry is a competitive one, though, and to succeed reps must be determined and aggressive. The company supports them with high-quality merchandise and the firm belief that the way to grow is to provide customers with the right products and top-grade service. The company, having celebrated its centennial in 1987, has a long history and is confident of a future as successful.

OXFORD INDUSTRIES, INC.

VITAL STATISTICS

Entry Level Salary for Sales: **$30,000**
Senior Level Salary for Sales: **$100,000+**

Benefits

medical/dental: **Medical, no dental**
life insurance: **Yes**
disability: **Yes**
travel allowance: **Yes**
company car: **Yes**
profit sharing plan: **No**
stock purchase plan: **Yes**

child care: **No**
retirement plan: **Yes**
savings investment plan: **Yes**
tuition assistance: **Yes**
relocation assistance: **Yes**
memberships: **Country club**

Corporate Culture Index   (1 = lowest, 10 = highest)

training: **9**
support: **9**
benefits: **9**

security: **10**
mobility: **6**
intangibles: **9**

Address: 222 Piedmont Avenue, N.E., Atlanta, GA 30308
Contact: Human Resources; telephone 404/653-1329

Oxford Industries, Inc., ranks 455th on the Fortune 500 list. In 1987 it had sales of more than $500 million, up 4% from 1986. Profits for 1987 amounted to $11 million, up a modest 3% from 1986.

Oxford Industries, Inc., designs, manufactures, markets, and distributes consumer apparel products for men, women, and children. It also offers related services to a wide range of apparel retailers. For some years now, the apparel industry has suffered slow growth, especially in earnings—and 1987 was no exception for Oxford. In its own words, "This is not satisfactory performance."

There are several reasons for the company's flat earnings for 1987. Most importantly, apparel industry conditions have remained difficult. The volume of imported textiles and apparel continues to grow, flooding the U.S. market. This leads to extreme competitive pressures that have a particularly strong negative impact on companies like Oxford with substantial domestic marketing bases. In addition, the retail end of the business is undergoing an unprecedented shakeup of repositioning, restructuring, and consolidation in the intense struggle for market share. More disturbing still is the growing trend of large manufacturers to go directly to foreign sources for the manufacture of their private label products.

So why would a rep want to work for this company? Because Oxford is trying hard to overcome these problems, and fortunately, it's succeeding. It engaged in its own restructuring in 1987, closing down a division and some apparel lines in an effort to improve operating costs and focus more sharply on its profitable and promising operations. The company was encouraged by the modest gains it enjoyed that year despite the costs of the restructuring, and it looks to the future with renewed confidence. Oxford divisions that performed well in 1987 were Our Polo for Boys, Merona, Lanier Clothes, Oxford Slacks, Women's Sportswear Separates, and Women's Branded Sportswear. In addition, BJ Design Concepts, which markets screen-printed apparel, had an outstanding year, and the acquisition of Mainsail gave Oxford a strong presence in the rapidly growing knit and fleece markets.

Oxford's domestic plants still produce the majority of its sales and have been operating at their highest level in recent years. Nevertheless, the company, encouraged by the U.S. trade policy, is actively pursuing opportunities in Mexico and the Caribbean countries. At present, several of Oxford's divisions have developed full-time foreign sources in this hemisphere, and this should lead the way for increased involvement of Oxford's other divisions as well.

It has also helped that Oxford's largest customer base, department and chain stores, has held its own in the battle for the consumer dollar, and the company has kept its leading position with these customers. Several Oxford divisions have also benefited from the trend among those retailers, who have traditionally emphasized branded merchandise, to increase their private label offerings. In a world of fierce competition and rapidly changing patterns of marketing and retailing, Oxford directs its energies toward identifying opportunities and vacating unpromising sectors. Oxford is banking on the variety and quality of its lines to meet the challenges of this volatile market.

Oxford also counts heavily on its small but well-trained sales force to keep it a major player in this competitive industry. The discussion here will focus on one of the company's divisions, Oxford Slacks, to give you a picture of what selling for Oxford entails. This division maintains a force of only eight reps (called "account executives"), and it chooses them very carefully. It looks for college graduates with a business background; prior selling experience is helpful but not necessary. In addition to the usual interviews, candidates also take a session with an industrial psychologist who uses a "predictive index" to identify those with the requisite traits for success in this field.

The training program itself is very thorough. It begins with two weeks of formal classroom instruction in Monroe, Georgia, covering orientation, company systems and procedures, product knowledge, the language of the fabric and apparel industry, marketing concepts, and selling skills. The major part of the training, though, requires new hires to observe an experienced account executive (AE) on the job for up to eight months. During this time, the new hire will also tour Oxford plants and learn about fabrics. At the end of training, new reps are assigned territories, which are made up along product lines rather than by geographical areas. For instance, an AE might be given all the accounts handling slacks in the Northeast.

AEs do not sell directly to retail outlets, but rather to the central buying offices of major department stores and specialty stores. Overall, however, Oxford sells to the entire spectrum of the apparel market—department stores, chains, discounters, and upscale direct marketers. Each AE, however, is assigned only a specific segment of the total market.

Salaries for trainees average about $30,000; senior AEs can earn six figures with a combination of salary and bonuses. Bonuses depend on meeting individual and group quotas. AEs work mostly in teams, and the company strongly encourages a sense of teamwork and group effort. Other benefits include: medical and life insurance, disability and retirement plans, a stock purchase plan, a 401K plan, a savings plan, tuition assistance, paid relocation expenses, and a company car.

AEs operate their territories like their own businesses. They plan their strategies, schedule their calls, and exercise a good deal of independent judgment in managing their territories. The competition is stiff, but Oxford has a variety of divisions and lines with good customer acceptance and recognition. The sales force is small and tightly knit, and it is as determined as the company to succeed.

PHILLIPS-VAN HEUSEN CORPORATION

VITAL STATISTICS

Entry Level Salary for Sales: **$30,000**
Senior Level Salary for Sales: **$125,000**

Benefits

medical/dental: **Yes**	child care: **No**
life insurance: **Yes**	retirement plan: **Yes**
disability: **Yes**	savings investment plan: **Yes**
travel allowance: **Yes**	tuition assistance: **Yes**
company car: **Yes**	relocation assistance: **N/A**
profit sharing plan: **Yes**	memberships: **Smokenders**
stock purchase plan: **Yes**	**Weight Watchers**
	Health clubs

Corporate Culture Index   (1 = lowest, 10 = highest)

training:	**10**	security:	**9**
support:	**9**	mobility:	**6**
benefits:	**10**	intangibles:	**9**

Address: 1290 Avenue of the Americas, New York, NY 10104
Contact: Vice President, Sales and Marketing Operations; telephone 212/468-7010

Phillips-Van Heusen ranks 473rd on the Fortune 500 list. In 1987 it had net sales of more than $500 million, up 34% from 1986. Profits, at $30 million, were 49% above those of 1986.

Phillips-Van Heusen is one of the nation's leading apparel and footwear manufacturers and marketers. In 1987 the company acquired G. H. Bass & Company, one of the finest brand names in the shoe industry, a move that it believes will have a major impact on the corporation's future. In addition to Bass, Phillips-Van Heusen has four other operating divisions, all described briefly here.

G. H. Bass & Co. comes to the company with an excellent reputation for high-quality footwear that has won long-term loyalty and esteem from its customers and retailers alike. Phillips-Van Heusen intends to maintain that tradition with careful management of production and pricing, improvement and expansion of the shoe company's retail and catalogue divisions, controls to ensure that Bass products will be distributed only to those retailers willing and able to present them in the fine image implicit in the name G. H. Bass & Co., and the selection of a new ad agency for the line.

The Van Heusen Company division markets the Van Heusen and Hennessy brands of men's shirts. In recent years, the trend in department stores toward private label garments instead of brand names has caused some trouble for this division. It responded aggressively by offering products of perceptible value with either classic styling or forward styling coupled with significant advertising support, which Phillips-Van Heusen is confident will keep the company a major factor in the market.

The Designer Group markets dress shirts under the name Geoffrey Beene nationally and Etienne Aigner regionally. This division achieved record results in 1987 and is expected to continue to grow. The Private Label Divisions comprise the Van Heusen Group's Pickwick division and the Private Label Sportswear Group's Somerset division. These divisions are positioned as major suppliers of private label merchandise to the larger retailers for use as their house brand products. They provide fashion leadership, quick response, superior inventory control, and optimal product cost for items in this ever-growing market. The Van Heusen Retail Division is a group of stores whose mission is to absorb the surplus branded merchandise of the company, thus leaving the Van Heusen Company with just about the "cleanest" distribution in the industry. In addition, the division is a profit center in itself and will continue to expand in locations that do not conflict with Van Heusen's branded accounts.

Phillips-Van Heusen has a small sales force, at present about 50 reps. Primary emphasis is on selling the company's line of shirts and sportswear to the "better" department stores and specialty stores concentrating on quality merchandise—no discount houses, in other words. The company expects that its Bass line of footwear will also be an important part of its business. The company looks for new sales reps who are knowledgeable in the retail or apparel industry, and its new hires usually have prior sales experience. A college degree is not necessary.

Training at Phillips-Van Heusen is primarily an on-the-job affair, with the trainee apprenticing under the supervision of an experienced manager. There is not much classroom work in the program, which comprises mostly a review of the retail and apparel industries (for newcomers), product knowledge (shirting), company policies and practices, and learning the company's computer inventory control system. Reps need to know—and know thoroughly—the industry and the role of shirting in it. There are two lines of shirts each year, and reps must be completely familiar with inventory, prices, styles, and so on.

The training takes place in one of eight regional centers, and sometimes in a series of different locations. The trainee works with an experienced rep, learning the products, the customers, how to write up orders, and so on. The training can last anywhere from six months to two years, depending on the experience and capacity of the new hire to absorb the business. The training is crucial because new reps are not assigned a territory until they are deemed capable of handling their own territory and a territory becomes available. It's in the best interests of trainees to master what they need to know as quickly as possible so that they can become eligible for the next territory that opens up.

Territory size can vary greatly. Because the territory consists of department stores and leading specialty stores, those with few such stores can be very large, whereas those with many can be very small. In the upper Midwest and mountain regions, for instance, a territory could include several states. In a key urban area with a high density of stores, the territory may be a small segment of the area. For example, in New York City, a rep might have only two accounts to cover. In any case, reps work alone and spend most of their time in the field calling on accounts.

Salaries for beginning reps are about $30,000; senior salespeople earn up to $125,000. Reps work on a salary-plus-commission basis, and at the higher end of the scale most of the reps' income will be derived from commissions. Other benefits include: medical and life insurance, disability and retirement plans, stock purchasing and profit sharing plans, a 401K plan, a savings plan, tuition assistance, and a company car.

The apparel industry is highly competitive, so the atmosphere at Phillips-Van Heusen is tense and aggressive. Promotion opportunities are limited, but there is some progression from less lucrative to higher income potential territories. The line is top quality, though, and there is good income potential for reps who have a flair for fashion and for the rough and tumble of retail selling.

AUTOMOBILES

In a country that sometimes seems like one big success story, the automotive industry may be the biggest success story of all. Long before Bruce Springsteen was born to run, Henry Ford's Model T was putting the American Dream in driveways and on the open road all across the country. American car manufacturers have literally changed the face of the earth. In recent years they have learned to respond to strong and unexpected challenges from abroad. As a result, sales are up, but the manufacturers are not out of the woods yet.

Eight major manufacturers produce automobiles in the United States. Only three of them, the Big Three we profile here, are American and they account for more than two-thirds of car sales in the United States, with total earnings of more than $7 billion. (Ford alone accounted for nearly two-thirds of that figure.) Each has, in recent years, attempted to carve out a distinctive niche for itself in the business. Chrysler has tried to compensate for its traditional third-place standing and comeback status by positioning itself to take the lead in the upscale market with coupes and convertibles as well as by maintaining its very strong truck sales. General Motors, whose sales have been sluggish in the past few years, is taking the lead in technological innovation with new high-performance models. Ford is focusing on product design and engineering, along with its traditional people and lifestyle oriented message.

The Big Three would do well to scramble. Competition is as keen as ever as sales of Japanese and some upscale European models are slipping due to high prices. This gives American automakers a window of opportunity that they should exploit while they can. Although new technologies and sharp price competition may keep demand alive for a while, many industry analysts predict that if the industry's current growth rate of 1% to 2% continues, the world market for new cars will be oversaturated by the mid 1990s. And with oil prices fluctuating dramatically all the time, the future is even harder to foresee.

American automobile salespeople are legendary figures, maybe even more famous than Lee Iacocca (who started out as a salesman himself). In recent surveys, automobile salespeople have received especially high marks for friendliness and appearance. There does, however, seem to be much room for improvement when it comes to knowing the product and mastering the ins and outs of financing. All the factors that add up to effective salesmanship are especially important in the automotive industry. With so many different manufacturers flooding the market with their makes and models, car buyers need salespeople who can provide reliable information on which the buyers can base their decision, as well as a friendly atmosphere that will let the buyers feel that they are making their own free choice and not being "hustled" into something.

One thing is certain: with all the challenges facing the automobile industry in the future, some companies are going to suffer, but some will come out on top. The salespeople on the front lines will have a key role to play in determining which companies make it.

TRADE ASSOCIATIONS

Automotive Affiliated Representatives 312/644-6610

PERIODICALS

Automotive Industries
Automotive News
Ward's Auto World
Ward's Automotive Reports

CHRYSLER CORPORATION

VITAL STATISTICS

Entry Level Salary for Sales: *$25,000–$26,000*
Senior Level Salary for Sales: *$50,000*

Benefits

medical/dental: *Yes*
life insurance: *Yes*
disability: *Yes*
travel allowance: *Yes*
company car: *Yes*
profit sharing plan: *No*
stock purchase plan: *Yes*

child care: *No*
retirement plan: *Yes*
savings investment plan: *Yes*
tuition assistance: *Yes*
relocation assistance: *Yes*
memberships: *On-site wellness program*

Corporate Culture Index (1 = lowest, 10 = highest)

training: *9*
support: *8*
benefits: *9*

security: *8*
mobility: *8*
intangibles: *9*

Address: 12000 Chrysler Drive, Highland Park, MI 48288-1919
Contact: Personnel; telephone 313/956-5741

Chrysler Corporation ranks 10th on the Fortune 500 list. In 1987 it posted record sales of more than $26 billion, a 17% increase over 1986. It also boosted its retail car and truck market share to 12.3% of the total, as compared to a market share of 11.7% in 1986.

The story of the Chrysler Corporation from the late 1970s to the mid 1980s reads like a cross between "Cinderella" and "The Little Engine That Could." Facing bankruptcy and with sales declining, costs increasing, and overcapacity mounting, the company seemed doomed to go under. Now, everyone knows how Lee Iacocca took over the floundering company, secured a loan guarantee from the U.S. Congress, and turned the picture around in a few years. At that time, Chrysler needed to do a major selling job: to itself, to persuade workers and managers that they could compete with both American companies and foreign imports; to the government, which had to approve the loan guarantee; and to the public, who had to be persuaded that Chrysler had the right product, at the right time, with the right price. The company got the right man for the job in Iacocca, who began his career as a salesman and who has never lost touch with the art of salesmanship.

For instance, when Chrysler came out with its K cars, it scored a major success against its domestic competitors and took the high ground against Japanese imports in the mid-sized market. But it might not have happened that way. At first, the K line was marketed like all domestic lines at that time, in a stripped-down model with even very basic add-ons increasing the sticker price. The Japanese, however, were offering Toyotas and Datsuns already equipped with a full complement of extras—at no added charge to the sticker price. When dealer sales reps complained, Chrysler listened, and the second edition of K cars included a number of high-priced options as standard equipment. The public took to the cars and to Chrysler, and the disaster was averted. Chrysler became known as a company that paid attention to salespeople.

Chrysler is still listening and is moving to bolster its domestic line in several directions. For example, it had no four-wheel-drive vehicle and was missing out on a major market. So, in 1987, Chrysler acquired American Motors, maker of the world's best-known four-wheeler—the Jeep. The merger has already helped Chrysler increase its share of the North American truck market substantially, and it is expected to do even more in the future. New Chrysler models will feature a two-door sports coupe, stylish new Dodge and Plymouth sedans, and a Chrysler luxury car. In addition, Chrysler management will continue to monitor costs carefully so that new products can be priced to meet the competition—domestic and foreign.

Turning Chrysler around and keeping it turned around require a really dedicated Chrysler sales staff. As with all the automotive companies, Chrysler reps (district managers) do not themselves sell their products to the public. Instead, they work closely with Chrysler dealerships to provide cars for their retail lots, to help make their businesses more efficient, and to assist their floor sales staff in moving Chrysler products. District managers are usually 26 to 28 years old when they begin, have at least a bachelor's degree, and possess some prior selling experience.

District managers undergo formal training for from six months to two years, depending on experience and education. Emphasis is on dealer operations, implementing marketing strategies, and making the best use of the extensive advertising campaigns that Chrysler, like the other domestic and import automotive companies, mounts in all media. Every year there are two-week district manager seminars on new model training, and constant informal training goes on throughout a district manager's career.

For its part, Chrysler goes to great lengths to provide support to its dealers and district managers. It now maintains 17 regional training centers for dealer service technicians. Also, at present, about 150 dealer showrooms have Chrysler's Computer Assistance Program, a computer program that in effect takes customers through the "building" of their dream car— "down to the color and trim." As mentioned, Chrysler also provides extensive advertising and promotion materials, gives clerical/administrative assistance to district managers, and maintains vigorous R&D and quality management to ensure that its products will be attractive, priced competitively, and in A-one condition when they reach the dealer's showrooms.

Salary for beginning sales district managers is about $25,000 to $26,000. Senior sales personnel earn about $50,000. The Chrysler sales staff is on a straight salary basis because the district managers are considered more part of the team than independent sales reps who are responsible for their own sales.

Other benefits provided by Chrysler include: full medical and dental insurance, group life insurance, a retirement plan, tuition assistance, and a company car. In addition, Chrysler offers a Salaried Employees' Savings Plan, which is a stock purchase plan, and incentive compensation awards for officers and key Chrysler employees who have made significant contributions to the success of the company.

The climate at Chrysler is group oriented. The challenges that the company has faced and will face can only be met with skilled, dedicated teamwork. From design, to manufacturing, to showroom selling, teamwork is the name of the game. Chrysler has worked hard to come to agreements with its unionized work force to allow for significant savings in production and overhead, making its products more competitive, and giving the company a strong financial posture in case the slow times return. Employees have rallied behind Iacocca and the changes he has stood for. They have an upbeat pride in their work and a strong sense of confidence in the company.

FORD MOTOR COMPANY

VITAL STATISTICS

Entry Level Salary for Sales: **$24,000 (BA), $30,000 (MA)**
Senior Level Salary for Sales: **$40,000**

Benefits

medical/dental: **Yes**
life insurance: **Yes**
disability: **N/A**
travel allowance: **N/A**
company car: **Yes**
profit sharing plan: **Yes**
stock purchase plan: **Yes**

child care: **N/A**
retirement plan: **Yes**
savings investment plan: **N/A**
tuition assistance: **Yes**
relocation assistance: **N/A**
memberships: **N/A**

Corporate Culture Index   (1 = lowest, 10 = highest)

training: **9**
support: **9**
benefits: **8**

security: **7**
mobility: **8**
intangibles: **8**

Address: The American Road, P.O. Box 1899, Dearborn, MI 48121
Contact: Personnel; telephone 313/322-3000

Ford Motor Company ranks 3rd on the Fortune 500 list. Its 1987 worldwide sales were over $71 billion, an increase of 14% over 1986. Its record $4.6 billion net income in 1987 made it the most profitable automobile company in the world.

Ford's performance in 1987 prompted David Cole, director of Automotive Studies at the University of Michigan, to proclaim it "the best managed auto company in the world." How it got that way from a way-behind also-ran as recently as 1980 is the story of a simple strategy that was carefully implemented. The main thrust of the strategy was threefold: to increase efficiency by lowering Ford's break-even point from a high of 4 million vehicles in 1979, and to improve on the quality of Ford's cars and the negative image the public had of Ford products.

The company cut costs by $5 billion from 1981 to 1987, lowering its break-even point to 2.8 million cars, the lowest of the Big Three (Ford, GM, and Chrysler). More importantly, it changed its corporate thinking. It went from a top-down, autocratic management style to one fostering teamwork and input from all sectors. Ford's biggest success, the Taurus, was the result of stylists, engineers, manufacturing experts, and assembly workers pooling their talents in "Team Taurus" to create a sleek, new, high-quality automobile. Ford, with the nation's best selling car in its economy Escort and the number two seller in Taurus, has clearly won the public's confidence. With continued emphasis on efficiency and quality, Ford will probably be a powerful force well into the next decade.

The sales and marketing people are expected to supply much of that muscle. Initial sales training for new Ford reps takes about sixteen weeks, nine in on-the-job training in the new hire's district and seven in classes covering such areas as analyzing dealers' financial statements and performance reports, reviewing case studies, and role-playing. After six months at Ford or the Lincoln-Mercury division, reps generally go on to a fifteen-week field manager training program. There they concentrate on dealer operations, credit, and zone management. The zone management position is an entry-level management job; zone managers act as prudent business consultants to dealerships. Interestingly enough, many senior managers are recruited from the ranks of the zone managers.

Ford's field manager training program, which includes working for several weeks at a dealership, has been recognized as one of the best in the industry. It also includes training at the Ford Training Institute, which offers 32 courses in advanced topics. The Ford Parts and Service Division offers a similar career development program covering topics such as customer relations, sales and service strategies, and other critical aspects of the dealer and parts and service operations.

Other company support for salespeople takes the form of administrative/clerical help, first-rate advertising and promotion materials, on-target product and market information, and many one- to four-day programs for dealers held at training centers in hotels and conference centers.

Employee benefits include medical/dental insurance and vision-care plans, life insurance, retirement and disability plans, profit sharing and stock purchasing plans, tuition assistance, and a company car. The company and certain of its subsidiaries also provide selected health and life insurance benefits for its retired employees. Nearly all of Ford's U.S. and Canadian employees may become eligible for such benefits if they reach retirement age while working for the company.

Ford sales trainees receive a salary, but no commission. The starting salary for a new sales hire ranges from $24,000 for a college graduate with a bachelor's degree to $30,000 for one with a master's. The salaries of the top-level sales reps average about $40,000. At that level, most are promoted to management. Promotion opportunities from sales are good at Ford. The company likes to promote from within, and, as mentioned, many senior managers began as zone managers.

No one needs to be told that selling automobiles in today's marketplace is competitive business. Ford fought its way to the top in earnings over a long, difficult period in the early and mid 1980s. It plans to stay there. Ford's marketing staff and salespeople have their work cut out for them. Although Ford offers new hires an exciting chance to join a classy corporation, it also presents the challenge of meeting the demands that such a company necessarily makes on its employees. Ford is very selective in choosing the candidates for its training programs. The BA/BS degree (preferably in finance) is the minimum requirement. Much more desirable is a graduate degree, such as an MBA, in marketing, business administration, economics, finance, management, or automotive technology. Generally, successful candidates will also have graduated in the top third of their class.

Ford sales reps travel a great deal for business and to take courses. Although Ford has branch offices all over the country, at least some part of a sales rep's career with the company will be spent in Dearborn, Michigan, and frequent trips to Detroit are commonplace. Those thinking about a career at Ford must understand that they are undertaking a major commitment.

The new corporate culture of the company, though, puts an emphasis on individual initiative. Ford sees its future in building teamwork and expanding employee participation at all levels. Ford understands that no one individual is responsible for designing, engineering, manufacturing, assembling, and selling a product. That product is the result of thousands of people working together. As a result, Ford instituted such plans as Participative Management (PM), Employee Involvement (EI), pay-for-performance, profit sharing, and employee education, development, and training. Ford is serious about the future, and it expects its employees to be, too.

GENERAL MOTORS CORPORATION

VITAL STATISTICS

Entry Level Salary for Sales: **$25,000–$27,000**
Senior Level Salary for Sales: **$50,000+**

Benefits

medical/dental: **Yes**
life insurance: **Yes**
disability: **Yes**
travel allowance: **N/A**
company car: **Yes**
profit sharing plan: **Yes**
stock purchase plan: **Yes**

child care: **No**
retirement plan: **Yes**
savings investment plan: **Yes**
tuition assistance: **Yes**
relocation assistance: **Yes**
memberships: **N/A**

Corporate Culture Index   (1 = lowest, 10 = highest)

training: **6**
support: **8**
benefits: **10**

security: **9**
mobility: **8**
intangibles: **10**

Address: 3044 West Grand Boulevard, Detroit, MI 48202
Contact: Corporate Headquarters in Detroit for the nearest Salaried Personnel office; telephone 313/556-5000

General Motors Corporation ranks 1st on the Fortune 500 list. In 1987 it posted sales of more than $100 billion, down 1% from 1986. The automotive giant of the U.S., GM is now in the process of restructuring and retooling for the 1990s.

General Motors Corporation is a huge manufacturing firm, best known for its line of passenger cars, but it is also a major producer of buses, trucks, locomotives, construction equipment, and more. It is involved in defense procurement, electronics, telecommunications, and data processing as well. For all its size, however, the mid 1980s have not seen GM at its best. It has kept up its sales and revenue, but its profitability has declined to the extent that in 1987 its profits ($3.5 billion) badly trailed Ford's ($4.6 billion), even though GM had about $30 million more in gross sales.

One of GM's problems is that since it doesn't have a runaway best-seller like Ford's Taurus, it has been unable to sell enough cars to keep its huge plant capacity running at peak efficiency. Thus it has had to adopt a two-pronged strategy: to cut costs by reducing its break-even number and bringing more of its gross revenue down to the bottom line, and to beef up sales. To accomplish this, GM first had to cut back on the size of its operations, closing down or merging unprofitable plants. Initially, GM was reluctant to do this because it was proud of its great size and because it felt that when there was an upturn in sales and it regained its dominant position in the market, the additional capacity would be needed.

Current management at GM, however, is dedicated to improving the company's profit picture and is restructuring operations to reduce overhead and manufacturing costs (which, at present, are the highest among the Big Three automakers). Moreover, management feels this can be done, while at the same time keeping up production and improving market share. To accomplish this means improving worker productivity, a project that is already under way as joint labor-management councils at each GM plant meet to map out cost-cutting strategies.

Along with these efforts, GM also plans increased marketing efforts. The company now offers Chevrolet's Corsica and Beretta at the lower end of the market, with Cadillac's restyled Eldorado and Buick's snappy Regal at the high end. Also on the way is a new Cadillac, a full-sized pickup truck, and a new line of GM-10 cars (popular, mid-sized models). GM is also determined to make its new models stand out: no cookie-cutter, look-alike cars here. Large cars are in again, but more sleek and stylish than before. As Charles M. Jordan, GM design staff vice president, says, "We're dedicated to having a strong image from a block away." It's with this attention-getting, freshly styled line of new products that GM hopes to regain its dominant market share and boost sales.

Crucial to the effort is old-fashioned salesmanship. GM is taking pains to give each of its five car divisions a distinct and separate image, so that they are positioned to compete more with rival car companies than with their sister GM divisions. In addition, GM is working hard to improve its relations with its dealerships, an effort that will naturally require a skilled and highly motivated sales force.

As with other car companies, GM's sales reps (district managers or DMs) do not sell directly to the end user but rather act as consultants to the dealers, looking over their books and suggesting what cars they should stock. A DM, who is one cut above an entry-level rep, must have a good head for figures and the ability to analyze a dealer's business with an eye toward finding ways to improve it. DMs must suggest a mix of cars that is right for the dealer's market; they must be aware of different models, sizes, colors, and so on, and they must be up on accessories—what's hot, what's not—to provide the dealer with a line that will move.

GM looks for top-quality college graduates, those with degrees in business or marketing. Many DMs go on to get MBAs. Also, because GM moves its reps around a good deal and they are constantly on the road anyway, candidates for these jobs must show they are ready for the fast pace and a life away from home. In the downsizing that GM is now going through to reduce costs and boost profits, training has been cut back to absolute basics. Elaborate classroom programs are out for the present and on-the-job training is in. So too are self-study programs, in many cases video programs that teach dealers, dealer reps, and service people about new GM models. With the return of better times, GM expects to resume more formal training programs, but probably not so elaborate as it had in earlier boom times.

Salaries at GM range from $25,000 to $27,000 for trainees, with senior salespeople averaging about $50,000. GM salespeople are on straight salary; however, in line with its drive to increase productivity, the company also offers several performance-related incentive plans, including a Performance Achievement Plan and a Stock Incentive Plan. Promotion opportunities are good, with a chance to move up in sales and perhaps on to other divisions. In the fiercely competitive world of auto sales, good performers are readily recognized and rewarded.

Benefits are also substantial, as one would expect from a major corporation, including: medical, dental, and life insurance; a disability plan; pension and post-retirement benefits plans; profit sharing and stock purchase plans; tuition assistance; paid relocation costs; and a company car. GM has a low turnover rate, an endorsement of the solid benefits and prospects it offers to its reps.

GM makes heavy demands on its personnel. The climate is corporate and dynamic. DMs must be adept at coping with change and new situations. Volatility, fast pace, and challenge are the hallmarks of a rep's job at GM.

BEVERAGES

It is said that man does not live by bread alone. There is ample proof of that in the $113 billion in sales that the beverage industry racked up in 1987. This year, Americans will drink a half billion more gallons of beverages than they did last year. Soft drinks and beer account for nearly 75% of those sales, with fruit juices a distant third, followed by bottled water, drink mixes, wine, and spirits. In recent years, sales of soft drinks and bottled water have grown steadily, sales of wine, spirits, and mixes have declined, and sales of beer and fruit juices have basically stayed the same.

Americans drink almost twice as many soft drinks (sweetened, carbonated beverages) as other drinks—more than 46 gallons per person last year. Soft drink sales have been climbing steadily through the 1980s and are expected to continue their upswing, though some experts think that sales will level off in the mid 1990s.

Americans drink an average of 24 gallons of beer, but only 1½ gallons of spirits a year. Liquor distillers are able to make up in high retail prices what they lack in volume, however. Although spirits are consumed by fewer people and in smaller quantities, they generate more money than all other beverages, except for soft drinks and beer.

In recent years, the sales of light-tasting, low-alcohol drinks such as wine coolers and prepared cocktails have grown faster than any other alcoholic beverages. Coolers alone now account for more than 25% of the total wine market.

The demand for alcoholic drinks varies widely from region to region.

For example, the past few years have seen a steady rise in the Southeast and an equally steady decline in the Southwest. As the years go by, Americans seem to be drinking less and less alcohol. Experts say this is because consumers are becoming more concerned about drunk driving, alcohol abuse, and general physical fitness.

These very same trends explain why the fastest growing product in the beverage industry as a whole is bottled water. Last year, consumption of bottled water grew by a whopping 12%, to nearly 5 gallons per person annually. Even so, bottled water still accounts for only 5% of the beverage market.

In all, the beverage industry will not see any major changes in the next few years. The best sales opportunities are likely to be found with the major soft drink manufacturers and with brewers, who, even if they don't grow, are assured a steady supply of customers.

TRADE ASSOCIATIONS

Brewers Association of America 312/782-2305
Carbonated Beverages Institute 212/986-0280
Distilled Spirits Council of the United States 202/628-3544
International Bottled Water Association 703/683-5213
National Beer Wholesalers Association of America 703/578-4300
National Soft Drink Association 202/463-6732

PERIODICALS

Beverage Retailer Weekly
Beverage World
Brewers Digest
Modern Brewery Age

ADOLPH COORS COMPANY

VITAL STATISTICS

Entry Level Salary for Sales: **$24,000**
Senior Level Salary for Sales: **$36,000**

Benefits

medical/dental: **Yes**	child care: **No**
life insurance: **Yes**	retirement plan: **Yes**
disability: **Yes**	savings investment plan: **Yes**
travel allowance: **Yes**	tuition assistance: **Yes**
company car: **Yes**	relocation assistance: **Yes**
profit sharing plan: **No**	memberships: **On-site wellness**
stock purchase plan: **Yes**	**program**

Corporate Culture Index   (1 = lowest, 10 = highest)

training:	**9**	security:	**9**
support:	**9**	mobility:	**9**
benefits:	**9**	intangibles:	**10**

Address: Golden, CO 80401
Contact: Human Resources; telephone 303/279-6565

Adolph Coors Company ranks 256th on the Fortune 500 list. In 1987 it posted sales of more than $1 billion, 3% over 1986. Profits during that period amounted to $48 million, down 19% from 1986.

Adolph Coors Company is a major brewer and distributor of beer in the U.S. In 1987 it had another record year with beer shipments of 15.6 million barrels, up 2.8% from 1986, spurred by the company's successful expansion into the New Jersey and New York markets. Net earnings were down, however, because of soft sales in several other states and ongoing expenditures to build and expand the business. Coors is well aware that in 1987 the brewing industry was faced with an excess of capacity, which put pressure on prices and made discounting an important business tool. Crucial to the continued success of the company's operations is increasing volume, and Coors is implementing a three-pronged sales strategy to do just that.

Coors is working to (1) strengthen the performance of its existing brands and, especially, capitalize on the success of Coors Light, (2) gain market share in new and existing markets, and (3) develop and introduce new products. This strategy means increased emphasis on attracting and keeping a dedicated marketing force and strong distributors. It also involves continued expansion into territories not covered by Coors before (in 1988 the company expanded into its 48th and 49th states, Pennsylvania and Delaware). New products are on the way too, with national roll-outs of four new brands—Coors Extra Gold, Herman Joseph's Original Draft, HJ Light, and George Killian's Irish Red. Backing all this up will be a significant increase in advertising budgets, adding up to the company's largest sales marketing efforts to date. The theme of all the campaigns is to position Coors products as the optimum beverages for fun and sociability.

Although Coors is known primarily as a brewer and derives the bulk of its income from that business, it also operates in two other areas: Coors Ceramics and Allied Businesses. Coors Ceramics supplies products for the technical ceramic markets, and it is the world's largest volume supplier of ceramic components made of engineered high-purity zirconia. Allied Businesses continues Coors's basic strategy of developing and diversifying earnings by using technologies from its existing operations. Golden Aluminum, created in 1980, collects and recycles used beverage containers, thereby assuring a constant supply of raw material for its aluminum-rolling mill. In 1987 more than 95% of the mill's raw material came from recycled beverage cans. Other allied businesses include: Coors Distributing Company, Coors BioTech, Inc. (producer of corn syrup, yeast products, and the like), Coors Energy Company (originally created to supply energy to Coors brewing operations), and Coors Transportation Company (originally created to transport Coors beer).

Coors maintains a sales force of about 115, who sell Coors products to beer distributors and some large retailers. The Coors rep introduces new products and helps distributors improve their business operations by arranging for "special events," assisting in straightening out a delivery route, installing displays for a price special, and so on. The reps view themselves as consultants to the distributors, and they need to have some business knowledge and marketing savvy. The size of their territories varies, but in some cases they may have to spend as much as 50% of their time on overnights. They work alone for the most part, but they can rely on pretty heavy advertising and promotional support from the company. The products are well known and well regarded, and there is a constant supply of new and improved products from the company's R&D group.

Training lasts anywhere from six months to a year, depending on the new rep's experience. Coors looks for reps with a college degree, generally one with a major in business or marketing. The company tends not to hire recent college graduates, however, preferring to take on sales reps who have some actual experience in selling and marketing. New hires are generally in their mid to late 20s when they come to Coors.

The training itself takes place in Golden, Colorado, and in the field. It stresses professional selling skills, learning the business of distributors, territory management, and the values and mission of the company. In addition, Coors has a well-thought-out program of advancement for its reps, moving them from B markets to A markets to AA markets, increasing responsibility and compensation along the way. A matching curriculum of self-study materials accompanies the corporate moves, so training is ongoing as reps progress up the ladder. Coors has a large turnover in reps, but not many moves, and even when reps do leave, it's usually to become general managers of distributorships, where they continue to do business with Coors.

Salaries for rep trainees average about $24,000, and senior salespeople's salaries average about $36,000. The salaries are enhanced with bonuses, but bonuses depend on sales and business conditions. The company offers a good package of benefits: medical, dental, and life insurance; disability and retirement plans; profit sharing and stock purchase plans; tuition assistance; paid relocation expenses; travel allowance; and a company car.

The brewing industry is highly competitive, as can be seen in the high-profile print and media advertising put out by the country's major breweries. Reps have to hustle and work hard to give their distributors an edge. It's not uncommon, for example, for Coors reps and sales managers to accompany distributor personnel on their deliveries in order to meet the retailers personally and monitor the marketplace for themselves. Coors employees are loyal to the company, and the company in turn makes every effort to provide the kind of support that merits such loyalty.

BROWN-FORMAN, INC.

VITAL STATISTICS

Entry Level Salary for Sales: ***$23,000***
Senior Level Salary for Sales: ***$50,000***

Benefits

medical/dental: **Yes**
life insurance: **Yes**
disability: **Yes**
travel allowance: **Yes**
company car: **Yes**
profit sharing plan: **N/A**
stock purchase plan: **Yes**

child care: **No**
retirement plan: **Yes**
savings investment plan: **N/A**
tuition assistance: **Yes**
relocation assistance: **Yes**
memberships: **No**

Corporate Culture Index   (1 = lowest, 10 = highest)

training: **7**
support: **8**
benefits: **9**

security: **8**
mobility: **9**
intangibles: **10**

Address: P.O. Box 1080, Louisville, KY 40201
Contact: Sales Department; telephone 502/585-1100

Brown-Forman, the seventh largest beverage supplier in the U.S., ranks 302nd on the Fortune 500 list. In 1987 it had net sales of $1.4 billion, up 9% from 1986.

Founded in Louisville, Kentucky, in 1870, Brown-Forman has grown into a diversified producer and marketer of high-quality consumer products best known for its premium labels: Jack Daniel's, Early Times, Martell, Canadian Mist, Old Bushmill's, Korbel, Fontana Candida, Bolla, Cella, and Noilly Prat, among others. Less widely known are Brown-Forman's more recent ventures into china, crystal, and glassware under the Lenox brand name, and premium-quality luggage under the Hartmann label.

The worldwide wine and spirits market is currently in the grips of what the company calls "evolving consumer attitudes and social values about the consumption of alcohol," but Brown-Forman continues to counter such ominous consumer trends by building on a powerful premium brand image to maintain and expand sales in this threatened market.

All things considered, the company has fared remarkably well during this difficult period, with its current income from wine and spirits at a level roughly twice that of 1980. Brown-Forman has stood its ground mainly by offering the most successful brands in the liquor business: Korbel, the nation's best-selling champagne; Jack Daniel's, America's best-selling premium whiskey; Bolla, America's premium wine—a track record maintained with the 1985 acquisition of California Wine Cooler, a leader in its own surging market.

Candidates are expected to be articulate, persuasive, and full of conviction, and to hold at least a BA degree. No sales experience or technical knowledge is required, however. Trainees go through a one-shot, ten-day training course at the company's Louisville headquarters (or alternatively at one of three training locations in Illinois, Massachusetts, or Mississippi). The course consists of videotaped sales presentations, classes in selling skills, and extensive one-on-one training in the field under the local district sales manager.

After training, new reps are evaluated by their district manager twice a month, with an eye toward promotion depending on their productivity. As new reps learn the ropes, they climb a predictable path from small territory to large, from minor to major accounts. Rapid promotion is possible because of the company's firm policy of hiring and promoting strictly from within. All management spots are filled by former reps.

Brown-Forman reps work on expense account, almost always alone, covering territories ranging in size from two rural states to one city neighborhood. Top management is accessible by a call to the district sales manager. The 3% to 6% turnover rate is relatively low for such a volatile industry and underscores the company's commitment to its sales staff's well-being. As elsewhere in the industry, reps rotate stock, set up displays, and do everything within legal limits to encourage wholesalers and retailers to buy their line of wines and spirits; this legally permissible conduct varies from state to state.

Reps take special pains to maintain a professional, dignified image, partly as a result of widespread image-pressure of the entire alcoholic beverages industry. The atmosphere is friendly and family-like (first-name-basis relationships are the rule), however, as befits an industry that thrives on conviviality.

The average trainee makes $23,000 a year plus a bonus of up to $4000. Senior salespeople routinely pull in $50,000, including a bonus of about 15% of sales. Brown-Forman's more than 150 reps sell solely to retailers and wholesale distributors, with strong support from their 15 branch sales offices around the country, which provide advertising and promotion materials; typing, filing, and other clerical assistance; and research.

Benefits include: dental and medical insurance, tuition assistance, life and disability insurance, stock purchase and retirement plans, a 401K plan, a travel allowance and company car, and paid relocation expenses. In addition, reps are entitled to discounts on Lenox china and Hartmann luggage, both Brown-Forman divisions.

Brown-Forman earns high marks for training, support, benefits, and job security as well as top marks for job mobility (promotion) and other intangibles. In an industry currently feeling the squeeze from MADD (Mothers Against Drunk Driving) and other such groups, Brown-Forman takes the top of the line wines and spirits to that large segment of the public still prepared to pay a premium price for premium taste.

THE COCA-COLA COMPANY

VITAL STATISTICS

Entry Level Salary for Sales: **$15,000–$16,000**
Senior Level Salary for Sales: **$30,000–$40,000**

Benefits

medical/dental: **Yes**
life insurance: **Yes**
disability: **Yes**
travel allowance: **Yes**
company car: **Yes**
profit sharing plan: **No**
stock purchase plan: **Yes**

child care: **No**
retirement plan: **Yes**
savings investment plan: **N/A**
tuition assistance: **Yes**
relocation assistance: **Yes**
memberships: **No**

Corporate Culture Index   (1 = lowest, 10 = highest)

training: **9**
support: **9**
benefits: **9**

security: **10**
mobility: **10**
intangibles: **10**

Address: 1 Coca-Cola Plaza, N.W., Atlanta, GA 30313
Contact: Personnel; telephone 404/676-2121 ext. 3931

Coca-Cola ranks 38th on the Fortune 500 list. The global Coca-Cola system provides full or part-time employment for more than a million people in 155 countries. Last year, retail sales totaled $50 billion.

Coca-Cola is, to say the least, one of the best-known companies in the world. It is the world's most recognized trademark and the center of the largest production and distribution system in the world. As the company noted in its most recent annual report, "The heart of the Coca-Cola Company is selling soft drinks to a thirsty world, one drink at a time, more than 524 million times a day, and counting."

But there's more to Coca-Cola than soft drinks. The company has been preparing itself for the 1990s by moving into new areas. It recently acquired Columbia Pictures, which it merged with Tri-Star Pictures to form the largest film company in the world. It was able to do this by taking advantage of the sound financial shape of the soft drink side of the business to finance entry into even more profitable ventures.

Coca-Cola's phenomenal success results not only from a high-quality product and solid financial management, but also from a top-notch sales force. Recently, *Sales & Marketing Management* magazine rated Coca-Cola's sales force as first in quality. Sales reps have played an especially important role as Coca-Cola has worked to overcome the disastrous introduction of "New Coke" into the market a few years back. While Max Headroom may be Coke's best-known salesman, he doesn't do it alone. Coca-Cola fields more than 750 sales reps across the country.

Coca-Cola looks for aggressive, high-energy people who can come up with new tactics and ideas. It likes to hire "generalists," who can understand a range of issues and deal comfortably with a wide variety of people (a college degree is a necessity). Coca-Cola provides training at every step of a rep's career to ensure success in his or her present position and proper preparation for the next.

The initial training lasts for three to six months and takes place in the field. It works like an apprenticeship—each trainee works one-on-one with a district sales manager. The trainee learns the daily ins and outs of the work, whether it's promoting new items, getting more shelf space, obtaining local advertising, or providing reliable marketing information back to Coca-Cola management. In addition, outside professionals teach classes on specific aspects of the business such as finance, selling skills, distribution, and management.

Trainees who complete the program are designated as territory managers and are assigned to a number of specific accounts (such as a specific fast-food chain) or to a geographic area. Either way, they deal with both wholesale distributors and retailers.

The size of a sales territory varies widely with population, and one rep could be responsible for the two Dakotas and Nebraska, whereas another might be responsible for just a few blocks in downtown Los Angeles. Reps generally work alone and usually spend one or two nights a week on the road. Financial and technical help is close at hand when they need it, and they are assured of as much advertising and promotional material as they need. The company regularly runs courses to teach reps new skills and keep them up to date with all company developments. This kind of training helps reps move up the corporate ladder. For example, one rep worked his way up from territory manager to district regional sales manager to vice president for the fountain division to senior vice president for marketing!

Salaries start at $15,000 and go as high as $40,000. Commissions can run as high as 25% of base salary and are strictly geared to "gallonage"— the more gallons of Coke you can sell, the greater your reward. Coca-Cola provides a full range of benefits: medical and dental insurance, a company car and travel allowance, tuition assistance, life insurance, retirement and disability benefits, a stock purchase plan, moving expenses, and child care.

Though Coca-Cola is an aggressive and dynamic company, it strives to maintain a warm and family-like atmosphere. Almost everyone works in shirt-sleeves, and people call one another by their first names. Coca-Cola has been around for nearly a century and sometimes seems as old as America itself. Yet its upbeat feel and innovative management along with the public's never-ending appetite for "the real thing" give it the feel of a young company with nothing but the future ahead.

PEPSICO, INC.

VITAL STATISTICS

Entry Level Salary for Sales: **$28,000**
Senior Level Salary for Sales: **$40,000**

Benefits:

medical/dental: **Yes**	child care: **Yes**
life insurance: **Yes**	retirement plan: **Yes**
disability: **Yes**	savings investment plan: **N/A**
travel allowance: **Yes**	tuition assistance: **Yes**
company car/truck: **Yes**	relocation assistance: **Yes**
profit sharing plan: **Yes**	memberships: **No**
stock purchase plan: **Yes**	

Corporate Culture Index (1 = lowest, 10 = highest)

training:	**8**	security:	**9**
support:	**9**	mobility:	**9**
benefits:	**9**	intangibles:	**9**

Address: Anderson Hill Road, Purchase, NY 10577
Contact: Personnel; telephone 914/253-2000

PepsiCo, Inc., ranks 29th on the Fortune 500 list. In 1987 it posted sales of $11.5 billion, up 26% from 1986. At the same time, profits of $605 million were 30% more than those in 1986.

PepsiCo, Inc., holds a leading position in three domestic U.S. markets: soft drinks, snack foods, and fast-food restaurants. With over 16,000 units, its restaurant system is the biggest in the world. Soft drinks are the largest selling product in supermarkets today, and the Pepsi brand is the "largest-selling brand of *all* brands, of any product, in all supermarket categories," according to PepsiCo's own findings. Frito-Lay, the nation's largest manufacturer and marketer of salty snacks, racked up its nineteenth consecutive year of sales growth in 1987 and has traditionally been PepsiCo's most profitable operating unit.

PepsiCo products have always been popular with teenagers and young adults. When the "baby boom" swelled these ranks, the company's sales naturally soared. Although many believed that as the baby boomer generation aged, demand for these same products would decline, that didn't happen. Instead, the maturing baby boomers have continued to eat the snack foods of their youth, and PepsiCo's sales show no sign of weakening.

To be sure, PepsiCo works very hard to keep its products contemporary and up to date, enabling the company to retain the brand loyalty of its customers over the years. The teen who drank Pepsi is now the 45-year-old adult who drinks Diet Pepsi. With snack foods, the trick is to continually offer new tastes to stimulate consumer interest but not to detract from sales of established favorites.

The demographics are also kind to PepsiCo's fast-food outlets. With more and more dual-income families and single people than ever before, the customer base of quick-food restaurants is expanding. Thus, in all its prime markets, PepsiCo sees excellent prospects for future growth by extending their lines, with no need for investing profits in unfamiliar industries or distantly related ventures. PepsiCo's strategy of continued growth in sales and profitability is based on servicing just those markets in which its expertise is strongest.

The route to a sales job at PepsiCo is just that—the job of route manager. The Frito-Lay division fields a sales force of more than 10,000 route managers who sell and deliver fresh products to more than 400,000 accounts. The route managers stock the Frito-Lay snacks directly onto the supermarket shelves; the only time supermarket personnel handle the products is when the customers bring them to the checkout counter. This labor-intensive system of sales and distribution gives the company several significant benefits. First, it ensures that all Frito-Lay products are fresh and in good condition on the shelves, which is important for customer satisfaction. Second, it provides the company with immediate inventory control information, allowing it to plan production and distribution more efficiently. Finally, it reduces supermarket labor costs, making Frito-Lay products that much more profitable.

Preparing for a route manager's job involves heavy on-the-job training, with the trainee and district manager going over the route, working through the training manuals and procedures, and so on. Initially, there is a week of classroom work on selling skills, route management, and other subjects. This is followed by field work and two weeks of study. Route managers must also learn to use the company's hand-held computers. The computers reduce paperwork, keep close track of orders, and allow managers more time to sell. The immediate feedback from the computers allows Frito-Lay to monitor sales quickly, immediately assess the effect of product promotions, and promptly adjust production and delivery as necessary.

Candidates for route manager positions do not need any specific educational background, although a college education is a definite plus. Selling experience is very helpful, but what the company looks for most is drive and determination. The hours are long and the work is hard. Route sales reps are out all day, selling, making deliveries, rotating stock on the shelves, setting up displays, and helping the retail outlet owners and managers move the product.

Salaries for beginning route managers average $28,000, with senior salespeople averaging around $40,000. Salaries are augmented by both bonuses and incentives, but the amounts and percents depend on the location, the types of accounts, and other factors. Other benefits are quite extensive: medical and dental insurance plans, group life insurance, disability and retirement plans, profit sharing and stock purchasing plans, child care, tuition assistance, paid moving expenses, and a company route truck. For additional support, there is Frito-Lay's—and PepsiCo's—commitment to new products and to keeping their brands fresh and contemporary. For instance, in line with today's concerns about health and fitness, Frito-Lay is looking for ways to offer snack choices that reflect nutritional preferences. It has already begun test-marketing a new low-oil concept in snacks. Light brands promise to offer the same snack taste, but with lower fat content, giving PepsiCo an opportunity to meet emerging consumer needs and give its sales force added punch.

More importantly, for those reps who show industry, perseverance, ability, and sales savvy, there are many opportunities for career advancement. Although route managers work mostly on their own, their work is closely monitored and doing well draws attention. In a company as large as PepsiCo, there are many places to go and many different kinds of accounts to sell. Sales personnel are tapped for management positions; the present Frito-Lay training director, for example, worked a route for three years before becoming national head of training. At PepsiCo, performance counts, and hard-working, hard-selling reps will be noticed.

JOSEPH E. SEAGRAM & SONS, INC.

VITAL STATISTICS

Entry Level Salary for Sales: **$20,000**
Senior Level Salary for Sales: **$35,000**

Benefits

medical/dental: **Yes**	child care: **No**
life insurance: **Yes**	retirement plan: **Yes**
disability: **Yes**	savings investment plan: **N/A**
travel allowance: **Yes**	tuition assistance: **Yes**
company car: **Yes**	relocation assistance: **Yes**
profit sharing plan: **Yes**	memberships: **Weight Watchers**
stock purchase plan: **Yes**	**Smokenders**
	Health Club dues,
	in NYC
	$150 annual liquor
	allowance

Corporate Culture Index (1 = lowest, 10 = highest)

training:	**8**	security:	**8**
support:	**8**	mobility:	**9**
benefits:	**10**	intangibles:	**8**

Address: 374 Park Avenue, New York, NY 10152
Contact: Personnel; telephone 212/572-7155

Joseph E. Seagram & Sons, Inc. ranks 192nd on the Fortune 500 list. In 1987 it posted sales of more than $2 billion, up 12% from 1986. Its 1987 profits, at $338 million, were up 37% from 1986.

Joseph E. Seagram & Sons is the U.S. group of the Seagram Company, Ltd., headquartered in Canada. The parent group has international interests as well, and its combined sales for 1987 amounted to more than $3.8 billion. The main product of the company is spirits, more specifically high-quality whiskies, although in recent years it has branched into the wine cooler business and into the nonalcoholic beverage industry with the purchase of Tropicana and its line of premium branded fruit juices and juice beverages.

In the U.S. the spirits industry, like the cigarette industry, is feeling somewhat defensive. With the current emphasis on health and physical fitness, spirits—and to a lesser extent wines—have had a certain amount of trouble holding their own as beverages of choice. Seagram has always advocated a policy of moderation in the use of wine and liquor, and it now promotes wines and spirits as an adjunct of the good life, a sign of sophistication and good taste. It concentrates on the concepts of quality and tradition in the use of its products and makes its appeals especially to upscale consumers.

Joseph E. Seagram markets spirits and wines, some of which are agency brands—products that Seagram does not own but for which it acts as selling agent—with the rest under its own labels. Among the major agency brands are: Jameson Irish Whiskey and wines from C. K. Mondavi, the Charles Krug Winery, and Mirassou Vineyards. Other international brands handled by Joseph E. Seagram include: Barton and Guestier wines, Chivas Regal 12-year-old Scotch, Mumm Champagne, Sandeman Port and Sherry, and the Glenlivet Single Malt Scotch Whisky. (*Note:* When the product is Scottish or Canadian, it is spelled "whisky"; when it is American or Irish, it is spelled "whiskey.") The Seagram Chateau & Estate Wines Company also handles Perrier-Jouët Champagne and wines from the dominant European vineyards.

Additional major Seagram brands on the U.S. market include, among others: Boodles Gin, Seagram's Extra Dry Gin, Lord Calvert Canadian Whisky, Seagram's 7 Crown Blended Whiskey, Seagram's Wine Coolers, Wolfschmidt Vodka, and wines from Mumm's Cuvée Napa, Sterling Vineyards, and the Monterey Vineyard. The Tropicana line represents an expansion of the company into nonalcoholic beverages.

The restructuring of Joseph E. Seagram's sales and marketing companies in 1987 strengthened the company's sales of its major spirits brands—particularly Chivas Regal, V.O., 7 Crown, and Seagram's Gin. At the same time, Seagram's Wine Coolers gained the number-one position in a still relatively new market. Sales of Perrier-Jouët increased substantially, making it the third highest selling champagne in the U.S. behind Mumm, with Brown-Forman's Korbel the leader. Nevertheless, and despite the wide variety of products on the market, whisky "remains at the heart of Seagram's business and worldwide prominence." Here Seagram meets a major challenge in finding how to use innovation and ingenuity to revitalize a mature market. One strategy is to encourage consumers to think of Chivas Regal, a premium scotch, not only as a drink for special occasions but also as one that makes any occasion special.

Seagram looks for new reps who are outgoing, aggressive, and bright. They are usually college graduates, but that is not necessary, nor is prior sales experience. Reps are trained in the field (there are seven regions) for six to nine months. The training involves three initial segments (company orientation, sales training, and merchandising), followed by a period of on-the-job-training in the field, and finally a session on advanced selling and merchandising. The training sessions continue throughout a rep's selling career at Seagram, and there is a definite career path that reps can follow from sales rep to state sales manager to regional sales manager to vice president of sales. Reps, of course, can keep selling if they want to, but Seagram hires people whom it considers to be promotable and it sets its reward system in such a way that management-track positions pay more than sales rep positions. Opportunities exist in marketing and merchandising, too, once the rep has been successful in the field.

Seagram reps sell in a three-tier marketing system, as do reps of other companies in the field. Seagram sells mainly to its distributors (including large chain stores and drugstores—where allowed by state law—and to state-controlled package stores as well), who sell to retail outlets, who sell to the individual customer. Reps, however, also make sales to retail stores, and, with the addition of wine coolers and Tropicana products, began calling on grocery chains and supermarkets, too. As with other retail selling, the reps must be able to set up displays, rotate stock, vie for optimum shelf space, and use the company's significant print advertising to increase sales. Reps work alone and make calls constantly. Territories are not generally large geographically, however, so there are few overnights.

Salaries for trainees average about $20,000 with another $2000 from the bonus plan, making a total of about $22,000. Senior salespeople make about $35,000 plus about another $5000 in bonuses for a total of $40,000. The bonus plan is based on several components: corporate objectives, division objectives, and "behavioral objectives." (Behavioral objectives involve personal goals set for the rep by the company.) Other benefits include: medical, dental, and life insurance; disability and retirement plans; profit sharing and stock purchasing plans; tuition assistance (100%); paid relocation expenses; a liquor allowance ($150 per year); and a company car.

The atmosphere at Seagram is corporate but friendly. It is a family-run business, but it stresses innovation and aggressiveness in selling as well as quality and tradition in its products. Although the line may not be for everyone, Seagram has a solid reputation, a classy array of products, and an industry which may lack runaway growth potential but which is, at the very least, recession resistant.

CHEMICALS AND PLASTIC PRODUCTS

Most of us think of chemistry as something having to do with beakers and test tubes. That's partially true, but it's not the whole story. The work of American chemical manufacturers may begin in the laboratory, but it ends up in virtually every home, farm, and workplace in the country. The chemical industry has many facets—it's intellectually stimulating and politically sensitive (owing to strict government regulation). And it's very profitable. In 1987, the American chemical industry saw an 8% increase in sales, to $26 billion, and a whopping 29% increase in net profits, to the tune of nearly $16 billion. And the future looks good.

Chemical manufacturers make many things: soaps, cosmetics, paints, perfumes, plastics, antifreeze, fibers, and fuels, to name a few. Nearly half of the industry's activity is accounted for by petrochemicals, chemical products derived from petroleum or natural gas. Declining oil prices have given a big boost to manufacturers of petrochemicals, which are key components of synthetic rubbers and fibers, plastics, and fertilizers.

As you can see, the chemical industry plays a major role in a heavily industrial economy. That's why it does well here in the United States and abroad, in both industrial and developing countries—so well that it's one of the few major American industries that regularly runs a trade surplus. And that's probably why its stocks have been especially attractive to foreign investors, who currently own 30% of the American chemical industry.

Intelligent chemical companies have diversified in the 1980s to protect themselves from OPEC's whims and from future industrial downturns. In particular, many have turned to consumer products, which will always be in demand, as a hedge against hard times. For example, Dow Chemical has made itself a household name with Saran Wrap, cleansers, and Ziploc storage bags, and Du Pont has been manufacturing Stainmaster carpets and biomedical drugs.

The chemical industry is heavily regulated by the federal government. Meeting government requirements eats up $2.5 billion industry-wide every year. Most of the programs regulating the industry are administered by the Environmental Protection Agency, which, despite the cutbacks of the Reagan years, is still going strong. Some phases of the industry that are subject to regulation are: treating and disposing of hazardous and toxic wastes (this includes cleaning up old and poorly designed waste dumps), introducing possibly dangerous chemicals into the workplace and testing and labeling them accordingly, and synthesizing chemicals from natural resources. This public-policy dimension is unique to the chemical industry, and it creates special challenges as industries try to work with, and not against, the government.

Research and development is an especially significant element of the chemical industry. In the past decade, R&D has grown by nearly 13% a year and now stands at nearly $10 billion industry-wide. This is one of the few industries where the work of scholars and researchers translates directly into new products and avenues for sales. With our scientific knowledge growing every day, new horizons emerge from the laboratory. A few decades ago, who had ever heard of silicon or even plastic?

In recent years, many chemical companies restructured and streamlined themselves so as to be leaner and more competitive in the future. Laboratories promise to discover and create as many new chemicals and chemical products as society can find use for. As one industry analyst recently put it, "The fun isn't over."

TRADE ASSOCIATIONS

American Chemical Society 202/872-4600
Sales Association of the Chemical Industry 212/686-1952

PERIODICALS

Chemical Processing
Chemical Week
Modern Plastics
Plastics World

AMERICAN CYANAMID COMPANY

VITAL STATISTICS

Entry Level Salary for Sales: **$31,000**
Senior Level Salary for Sales: **$50,000**

Benefits

medical/dental: **Yes**
life insurance: **Yes**
disability: **Yes, short and long term**
travel allowance: **Yes**
company car: **Yes**
profit sharing plan: **Yes**
stock purchase plan: **Yes**

child care: **No**
retirement plan: **Yes**
savings investment plan: **Yes**
tuition assistance: **Yes**
relocation assistance: **N/A**
memberships: **Smokenders**
Weight Watchers
On-site fitness
center

Corporate Culture Index   (1 = lowest, 10 = highest)

training: **8**
support: **8**
benefits: **10**

security: **9**
mobility: **8**
intangibles: **10**

Address: One Cyanamid Plaza, Wayne, NJ 07470
Contact: Manager, Personnel Administration; telephone 201/831-2000

American Cyanamid Company ranks 106th on the Fortune 500 list. In 1987 it enjoyed sales of more than $4 billion, up 9% from 1986. Profits for the same period were $276 million, an increase of 36% from 1986.

American Cyanamid is a leading research-based biotechnology and chemical company. It develops, manufactures, and markets medical, agricultural, chemical, and consumer products on a worldwide basis. It operates 19 research laboratories and about 100 plants, and its 19 divisions sell more than 3000 products in more than 135 countries. Cyanamid has more than 34,000 employees worldwide, with about one-third of them working outside the U.S. The company operates four business groups: Medical, Agricultural, Chemicals, and Shulton (consumer products).

The Medical Group comprises several divisions, of which Lederle Laboratories is the largest. Lederle discovers, manufactures, and markets prescription pharmaceuticals, generic compounds, vaccines, vitamins, and nutritional supplements around the world. Its major research efforts are in the areas of anticancer drugs, cardiovascular drugs, and antibiotics. With $1.6 billion in sales, the Medical Group contributes about 40% of Cyanamid's revenue and is the company's most profitable business.

The Agricultural Group concentrates its operations in three major commercial areas: crop protection chemicals, animal nutrition and health, and vegetation and pest control management. The Chemicals Group produces more than 2000 different substances used in 14 major industries, ranging from aerospace and automotive to plastics and paper manufacturing. Shulton markets some of the world's best-known consumer products, including Old Spice (men's fragrances and toiletries), Pierre Cardin fragrances, Pine Sol liquid cleaner, Breck hair-care products, and Combat roach killer.

With so many disparate businesses, sales reps at Cyanamid can find just about any kind of selling niche. Training, compensation, and markets will vary with different divisions and product lines, but in general Cyanamid trains its reps to work and think independently. Sales reps receive formal instruction as well as on-the-job training. This discussion concentrates on the position of sales rep in the Chemicals Group. Selling for the Medical Group is similar to selling for any other pharmaceuticals company marketing prescription drugs, and selling for the consumer group is similar to selling for other mass consumer product manufacturers.

The Chemicals Group, a billion-dollar business in 1987, has been troubled with increased competition from abroad and with the need to upgrade old manufacturing plants to comply with new environmental laws. It does not have the profit margins that Cyanamid is looking for, but it has moved ahead with its growth strategies, which are based on taking advantage of its new technologies and on modernizing plants and equipment to lower costs and increase profits. Another facet of the strategy is to promote sales with aggressive marketing.

Some of the division's main products are resins and adhesives, "ingredient products," that can be used in car paint, for instance, or paper or appliances or beer cans. The sales force of 200 is divided into industry groupings, and a rep might sell only paint to the automotive industry or paper chemicals to the paper industry. A rep might write up an order for a train-load of materials for Ford or Du Pont, for example. Reps tend to work alone, but in some areas or on some special accounts there is team selling. Reps' territories vary in size, from a local area to a territory covering several states. Reps generally call on retailers and wholesale distributors, and they commonly demonstrate certain products, especially ones used in the paper industry and in water treatment facilities.

Candidates for the sales rep position in this division need to have a college degree with a technical background in, for example, chemistry or chemical engineering. Prior selling experience is helpful, but it is not necessary. All reps undergo a four-week training program given at headquarters in Wayne, New Jersey, that focuses on company policies, safety, and sales skills. In addition, there is one to six months of technical training with a concentration on product knowledge and industry information before a rep is given a sales assignment.

Advancement opportunities are excellent at Cyanamid, with a definite career ladder in the Chemicals Group: from sales rep to assistant to the marketing manager, regional manager, business manager, and general manager. Company policy encourages promotion from within. Additional support takes the form of first-rate ad and promotion materials, administrative/clerical help, when possible, and an especially strong commitment to R&D to bring out new and improved products. Increasingly, the division is becoming known for its high-tech contributions to the aerospace industry, and Cyanamid policy is aimed at getting into the high-risk, high-reward, high-tech business, where it believes its heavy commitment to R&D will really pay off.

Average starting salary for sales rep trainees is about $31,000, with senior salespeople averaging about $50,000. Bonuses can go as high as 40% of salary, but they depend on three factors: regional profitability, overall sales growth, and meeting specific, individual objectives. Other benefits include: medical, dental, and life insurance; disability and retirement plans; a stock purchase plan; a profit sharing plan (dependent on company performance); a 401K plan; tuition assistance (up to 100%); and a company car.

Cyanamid has a corporate, strict, formal atmosphere. It is high-tech and professional, but it is now more people-oriented than before, more open to discussion of corporate policies, and more receptive to new ideas. With its numerous career paths, diverse markets, and devotion to R&D, it offers its reps solid prospects for future growth.

CONSTAR INTERNATIONAL INC.

VITAL STATISTICS

Entry Level Salary for Sales: **$25,000**
Senior Level Salary for Sales: **$40,000–$50,000**

Benefits

medical/dental: **Yes**	child care: **No**
life insurance: **Yes**	retirement plan: **Yes**
disability: **Yes, short and long term**	savings investment plan: **N/A**
travel allowance: **Yes**	tuition assistance: **Yes**
company car: **Yes**	relocation assistance: **Yes**
profit sharing plan: **No**	memberships: **No**
stock purchase plan: **No**	

Corporate Culture Index   (1 = lowest, 10 = highest)

training:	**10**	security:	**9**
support:	**9**	mobility:	**8** *(low turnover)*
benefits:	**8**	intangibles:	**9**

Address: P.O. Box 6339, Chattanooga, TN 37401-6339
Contact: Human Resources; telephone 404/691-4256

Constar International Inc. enjoyed sales of more than $450 million in 1987, up 15% from 1986. Net profits for 1986, at $9.6 million, were up only 2% from 1986, trailing 1985's $10.7 million.

Constar International Inc. not only changed its name in 1987, it also refocused its energies. In that year, the company completed the sale of Dorsey Trailers, a business it had been in for more than 27 years, and changed its name from the Dorsey Corporation to Constar International. The switch signaled a shift of the company's resources to maintaining and enhancing its leadership in the plastic packaging industry, where its mainstay is Sewell Plastics, a wholly owned subsidiary. Another of Constar's interests is the Bickford Family Fare chain of restaurants, a New England-based operation that the company believes has solid prospects for future growth.

Constar's main business is producing plastic containers, which accounts for over 90% of the company's sales. Sewell Plastics is the country's largest maker of plastic containers, and because of its innovation, quality, and service, it is the preferred supplier for a growing list of major customers.

Constar's strategy is to pursue its leadership in the plastic container area, developing new products and improving its services. With the addition in 1987 of plastic bottle plants purchased from Owens-Illinois, Constar established itself as a leading supplier in a seemingly endless growth market; the thirst for soft drinks in plastic bottles seems all but unslakeable. In addition, many other consumer items like salad dressings, mustard, coffee, peanut butter, barbecue sauce, liquor, and motor oil are now packaged for the first time in plastic containers, which has made the management at Sewell very happy.

Constar now has 23 strategically located production facilities in 16 states from which it can effectively supply its customers' needs on a nationwide basis. These production facilities are backed up by a sophisticated technical, engineering, and product development team based in Atlanta, whose job is to devise still more effective, attractive, and cost-competitive plastic containers. Constar now produces plastic packaging from many different kinds of plastic materials, like polyethylene, polypropylene, and polyvinylchloride. Plastic soft drink containers are made from PET, which is one of the most popular of all plastic materials, and Constar's R&D group is a leader in the development of technological advances for its use.

One cloud on the plastic packages horizon involves environmental issues. Not being biodegradable, plastic presents a real problem of disposability. Constar is a leader in fostering the recycling of plastic products, which, some may be surprised to learn, have a number of uses in their recycled state. For example, recycled soft drink bottles can be made into such items as paint brushes and fiberfill for pillows, sleeping bags, and ski jackets, and can be used in the production of bathtubs, lumber, floor tiles, and automobile parts. Sewell Plastics is actively engaged in this process and, as a member of several plastic recycling industry groups, is pursuing the goal of recycling 50% of the soft drink containers sold in the U.S. by 1992, as compared to 20% in 1987.

Constar reps call on large manufacturers such as major bottlers, soap and bleach factories, beverage companies, and the like. Reps get to know their customers, learn their needs, and propose suitable Sewell containers. Where necessary, reps obtain specs for customized bottles from the customer and use the production people at Sewell to develop a product that fills the bill. Reps build partnerships with their customers that eventually turn into long-term sales relationships. They normally do not have to demonstrate Constar products; customers know pretty much what they need and the rep's job is to learn each customer's particular requirements and fill them.

Constar looks for new reps who are college grads, preferably with a technical degree. Sales experience is not necessary, but technical knowledge is very helpful. Reps will be dealing with customer specs for plastic packaging—weight and thickness requirements, strength, and special properties dictated by the substances the bottle will contain, for instance; so they must be comfortable with these kinds of problems and be able to handle them effectively.

Training is a lengthy process which takes place on and off for two years with limited sales calls (on-the-job training) in between. Reps are rotated through many different departments of the company. The initial six months of training takes place at headquarters in Chattanooga, followed by stints in the sales service department and at a plant where the bottles are made.

Salaries for sales trainees average about $25,000, with senior salespeople earning from about $40,000 to $50,000. In addition, the company offers "incentives" based on achieving certain goals and quotas. Constar prefers incentives to commissions because it feels that commission reps might not provide the level of service it expects. The company does, however, provide first-rate technical support, and the turnover among reps is low.

Other benefits include: medical, dental, and life insurance; disability and retirement plans; a 401K savings plan; paid relocation expenses; tuition assistance of 100%; and a company car. The company does prefer to promote from within, but because it is still relatively small, there is not a lot of room for growth—yet. Given the demand for plastic bottles and packages, though, and the fact that this demand seems largely resistant to swings in the economy, Constar appears to be a good bet for the long haul.

THE DOW CHEMICAL COMPANY

VITAL STATISTICS

Entry Level Salary for Sales: *$26,000–$30,000*
Senior Level Salary for Sales: *$55,000–$60,000*

Benefits

medical/dental: **Yes**
life insurance: **Yes**
disability: **Yes**
travel allowance: **N/A**
company car: **No**
profit sharing plan: **No**
stock purchase plan: **Yes**

child care: **Yes**
retirement plan: **Yes**
savings investment plan: **N/A**
tuition assistance: **Yes**
relocation assistance: **Yes**
memberships: **Yes, for senior sales personnel**

Corporate Culture Index (1 = lowest, 10 = highest)

training: **10**
support: **9**
benefits: **9**

security: **10**
mobility: **8**
intangibles: **9**

Address: 2030 Williard H. Dow Center, Midland, MI 48674
Contact: University Relations and Recruiting; telephone 517/636-2177

The Dow Chemical Company ranks 24th on the Fortune 500 list. Sales in 1987 went over $13 billion, up 20% from 1986, positioning Dow as the second largest chemical producer in the U.S. (exceeded only by Du Pont).

Dow products, from Saran Wrap to the polycarbonate plastics used in compact discs and car parts, pervade the country. The company's main business, however, has been in basic commodity chemicals and plastics, which used to account for 80% of its output. In the 1980s Dow moved strongly into what it believes is its future—engineered plastics and more advanced chemicals. To this end, in 1986, for the first time, Dow split its sales 50/50 between basic and specialty products.

When the oil crunch hit in the 1970s, with costs going through the roof, Dow found it hard going to keep up high production of basic petroleum-based plastics. However, when oil prices dropped back into the $19 to $20 per barrel range, there was a resurgence in the plastics market. More to the point, Dow found that the trend for success in this marketplace lay in engineered plastics that sold for $10 to $12 a pound rather than the ordinary 59-cents-a-pound plastics. Pursuing this more highly developed type of product, Dow moved into polycarbonates. The policy seems to be working because in 1987, Dow's second quarter sales were the best of any three-month period in the company's history.

This is not to imply that Dow is neglecting its basic consumer and pharmaceutical markets. It is still a giant in household products (Ziploc bags, Saran Wrap, cleansers, and so on). Pharmaceuticals still lead Dow's Consumer Specialties division with $934 million in sales for 1986. These include both prescription drugs and over-the-counter items like chewing gum, allergy preparations, and antihistamines. The thrust is for the company to pursue its huge basic market (consumer and industrial) with ever more sophisticated, upscale products while establishing itself as a leader in all new high-tech chemical areas.

To accomplish this, Dow needs a highly trained, sophisticated sales force, able to handle a wide variety of products in a number of different markets. In addition, a Dow sales rep routinely has responsibility for accounts worth $5 to $10 million. A single order that a sales rep writes up may be delivered in a freight car. Thus Dow is looking for candidates who can take on varied responsibilities, can be innovative in meeting new situations, and can cope with very competitive markets.

To train new reps to carry out these functions, Dow has instituted a comprehensive sales training program that lasts for a year. There is no expense involved for the new hire, and the training takes place both at the headquarters in Midland, Michigan, and in the field. The first three weeks of orientation are at Midland. Then the program alternates between several months in the office and several months in the field. There are some classes, but much of the training is conducted on a one-on-one basis.

The program is carefully monitored all along the way, with evaluation of the new hire taking place every three months by a three-person team. The evaluations serve a dual purpose. They provide feedback to the reps on how well they are mastering the material and techniques taught. They also provide for career tracking, since after the first year, trainees are allowed to choose the division in which they wish to work. They are exposed to different kinds of accounts so that they can become familiar with the range of Dow products and markets; it is then up to them to choose which areas they want to pursue.

Dow does not require any special technical knowledge or sales experience from its sales trainees. It does look for a college degree (BA/BS), generally in business or a technical subject (a college background in chemistry, technology, or business is a definite asset). A liberal arts major with drive and talent, however, will be in the running, too.

Because Dow is competing with other blue-chip companies for the best graduates, it offers an attractive starting salary ranging from $26,000 to $30,000. The salary for senior account managers ranges from $55,000 to $60,000 plus a bonus of 5%–7%. The reps generally work on their own, but in some cases a service technician is brought in to help close a sale, or another sales rep from a distant state may be flown in to help nail down a contract. As you can see, Dow considers sales the work of many hands, not just the product of the one who wrote the order. That's why the position is completely salaried with no commissions. A "company performance" bonus and a contingency bonus are awarded if the company as a whole does well.

Sales reps normally cover a territory comprising two states and must expect to spend two nights a week on the road. They receive an expense account and a company car. Dow reps generally do not install or demonstrate products; their customers usually know what they want. Reps sell from a catalogue, but they are expected to instruct their accounts on new chemicals and their uses. They are also expected to service their existing accounts and to secure new ones in their territories. They are responsible for making their territories grow.

Benefits are excellent. They include: medical, dental, life, and disability insurance; retirement plans; tuition assistance; profit sharing; a stock purchase plan; and child care. Other support, such as administrative help, promotion materials and new product information, and leading research staffs, gives reps a big edge in selling and in teaching customers about new Dow products.

Dow is a major corporation and it makes major demands on its employees. It looks for an aggressive and dynamic sales force capable of succeeding in a competitive marketplace. It knows the image it wants to project and expects its employees to follow through, as in the case of its dress code. At the same time, Dow recognizes and rewards talent. It promotes *totally* from within. It is ready to commit significant company resources to help a rep complete an important sale. It offers top-grade benefits and competitive salaries. What's the bottom line? Sales force turnover is low, a telling fact that speaks of the satisfaction of the sales reps.

E. I. DU PONT DE NEMOURS AND COMPANY

VITAL STATISTICS

Entry Level Salary for Sales: **N/A**
Senior Level Salary for Sales: **N/A**

Benefits

medical/dental: **Yes**	child care: **Flexible spending account**
life insurance: **Yes**	
disability: **Yes**	retirement plan: **Yes**
travel allowance: **Yes**	savings investment plan: **Yes**
company car: **Yes**	tuition assistance: **Yes**
profit sharing plan: **No**	relocation assistance: **Yes**
stock purchase plan: **Yes**	memberships: **No**

Corporate Culture Index   (1 = lowest, 10 = highest)

training:	**9**	security:	**10**
support:	**9**	mobility:	**9**
benefits:	**9**	intangibles:	**10**

Address: 1007 Market Street, Wilmington, DE 19898
Contact: Professional Staffing, Employee Relations Department; telephone 302/774-1000

E. I. du Pont de Nemours ranks 9th on the Fortune 500 list. In 1987 it posted more than $30 billion in sales, an increase of 12% from 1986. Profits of $1.7 billion for that period were up 16%.

With the development of nylon in 1938, du Pont ushered in the new age of synthetic fibers and materials science that has changed and is still changing the way we live. It is not just the flood of new products with new applications that distinguishes du Pont, however. It is the company's long-time concentration on applying advanced technologies to solve increasingly complex materials problems that sets it apart and accounts for its enormous success. R&D (research and development) has been—and still is—a major driving force behind du Pont's growth. The company has regularly been ranked with the top companies in the world in total R&D

expenditures, and it also scores near the top in research expenditures as a percentage of sales. It is the largest chemical company in the U.S.

Du Pont, moreover, was well positioned to take advantage of the shift in recent years to global markets. It manufactures in more than 35 countries and markets in more than 150. Today, about 40% of its total sales originate abroad, and it expects that figure to balloon to about 50% in the 1990s. In addition, it supports pioneering research in a number of important areas: agricultural and industrial chemicals, biomedical products, coal, fibers, industrial and consumer products, petroleum (exploration, production, refining, marketing, and transportation), and polymer products.

R&D is a vital part of du Pont's success, but it by no means explains the whole of it. Other companies have excellent research facilities as well. To ensure its continued success in the modern competitive world, du Pont has moved to forge close links between its research and its marketing people. It saw that, as today's customers demand ever more sophisticated materials, the lead time between discovery and application grows ever shorter. True, chemical companies need major research capabilities to be competitive, but they also need to have market-responsive research that is flexible and attuned to changes in the market and different customer needs.

All modern chemical companies face the same problem, but du Pont tries to create products that fit its customers' desires and needs, rather than trying to fit its customers into what it does best. Nowhere is this realignment of priorities more evident than in the way the company selects its sales staff.

The typical du Pont sales rep is quite atypical as far as sales reps go. Du Pont reps are generally older, in their late 20s at least, and more likely are in their early 30s. This is the result of a requirement that they spend three or four years in the company *before* being tapped for sales. The reps are also more highly educated and trained than most other sales reps. They frequently have engineering degrees and have worked in a du Pont plant or in R&D as a technician. Part of every manager's job at du Pont is to be on the lookout for bright, outgoing, people-oriented researchers and scientists who might have real sales potential. As a result, sales at du Pont is not an entry-level position but a career path that a skilled technician with the right qualifications may choose. A technical background is a must (acquired as an engineer in any one of a variety of specialties, including biochemistry, pharmacology, and statistics).

Training for the position of sales rep is quite extensive, even on top of the years the candidate has already put in working for the company. Reps are trained for at least 150 days before they ever set foot in their territories. The training programs vary, however, according to the product lines and markets the rep will serve. In addition to getting down to the nitty gritty of sales (pricing, the legal aspects of selling, using the company's dictation system), the training is focused on orienting the new rep to du Pont's approach to selling. Reps learn the vital importance of developing close customer relationships. As valuable as the immediate sale is, more important to du Pont is that the rep become a consultant to the customer, one who can bring the vast resources of du Pont to bear on that customer's needs and concerns. Because du Pont reps have spent such a long time with the company before selling, they know what the company can do, what buttons to push to get things done, and where to look for exactly the right solution to a particular problem. As a result, du Pont reps are able to offer their accounts not just an enormous laundry list of products, but also incredible expertise and understanding.

Salaries for reps are directly related to the industries they service, and du Pont services a broad array. Compensation, however, is at the top end of the industry average because du Pont knows the value of its reps and is willing to pay them well. The compensation plan also includes "incentives" designed to reward selling both for today and in the future, in an attempt to escape the tyranny of short-term awards for quick sales. For instance, the company will reward the sale of a truck-load of semiconductors this week, and it will also reward the rep for the *idea* of using the same semiconductors for a product still on another customer's drawing board. Other benefits include: medical, dental, and life insurance; disability and retirement plans; a stock purchase plan with savings; tuition assistance; paid relocation expenses; and a company car.

Most reps have a home office, and their territories vary greatly in size. They spend most of their time on the road, however, which in some cases can mean many overnights. Reps work mostly alone, but they do also work in "business teams." They focus on their customers, not only selling them du Pont products, but also lending them du Pont's expertise. All this, plus the low turnover and high promotability, makes du Pont a great place to be a rep.

HOECHST CELANESE CORPORATION

VITAL STATISTICS

Entry Level Salary for Sales: **$24,000**
Senior Level Salary for Sales: **$50,000**

Benefits

medical/dental: **Yes**	child care: **No**
life insurance: **Yes**	retirement plan: **Yes**
disability: **Yes**	savings investment plan: **N/A**
travel allowance: **Yes**	tuition assistance: **Yes**
company car: **Yes**	relocation assistance: **Yes**
profit sharing plan: **Yes**	memberships: **No**
stock purchase plan: **No**	

Corporate Culture Index (1 = lowest, 10 = highest)

training:	**9**	security:	**7**
support:	**7**	mobility:	**7**
benefits:	**8**	intangibles:	**8**

Address: Route 202-206 North, Somerville, NJ 08876
Contact: Human Resources; telephone 201/231-3225

Hoechst Celanese ranks 6th in the chemicals industry and 91st on the Fortune 500 list. In 1987 the company earned $169 million on sales of $4.6 billion, up 347% from 1986.

The Hoechst Celanese Corporation was formed in 1987 from a merger of American Hoechst with Celanese Corporation. Now, the company is a subsidiary of the West German chemicals conglomerate Hoechst AG, a leading producer of man-made fibers, films, chemicals, and other synthetic materials.

At the heart of this company's success lies one of the most advanced R&D efforts in operation, a performance in the applied sciences that has led to the development of man-made fibers that feel like the real thing, but are more stain-resistant, fire-proof, and clearly superior to natural fibers in a whole host of industrial applications.

In its 1987 annual report, Hoechst called its corporate philosophy "High Chem," which the company defined as "the synergistic blending of chemistry and other sciences, with the objectives of improving the quality of life, preserving the environment, helping to shape the future of mankind" and last but not least, making a huge profit.

Hoechst's various divisions comprise a number of world leaders in their respective product categories: The Chemical Group, American's number-one supplier of basic organic chemicals; Fibers and Film, the world leader in high-denier polyester filaments used in seat belts, fabrics, tire cord, and other webbings; Textile Fibers, makers of Trevira polyester and Celebrate acetate, the most popular brand-name synthetic fibers on the market today; and Life Sciences, producers of a wide range of advanced pharmaceutical products.

At the heart of this effort to synthesize practically everything are the miracles of modern chemistry. So it's not altogether surprising that some prior sales experience is helpful but not a prerequisite for a rep, whereas a college degree most certainly is.

The highly organized training program lasts 18 months, with classes conducted at the New Jersey headquarters, followed by on-the-job training in the field at various regional offices. Training continues at regular intervals after this preliminary course, with a view toward promotion to top management within the company, a firm corporate policy. An average sales trainee's salary runs $24,000, whereas a senior executive can pull in more than $50,000. There is also a quarterly bonus based on performance.

Other benefits include: medical and dental insurance, tuition assistance, life insurance, disability, retirement, travel allowance, profit sharing, 401K, relocation expenses, and company cafeteria.

The amount of time a rep spends on the road varies from product to product and territory to territory. In pharmaceutical sales, reps call on doctors to explain and sometimes demonstrate wares. Pharmaceutical reps frequently train physicians in the proper use of the company's most recent products.

Sales supports, critical in a field that relies on up-to-the-minute information, consists mainly of distributing the latest advertising and promotional materials at bimonthly sales meetings with regional sales managers.

Since this is a company known for its highly trained, highly educated, thoroughly professional sales staff, a polished appearance is par for the course, along with an extremely disciplined sales effort.

With such esoteric products as laser-driven fiber optics, high-storage optical recording disks, and a liquid crystal polymer designed to replace metal in a whole host of products, salespeople have their work cut out for them. This is fast-paced, demanding work. With products like these, you can take that BS degree from the shelf, dust it off, and start selling your customers high-density polymer yarns suitable for—well, that's your job to know and theirs to find out.

MONSANTO COMPANY

VITAL STATISTICS

Entry Level Salary for Sales: **$24,000–$32,000**
Senior Level Salary for Sales: **$50,000–$59,000**

Benefits

medical/dental: **Yes**
life insurance: **Yes**
disability: **Yes**
travel allowance: **Yes**
company car: **Yes**
profit sharing plan: **No**
stock purchase plan: **Yes**

child care: **No**
retirement plan: **Yes**
savings investment plan: **N/A**
tuition assistance: **Yes**
relocation assistance: **Yes**
memberships: **Yes, for sales managers**

Corporate Culture Index (1 = lowest, 10 = highest)

training: **9**
support: **8**
benefits: **9**

security: **8**
mobility: **8**
intangibles: **8**

Address: 800 North Lindberg Boulevard, St. Louis, MO 63167
Contact: Personnel; telephone 314/694-1000

Monsanto Company ranks 55th on the Fortune 500 list. In 1987 it posted sales of more than $7.6 billion, an 11% increase over 1986 and the company's largest annual increase since 1979.

Monsanto Company is a major manufacturer of chemical products for industrial, agricultural, and consumer use. It comprises six business units operating in different product areas: Monsanto Agricultural Company (herbicides and fungicides), Monsanto Chemical Company (plastics and chemicals for industrial use), G. D. Searle & Company (pharmaceuticals), Fisher Controls International, Inc. (control systems for manufacturing plants), the NutraSweet Company (artificial sweeteners), and Monsanto Electronic Materials Company (silicon for the semiconductor industry). Of these, the Agricultural and Chemical companies accounted for two-thirds of total Monsanto sales in 1987.

The company's strategy for the next decade emphasizes research and development of new products and expanded uses for existing products in each of the business units. For instance, the Agricultural Company has greatly expanded the uses of herbicides from traditional row crops to forestry management, plantation crops, lawn and garden care, and more. The Chemical Company successfully promoted its Saflex interlayer, used in automobile safety glass for 50 years, for architectural uses, to give greater safety to a variety of structures. With a major seller in Calan SR, a hypertension medication, Searle increased its R&D on new products and is vigorously pursuing efforts to license and market compounds developed by other companies. NutraSweet Company is introducing Simplesse, a natural fat substitute that will find uses in many new types of low-cholesterol and low-calorie food products. Fisher is developing a new flowmeter and new processing instrumentation products, and Monsanto Electronic is trying to increase profits by stressing service and superior product quality. As Earle H. Harbison, Jr., CEO of Monsanto Company, says, "Monsanto is becoming increasingly knowledge-intensive rather than capital-intensive as we seek to introduce a steady stream of new products to the market."

To ensure that these new products find acceptance in the marketplace, Monsanto needs a technically savvy, trained, and motivated sales force. The training program for new hires lasts six months and takes place at headquarters in St. Louis, Missouri, and in the field. It has both formal and informal components, with classroom sessions devoted to developing product knowledge and selling skills. The informal, often one-on-one sessions involve visiting plants and on-the-job training with experienced reps.

The primary emphasis of the training is on orienting new reps to the company, its products, and its organization. Because the various operating companies of Monsanto deal with such different products and selling situations, the new hire has an opportunity to get acquainted with a number of different kinds of accounts in different industries. For instance, a Monsanto rep might end up selling herbicides to agribusinesses, chemical products and plastics to major auto makers, pharmaceuticals to the health-care industry, silicon to the semiconductor industry, or plant monitoring systems to complex manufacturing operations.

In any case, new reps will need some degree of technical expertise. Monsanto looks for college graduates with majors in chemistry and a good business sense that has been developed through college courses in marketing. Liberal arts majors, however, are not out of the running. Monsanto believes that specific product-related technical expertise can be learned in training and on the job with a mentor. However, the new rep must demonstrate the ability to grasp the material and also show good interpersonal skills and motivation. Prior sales experience is not necessary, but it is helpful.

After training, Monsanto supports reps in the field by providing excellent sales and promotional materials and assistance with clerical and administrative chores where possible. Reps' territories vary in geographical size, depending on population density. For instance, a territory might amount to as many as three states or just one large metropolitan region. For the larger territories, some travel is necessary, possibly up to three nights a week. Reps generally work their territories alone, but they can call for assistance if an account requires special help. Monsanto also provides a company car and an expense account.

Salaries for sales trainees range from $24,000 to $32,000. Those with engineering or chemistry degrees are at the top end of the scale; those with liberal arts degrees are at the lower end. The average salary for senior sales executives ranges from $50,000 to $59,000 and up. Generally, Monsanto reps are on a salary-only basis, but some product lines do offer incentives for meeting and exceeding sales quotas. Cash awards for achievement are also available; supervisors can recommend reps for these, based on their productivity and performance.

Other benefits include: full medical and dental insurance, group life insurance, disability and pension plans, a stock purchase plan, paid moving expenses, and full tuition reimbursement. Promotion opportunities are good at Monsanto; the company likes to promote from within. Moreover, turnover among sales personnel is low, indicating that Monsanto reps find their careers at the company satisfying and rewarding.

The climate of the company is corporate and conservative, but management is definitely people-oriented. Monsanto is moving from a rather strait-laced ambience to a more open, informal one, enhancing its image as a dynamic innovator in the industrial chemical field.

UNION CARBIDE CORPORATION

VITAL STATISTICS

Entry Level Salary for Sales: **$28,000–$32,000**
Senior Level Salary for Sales: **$45,000–$60,000**

Benefits

medical/dental: **Yes**
life insurance: **Yes, basic and supplementary**
disability: **No, salary continuation**
travel allowance: **Yes**
company car: **Yes**
profit sharing plan: **No**
stock purchase plan: **Yes**

child care: **Yes**
retirement plan: **Yes**
savings investment plan: **Yes**
tuition assistance: **Yes, 75% undergraduate, 100% graduate**
relocation assistance: **Yes**
memberships: **No**

Corporate Culture Index   (1 = lowest, 10 = highest)

training: **9**
support: **9**
benefits: **10**

security: **9**
mobility: **9**
intangibles: **9**

Address: 39 Old Ridgebury Road, Danbury, CT 06817-0001
Contact: Personnel Development Laboratory (22 Saw Mill River Road, Hawthorne, NY 10532); telephone 914/789-5900/5901

Union Carbide is the fourth largest chemical company in the U.S., ranked 59th on the Fortune 500 list. In 1987 sales increased 9% to $6.9 billion, while profits rose 13% to $900 million.

In 1987, its seventieth year of operations, Union Carbide embarked on a massive corporate restructuring plan designed to take advantage of a general boom in the chemicals industry. With the company's plastics and chemicals units operating at or near capacity, management systematically tightened its focus on three basic activities: chemicals and plastics, industrial gases, and carbon products.

The company's products start out as raw chemical materials, which are then sold to manufacturers to be transformed into soap, shampoo, a desk chair, an auto body, or any one of a thousand synthetic materials we use every day.

Since such complex organic compounds are best understood by chemical engineers (or the seriously scientifically inclined), Union Carbide prefers candidates for sales positions to have a strong scientific background, as well as what the company calls "spice," "persistence," "interest," and "integrity." If this sounds like the formula for an ideal sales rep, remember that Union Carbide is a chemical company, after all.

Union Carbide is often in the lead in its product categories, whether developing a new skin care conditioner (Quatrisoft) out of plant-derived cellulose or a moisturizing cream based on Polymer HA-24. It even has a moisturizer made from crushed crab shells. These are all the inventions of a sophisticated R&D staff, which is always prepared to field technical questions. The sales-strategic issues are handled by the product manager.

The 250+ chemical sales reps rarely train customers or demonstrate products, except when the chemical processes involved are impressive enough to help clinch a sale. Reps spend two or three days on the road every week, traveling alone, on expense account, drawing just salary; UC pays no bonus or commission. The latest advertising and promotional materials are supplied to reps on a timely basis. Administrative, clerical, and research support are also amply provided by home base.

For two decades, sales training has been conducted in bucolic, campus-like surroundings at the Personnel Development Laboratory (PDL) in Hawthorne, New York. Here, UC salespeople from all over the world are trained to sell chemicals in a program comprising a series of workshops: Basic Selling Skills, High Performance Selling, Negotiation, Customer Service, and Industrial Marketing. Success in this program is critical to advancement.

An average salary for a sales trainee runs between $28,000 and $32,000. A senior executive takes home from $45,000 to $65,000. Benefits include: full medical and dental insurance, tuition assistance (75% undergraduate; 100% graduate school), a company car (but no car allowance), life insurance and disability plans, a retirement (noncontributing) savings program, a stock purchase plan, and—unusual for a Fortune 500 firm—flex-time plans for dependent child care.

The sales atmosphere at UC is corporate and highly professional. Like many a large organization dedicated to promoting sophisticated industrial products, this means that a suit (maybe even a white lab coat) is part of your uniform. UC is a perfect place for a chemical engineer who would just as soon sell chemicals as design them. Fine promotional opportunities, superb benefits, and first-rate training all make this company a name to be reckoned with.

W. R. GRACE & COMPANY

VITAL STATISTICS

Entry Level Salary for Sales: **$25,000+**
Senior Level Salary for Sales: **$55,000+**

Benefits

medical/dental: **Yes**	child care: **No**
life insurance: **Yes**	retirement plan: **Yes**
disability: **Yes**	savings investment plan: **Yes**
travel allowance: **Yes**	tuition assistance: **Yes, 75%**
company car: **Yes**	relocation assistance: **Yes**
profit sharing plan: **No**	memberships: **No**
stock purchase plan: **No**	

Corporate Culture Index   (1 = lowest, 10 = highest)

training:	**9**	security:	**9**
support:	**9**	mobility:	**9**
benefits:	**8**	intangibles:	**9**

Address: Grace Plaza, 1114 Avenue of the Americas, New York, NY 10036-7794
Contact: Corporate Personnel; telephone 212/819-5500

W. R. Grace & Company ranks 81st on the Fortune 500 list. In 1987 it had sales of more than $4.5 billion, up 21% from 1986. Profits of $173 million for 1987 contrast strongly with a loss in 1986 due to costs of restructuring.

W. R. Grace is an international specialty chemical company with interests in other fields as widely diversified as energy production (for example, gas, crude oil, coal) and energy services (for example, contract drilling). Recently the company has also decided to increase its presence in the health care industry (which is compatible with Grace's specialty chemical business).

Grace went through a major restructuring in 1986 in order to create a leaner, more efficient, and more focused company. Now, the company is looking for ways to exploit its first-rate research and development capacities by expanding its interests in chemical-related industries while eliminating its involvement in certain underperforming areas, such as its retail business and its fertilizer business.

Grace's core business at present is the Grace Specialty Chemical Company (GSC), which recently accounted for 60% of the company's total sales and 80% of its operating income. GSC is the world's largest specialty chemicals firm, and it honed its leading edge with a line of technologically superior products and services that can be fine-tuned to the specific needs of individual customers across a wide spectrum of industrial markets. In fact, GSC provides products and services in eight distinct areas: packaging, energy and transportation, construction, general industry, graphic arts, chemical intermediates, water treatment, and electronics.

GSC itself is an international company with sales of nearly $3 billion generated by 90 different product lines. It maintains manufacturing operations in 25 countries and sales offices in 17 more, and about 48% of its sales comes from outside the U.S. For management purposes, GSC is organized into 13 decentralized divisions that are responsible for the company's product lines on a geographical basis. The individual business units within a division are also largely decentralized, each with its own marketing, manufacturing, and product development capabilities. Such an arrangement keeps the different units in close contact with their customers and with industry developments and trends, an important consideration in servicing specialty markets.

With such a diverse group of companies and products, it's hard to pin down just what a Grace sales rep does. To get some idea of the training and responsibilities of a rep, we'll concentrate here on one of the major industries serviced by GSC—packaging—and the principal Grace product for that industry—flexible packaging under the Cryovac trademark. "Flexible packaging" refers to the clear plastic film used to wrap foods such as meat and cheese for display in supermarkets and other food outlets. GSC has developed the process of combining several different plastic materials to create wraps with a wide range of desirable properties. The appeal of GSC packaging lies in its specialized nature; for instance, some specific wraps are suitable for packaging bread, citrus fruits, and other fresh produce, and other wraps are more suitable for packaging meat. GSC is so successful because it is able to create innovative packaging that answers the needs of whole classes within the food industry.

Reps selling GSC packaging must understand both the capabilities of their own R&D people and the needs of the customers they service, primarily food processors. They are not selling a single product, but rather a total packaging approach that includes design, selection of materials and machines, installation and start-up of equipment, operator training, and after-sale service support. Reps call on the accounts in their territories, demonstrate GSC products, and look for a way that GSC expertise can help that account solve its packaging problems. Technical support personnel are always ready to help; for instance, they will fly quickly to meet with a customer who is having trouble with a product or a piece of equipment. Likewise, the R&D people are ready to develop a customized solution to an individual customer's packaging needs. If it proves successful, GSC will also roll out a nationally distributed product along the same lines. This is one of the ways GSC stays on top of changing conditions.

Training for a GSC sales rep is typically composed of a week in school at Cryovac Division headquarters in Duncan, South Carolina, followed by several weeks selling in the field. Then, it's back to school for another week, and so on, for about a year. The training covers laminants, service, selling, manufacturing, and other technical topics. GSC looks for college grads who have some experience in packaging, but it can be gained through college courses. Sales experience is a big help, too. GSC policy is to survey all present employees before filling a position, so reps can move up to positions in marketing, manufacturing, or even R&D.

Salaries at GSC, and at Grace in general, vary with the division and unit. Generally, trainees at GSC average $25,000 and up, with senior salespeople averaging $55,000 and up; bonuses and commissions vary with the unit and product line. Reps also enjoy excellent technical assistance, first-rate R&D, good promotional materials, and help with clerical chores. Other benefits include: medical, dental, and life insurance; disability and retirement plans, tuition assistance up to 75%, paid relocation expenses, and a company car.

GSC—and Grace as a whole—is a customer-driven firm. The extensive research and technical resources of the company are there to find answers to customers' problems. GSC reps sell solutions; if the company doesn't have a product that solves the problem, it will create one. The GSC rep is a major player in that game.

COMPUTERS, SOFTWARE, OFFICE EQUIPMENT, AND TELECOMMUNICATIONS

A few decades ago, the very idea of computers was nothing more than a glimmer in the minds of a few eccentric mathematicians. Now, as we move toward the twenty-first century, computers have revolutionized the human landscape and we can only just imagine what new horizons may lie ahead.

This phenomenal development is mirrored in the growth of the computer industry, which in the last 15 years has grown by a staggering 32%, more than any other industry (the second fastest growing industry is semiconductors, which has grown by 29%, with optical devices a distant third at 15%). In 1988, the industry generated nearly $40 billion in sales, up 22% from 1987, ending a two-year slump.

IBM, or "Big Blue," still dominates the field, but it now must share its dominance with upstart Apple and with Japanese manufacturers. The competition is especially stiff when it comes to developing computer graphics for the office. Apple, which has a history of introducing new concepts into the field, has the lead there, although IBM is catching up.

The term "computers" covers a wide range of products, each of which offers different prospects for the future. The software industry has been growing at a faster rate than the equipment (or hardware) industry for some time. Software sales climbed to $37 billion worldwide in 1987, a 23% rise from the previous year. More research and development currently goes into software than into any other facet of the industry.

The growth of software attests to the growth of personal computers. Most cost less than $15,000 and can perform many of the functions of larger computers. Four million personal computers were sold in 1987, most to businesses, the rest to schools and homes, for a total of $4 billion.

Supercomputers are especially fast systems that can perform very complex scientific and engineering tasks. Most have been purchased by governments, although in recent years more and more private businesses have bought them as well. A grand total of 60 units were sold in 1987, up 16% from 1986, for a total of $660 million.

Mainframes are the large, all-purpose computers most in demand by corporations. To give you an idea of their speed, their performance is measured in mips (millions of instructions per second), with the more sluggish machines operating at a mere 100 mips! Mainframe sales rose 5% in 1987 to nearly $10 billion. Lately, the handful of American manufacturers of mainframes have had to face stiff competition from Japan.

Perhaps the most exciting development in the field is AI (artificial intelligence). Simply and mind-bogglingly put, AI tries to develop computer systems that can reason like humans! Though research has been going on for decades, commercial uses of AI are very new. AI systems that can create languages and see are being used in medical research, oil exploration, and military weapons development. AI sales came to $807 million in 1987, an increase of 34% from the previous year. AI promises to be a boom sector of the American computer industry. Nearly half of the Fortune 500 companies are investing in AI research. Even the Japanese buy almost all of their AI systems from American companies.

And there's more. Computer technology has become linked with communications and other office equipment—which have become highly sophisticated in themselves. In fact, some companies have put computers, business machines, and telecommunications equipment all under one corporate umbrella. AT&T is one of these all-inclusive companies, but even those that aren't can still be big and prospering enterprises in this age of ever-emerging technologies: facsimile (fax) machines, cellular phones, word processors, voice mail equipment, and a host of other devices that keep cropping up on the business landscape. Offices and procedures are being transformed everywhere. Moreover, because of these technological developments, the office has become portable. Executives can have teleconferences from Amtrak Metroliners, attorneys can write briefs on lap-top systems aboard airplanes, and Washington officials can shred documents in limousines (well, not yet, anyway!).

Database accessing, electronic mail, and next year's advance in photocopying technology—the list isn't endless, it just seems so. What the expansion of products and services means is steady growth. Telecommunications revenues for 1988 are expected to have boosted 8.4% over those of 1987. Wider profit margins and more jobs should be the result.

There will be more network architects and fiber optics transmission engineers—and more people to sell their wizardry around the world.

TRADE ASSOCIATIONS

Institute of Electrical and Electronics Engineers (IEEE)
212/705-7900

PERIODICALS

A+ The Independent Guide for Apple Computing
Byte
Communications Week
Computer + Software News

AMERICAN TELEPHONE & TELEGRAPH (AT&T)

VITAL STATISTICS

Entry Level Salary for Sales: **$28,000–$32,000; $45,000 with an MBA**
Senior Level Salary for Sales: **$100,000+**
Incentives: **Yes**

Benefits

medical/dental: **Yes**
life insurance: **Yes**
disability: **Yes**
travel allowance: **N/A**
company car: **Yes**
profit sharing plan: **Yes**
stock purchase plan: **No**

child care: **No**
retirement plan: **Yes**
savings investment plan: **Yes**
tuition assistance: **Yes**
relocation assistance: **Yes**
memberships: **Smokenders**
Weight Watchers
Wellness program
Aerobics

Corporate Culture Index   (1 = lowest, 10 = highest)

training: **10**
support: **9**
benefits: **10**

security: **9**
mobility: **9**
intangibles: **10**

Address: 550 Madison Avenue, New York, NY 10022-3297
Contact: Personnel; telephone 212/219-7701

AT&T operations combine information movement and management: providing communications products, systems, and services to the global telecommunications marketplace. Ranked 2nd in the Fortune 500 listings for the electronics category, it is the eighth largest corporation in the U.S. In 1987 profits topped $2 billion on worldwide sales of $33 billion, a 1% increase from 1986—not bad, considering the breakup of AT&T as a utility company.

In 1984, a federal anti-trust action required that AT&T divest itself of three-quarters of its estimated $150 billion in assets. AT&T has thus been an old dog made to learn new tricks. Learning to compete in international sales has been arduous, but the company is back.

"AT&T is now in sales," AT&T's TV ads proudly proclaimed. As the company struggled to merge its long-separate computer and long-distance operations, its "instant sales force" began to get its complex balancing act together. And in 1987, record earnings, cost reductions, and higher sales finally paid off in higher profits.

"Imagine what it's like to be a hundred-year-old company that never sold," comments John McQuarrie, vice president for the Components and Electronic Systems division. "We didn't have anything close to a marketing organization." But with new stress placed on developing long-term relations with corporate clients, sales soared beyond even management's wildest dreams to just under $34 billion.

AT&T's sales effort now comprises Telecommunications Services (accounting for half of its revenue stream); Data and Consumer Products, which sells, installs, and rents communications and computer products for office and home use; and the Telecommunications Network Systems Division, selling switching systems and transmission equipment, which contributes roughly a fifth of total earnings.

Company training programs combine informal workshops with comprehensive on-the-job training. In a new rep, AT&T is looking for curiosity and an ability to make AT&T's business and the client's business grow. Since AT&T's products and services are constantly evolving, reps need to be able to stay abreast of trends in telecommunications.

A college degree is required, and some prior sales experience is helpful. Training takes 18 weeks out of the first 18 months, as reps start out as apprentice account executives, before graduating to become qualified, certified account executives in their own right.

The classroom curriculum consists of product knowledge (computers, PBXs, long-distance services), selling skills, customer service, and advanced selling skills. Some instruction is computer assisted, in keeping with a companywide effort to integrate data processing capability into operations at all levels. As a result, reps are given a high level of technical support, in addition to standard advertising and sales materials, administrative aid, and research assistance.

Account executives are trained to track the flow of information handled by the consumer (both voice and data transmission) as a means of determining effective solutions to a customer's present and future information needs.

The emphasis here is on building long-term relationships, not just on making a quick sale. Clearly, the company's major strength is its reputation as a solid, permanent fixture on a highly volatile scene. It's an image reps deliberately build upon when selling premium services at premium prices.

An account executive (AE) can climb a clearly defined promotional ladder to sales manager, to marketing and general management. The average salary (estimated) for a sales trainee runs from $28,000 to $32,000; some account executives with MBAs earn $45,000 to start. Senior sales executives clear $100,000, in addition to various incentives.

Territories vary in size from a thinly populated state to a few floors in a large metropolitan office tower. Some account executives work with one major customer (Sears Roebuck or Chemical Bank), whereas others manage a diversified portfolio of smaller accounts, hopping from one to the next.

Territories are rarely large enough to justify much overnight travel, although when an AE works on a national account, travel between company locations is essential. Reps usually work alone, but rely heavily on a strong technical support team prepared to play backup when help is needed.

The vast AT&T sales force numbers some 5000–7500, each of whom is provided with access to top management via the local branch manager, Bell Labs, or technical support.

The "Information Age" is an era during which AT&T has managed to remain a front-runner, contrary to much popular expectation. No longer is the sleeping telecom giant waiting to be aroused by a stern federal judge commanding: "Thou shalt go out and sell!" It's a company large enough to be both "corporate" and "laid-back," "family-like" and "dynamic," according to management.

Benefits include: medical and dental insurance, tuition assistance, a company car (no allowance), group life and disability insurance, a retirement/pension plan, profit sharing, and a stock purchase plan.

From the bad old days when a monopolistic Ma Bell embraced legions of dutiful employees in a vast, protective net, AT&T has been transformed into a lean, mean operation, conferring all the excitement of a new organization with the name-recognition and security of a favored classic.

APPLE COMPUTER, INC.

VITAL STATISTICS

Entry Level Salary for Sales: **They do not hire trainees**
Senior Level Salary for Sales: **$75,000–$200,000**

Benefits

medical/dental: **Yes**	child care: **Yes**
life insurance: **Yes**	retirement plan: **Yes**
disability: **Yes**	savings investment plan: **N/A**
travel allowance: **Yes**	tuition assistance: **Yes**
company car: **Yes**	relocation assistance: **Yes**
profit sharing plan: **Yes**	memberships: **On-site fitness**
stock purchase plan: **Yes**	**center**

Corporate Culture Index (1 = lowest, 10 = highest)

training:	**7**	security:	**10**
support:	**9**	mobility:	**8**
benefits:	**10**	intangibles:	**10**

Address: 2052 Mariani Avenue, Cupertino, CA 95014
Contact: Manager, Sales Training; telephone 408/996-1010

Apple Computer ranks 152nd on the Fortune 500 list. In 1987 the company posted sales of $2.6 billion, a stunning 40% increase from 1986. At the same time, profits jumped a comparable 41% to a total of $219 million, ranking Apple eighth in the computer industry, just after Wang.

Every computer-literate person in America has heard the story by now: how boy geniuses Steve Jobs and Steve Wozniak founded Apple Computer in a garage only a little over a decade ago. These two brilliant, off-beat entrepreneurs brought their fledgling two-man start-up directly into the ranks of America's Fortune 500 companies without passing "Go," and they certainly ended up collecting a lot more than $200.

Apple's daringly original vision was to put a low-cost, user-friendly, personal computer into the hands of just about everybody. They haven't succeeded yet. But Apple's innovative graphics and imaginative architecture have permanently changed the face of modern computing.

Today, with well over $2 billion in assets and a work force of some 5000 people, Apple is in the throes of a dramatic shift in focus, away from the personal and educational markets and toward the corporate user. This abrupt turnaround follows the departure of founder Steven Jobs, ironically dethroned by marketing whiz John Sculley, whom Jobs had coaxed to Apple from PepsiCo with the now famous question: "Do you want to sell sugared water for the rest of your life or do you want to change the world?" Two weeks later, Sculley joined Jobs. Two years after that, Jobs was out.

Though some old-timers freely bemoan the passing of the old anti-corporate atmosphere fostered by Jobs ("Now you either blend in or you're history," as one disgruntled former design engineer put it to *Business Week*), the new Apple still provides free popcorn and Friday afternoon beer blasts. (They even had a party for the Grateful Dead, who write songs on a Macintosh, at the "Campus" headquarters in Cupertino, California!)

Apple's highly experienced sales force has been reorganized to take on a new challenge: competing with IBM and IBM compatibles in their traditional domain, the large corporate office. Although Apple remains forceful in its historical stronghold, the educational market, that market is growing only a lackluster 5% a year, while the home market remains heavily dominated by IBM and IBM clones. This leaves corporate America as Apple's only realistic target.

Two major factors have enhanced Apple's belated appeal to American business: an enormous boom in desk-top publishing (where Apple has a clear technological lead over IBM) and customer confusion on the part of IBM users as to whether to spring for IBM's new Personal System 2, wait and see what develops, or try something new—like an Apple.

Nowadays, over 1,000 Apple reps are targeted to raid the executive suite by "the back door." They are being told to appeal directly to the end user (often a middle manager), bypassing conservative computer managers who still favor IBM and related technology.

As of the end of 1987, Apple was selling *directly* to only 75 major corporate accounts. 80% of all sales to business is still routed through large corporate customers. To beef up its secondary sales market, Apple has been teaming up its salespeople with reps from large retail outlets. John Sculley is also recruiting sales managers from IBM, DEC, Data General, and other rivals to help break into large corporate accounts.

Apple hardware and software may be easy to learn, but Apple is no place to learn the computer sales game. All reps must have extensive prior computer sales experience, good presentation skills, high technical proficiency, and a college degree.

SWAT (Selling with Apple Training), an ongoing one-week training program conducted at Apple's Cupertino headquarters, is constantly being revised to meet the needs of a changing market. The program includes company orientation, history, goals, culture, and a good deal of hard product knowledge. Reps generally stay in the division they were originally hired for, whether it is the K–12 team, which sells directly to schools (here former teachers do particularly well); the Higher Ed team, staffed to a large extent by professional reps hired away from other companies; the Business/Corporate account team, heavily dominated by extremely experienced reps; or the Government team, specially trained to adapt Apple technology to the needs of government data processing.

An experienced rep can clear up to an outstanding $100,000 a year. There is no average salary. Reps are frequently promoted to senior management, and Apple is doing its best to create headquarters positions to attract reps who want to come in out of the cold. Still, most prefer to stay in the field.

The corporate staff may be described as laid-back, but Apple's sales force prides itself on being hard-driven by a strong work ethic. Reps work alone, covering territories that vary widely in size (from ten urban blocks to four rural states). Turnover is only 5%, which speaks well of Apple's commitment to reps in terms of benefits and support systems. Benefits are generous, with a medical/dental insurance plan, tuition assistance (100% up to $2000 per year), a company car (no extra allowance), life and disability insurance, relocation expenses, retirement (401K) and stock purchase plans, and profit sharing.

Apple needs alert, flexible people, capable of responding creatively to sudden change. Reps frequently train customers in the use of rapidly advancing technology. Working for Apple is not for everyone, but it is for those who want to sell on the cutting edge.

CONTROL DATA
CORPORATION

VITAL STATISTICS

Entry Level Salary for Sales: **$45,000 ($30,000 salary, $15,000 commission)**
Senior Level Salary for Sales: **$80,000–$100,000**

Benefits

medical/dental: **Yes**	child care: **Yes**
life insurance: **Yes**	retirement plan: **Yes**
disability: **Yes**	savings investment plan: **Yes**
travel allowance: **Yes**	tuition assistance: **Yes**
company car: **Yes**	relocation assistance: **Yes**
profit sharing plan: **Yes**	memberships: **Weight Watchers**
stock purchase plan: **Yes**	**Wellness program**

Corporate Culture Index   (1 = lowest, 10 = highest)

training:	**9**	security:	**9**
support:	**9**	mobility:	**10**
benefits:	**10**	intangibles:	**10**

Address: 8100 34th Avenue South, Minneapolis, MN 55440-4700
Contact: Headquarters Staffing; telephone 612/853-5110

Control Data, the sixth largest computer manufacturer in the U.S., ranks 125th on the Fortune 500 list. Its 1987 sales climbed just 1% to $3.6 billion, with profits just under $20 million, compared to a $265 million loss in 1986.

In 1988 Control Data returned to profitability. This Minneapolis-based computer hardware and data services firm successfully focused on its traditional strengths in scientific computers, engineering computers, and supercomputers, while aggressively expanding its data services division (Ticketron and state lotteries). A company once known for its disk drives has spun off that low-profit-margin sector into its own stand-alone subsidiary.

Control Data is an engineering-driven company, as opposed to the classic customer-driven computer company: IBM. Control Data develops products to accomplish specific tasks better than anyone else, whereas IBM waits for a market to develop and then jumps in with its own version.

If you think being a "techie" or "computer jock" is the proper background to sell computers, think again. "Selling mainframes for Control Data is a serious business," insists Bill Robinson, an experienced Control Data rep. "Most computer jocks want to talk about how slick a piece of hardware is. That's not what we do at Control Data."

What they do at Control Data is sell computers. Some sales experience and computer literacy are a must. Robinson reports that nearly everyone in his sales training class was a recruit from some other sales position, but not necessarily from within the computer industry.

After five weeks in "boot camp" at Minneapolis headquarters, sharpening selling skills, boning up on new industry applications, and "living the technical culture," new recruits are sent cold-calling into the field for a month. After that, they return to Minneapolis for a period of evaluation, testing, and field-experience analysis.

Reps are often assigned "horizontal" lines of accounts—banks in Virginia or schools in Montana—at the discretion of the district manager. For reps with ambitions to climb up to management, a "management" track attracts those willing to balance budgets and people, whereas a separate "consultant" track appeals more to people intrigued by the hardware side of the business.

Reps spend one or two nights a week on the road, covering territories typically consisting of part of a state. The average Control Data customer may be an aerospace company, a utility, a manufacturer interested in computer-aided design (CAD), a school, a petrochemical company, or a hotshot R&D outfit.

Sales are mainly to "technical decision-makers," those responsible for acquiring workstations, mainframes, and supercomputers. Sales reps are very well supported by a technical staff prepared to handle all the purely technical problems on accounts, leaving reps free to sell. In general, reps need to know more about the "what for" of computer operations than the "how to": the functions, features, and benefits of Control Data's products as compared with those of DEC, NEC, or IBM.

Selling high-ticket, sophisticated, multimillion-dollar computers is largely a team effort, involving the cooperation of any number of experts in closing a sale. Certain sales may require third-party consultants to come up with the correct hardware configuration for a specific application.

The average salary for a sales trainee is relatively high ($30,000 base salary plus a $15,000 commission). Nearly all have prior sales experience. Senior sales staff earn between $80,000 and $100,000, along with commissions that can reach 50% of base salary (the typical ratio of salary to commission is 40:60%, with no income cap). There are no bonuses.

Benefits include: medical, dental, group life, and disability insurance;

tuition assistance (if job related, 100% with C average or better); a company car but no allowance; a retirement/pension plan; a profit sharing and stock purchase plan; a voucher savings plan for child care; and an adoption benefit up to $2000.

Control Data has always been strong in scientific computing. With a much-heralded Transparent Computing Environment coming on line—an interface linking different levels of computing into a single operating environment—Control Data is moving to integrate scientific computing with more basic computer operations, making it a more well-rounded company.

It takes a technically sophisticated, highly motivated person to keep up with the Joneses when it comes to computers. But as both salary and benefits packages show, a whole host of intangibles (training, job security, mobility, and promotion) make Control Data an excellent organization in America's most competitive industry.

DIGITAL EQUIPMENT CORPORATION

VITAL STATISTICS

Entry Level Salary for Sales: **$25,000**
Senior Level Salary for Sales: **$70,000**

Benefits

---

medical/dental: **Yes**
life insurance: **Yes**
disability: **Yes**
travel allowance: **Yes**
company car: **Yes**
profit sharing plan: **No**
stock purchase plan: **Yes**

child care: **No**
retirement plan: **Yes**
savings investment plan: **N/A**
tuition assistance: **$650 per year**
relocation assistance: **Yes**
memberships: **Yes**

Corporate Culture Index   (1 = lowest, 10 = highest)

---

training: **8**
support: **8**
benefits: **10**

security: **8**
mobility: **9**
intangibles: **10**

Address: 146 Main Street, Maynard, MA 01754
Contact: Manager of Recruiting; telephone 508/264-1285

Digital Equipment Corporation ranks 38th on the Fortune 500 list. In 1987 it posted sales of over $9 billion, an increase of 24% over 1986. At the same time, its profits jumped an impressive 84% over 1986 figures, reaching more than $1 billion.

Digital Equipment Corporation was founded in 1957 by three MIT engineers with the idea that companies needed smaller, easier-to-use computers than the large mainframes that dominated the market at that time. The minicomputer was hugely successful, and now DEC designs, manufactures, sells, and services a wide range of products in the interactive computer industry. It has been particularly successful in the communications area with its new VAX generation of computers that have generated much new business from the insurance and financial services industries. For instance, at present close to 50% of DEC's sales comes from its commercial clients, up 10% from 1984.

What gave DEC this big edge was the creation of a single computer design for its entire line of minis of all sizes. That allowed them to be linked up into companywide networks, all controlled by Digital's proprietary VMS software operating package. This development allowed DEC to expand its VAX minicomputer sales into the larger commercial market from its earlier, more narrow technical and scientific base. Ken Olsen, DEC's president and one of its founders, sees it this way: "The real problem is how to make our customer's whole enterprise more productive." For Olsen, this means companywide networks.

As a result, the future appears to be one of increasing competition for DEC's VAX minicomputers. The shift toward personal computers in the marketplace has caught DEC in a soft spot; it does not have a comparable line of PCs. Relying as it does on its VAX systems, DEC is in danger of missing out on the growing trend toward "open systems": networks controlled by standardized software that are able to link up many different brands of computers. Even without a completely workable open system in place, "Networks of personal computers are being substituted for minicomputers," says Amy D. Wohl, an office-computing consultant.

DEC, however, feels up to the challenge. The company is sticking to its VAX guns and its marketing strategy of service and customer-oriented networks. This means that DEC sales reps must work closely with customer firms to understand their data processing and communications problems and then devise DEC solutions that are effective and easy to implement. The DEC rep must be technically knowledgeable, understand sales, and be able to deal with customers' top management and engineering staff, as well as with those actually inputting data. The DEC rep is a problem solver, and DEC itself is less in the business of selling machines than it is in the business of selling systems that answer a customer's needs. To this end, DEC reps usually work in teams, using support people, engineers, consultants, and others to ensure that the customer gets the right system for the job.

Sales training at Digital is intense, with an emphasis on real-world situations. The "basic training" for an inexperienced rep generally lasts six months and concentrates on product knowledge and selling skills. For new reps with selling experience this might be cut to three months. It takes place in Maynard, Massachusetts, and Hudson, New Hampshire. Digital's entire education effort, though, is quite large. It involves teaching more than 523 different courses for employees and customers worldwide. DEC also offers a tremendous amount of computer-assisted, self-study materials and instruction. Continuing education and development at Digital is very dependent on individual initiative. This reliance on the individual is reflected in the kinds of trainees DEC is looking for. The company rarely hires graduates fresh out of college (a college degree or its equivalent is mandatory). It is looking for people with a technical education and preferably with some business or selling experience as well.

The average salary for a sales trainee at Digital is around $25,000 or more, depending on education and experience. For senior sales executives, salaries average $70,000 and go up from there. DEC is generally a salary-only company, but there are bonuses, which are limited to the top 20% of the sales force. Other benefits include: medical/dental insurance plans, group life insurance, disability and retirement plans, a stock purchase plan, a company car, tuition reimbursement, and paid moving expenses.

The company's climate is a friendly one (all employees are on an informal, first-name basis), as might be expected when so much of the selling is done by teams working closely together. Still, DEC is in a very competitive industry, and its reps are accustomed to dealing with the highest echelon of management in some of the largest corporations in the country. Reps are expected to dress conservatively and be able to work with the whole range of a client's staff from the CEO down. Territories are fairly small, however, and travel is usually limited to occasional one-night trips.

Employee turnover is on the low side, which speaks well of the commitment that Digital's reps feel toward the company. The company in turn shows its commitment to its reps by its policy of promoting from within —it is quite common for sales personnel to move up to top management if they show the aptitude. Also, Digital provides backup support to its sales staff with first-rate sales and promotion materials for its products, by assisting reps in administrative/clerical chores where possible, and especially by conducting research to keep DEC systems at the top of the industry.

HEWLETT-PACKARD COMPANY

VITAL STATISTICS

Entry Level Salary for Sales: **$25,000**
Senior Level Salary for Sales: **$50,000+**

Benefits

medical/dental: **Yes**
life insurance: **Yes**
disability: **Yes**
travel allowance: **N/A**
company car: **Yes**
profit sharing plan: **Yes**
stock purchase plan: **Yes**

child care: **No**
retirement plan: **Yes**
savings investment plan: **Yes**
tuition assistance: **Yes**
relocation assistance: **N/A**
memberships: **Smokenders**
Weight Watchers
Wellness program
On-site fitness center
Computer classes for employees

Corporate Culture Index (1 = lowest, 10 = highest)

training: **9**
support: **9**
benefits: **10**

security: **9**
mobility: **9**
intangibles: **10**

Address: 3000 Hanover Street, Palo Alto, CA 94304
Contact: Manager, Corporate Staffing; telephone 415/857-1501

Hewlett-Packard Company ranks 49th on the Fortune 500 list. In 1987 it posted sales of more than $8 billion, up 14% from 1986. Profits, at $644 million, were up 25% from 1986.

Hewlett-Packard Company designs, manufactures, markets, and services computing and electronic measuring equipment for use in industry, business, science, engineering, health care, and education. The company's more than 10,000 products include: computer systems and peripherals, testing and measuring instruments, hand-held calculators, integrated instrument and computer systems, medical electronic equipment and instrumentation systems, and systems for chemical analysis.

H-P's continued growth in this world-competitive, high-tech market is predicated on its unswerving commitment to research and development. Every year, H-P invests about 10% of its net revenues in R&D (amounting to $900 million in 1987), an approach that enables the company to stay in the forefront of technology and maintain a steady flow of new and useful products. For instance, in 1987 well over half of H-P's orders were for products that had been introduced during the preceding three years.

Although the company is research-driven, it is also market-oriented. H-P basically sells solutions to its customers' problems. Its systems allow decision-makers in both business and technical fields to access essential information, to put it in meaningful form, and thereby to improve their personal and business effectiveness. The company, however, recognizes that, considering all the markets it serves, it can't possibly discover all the answers on its own. It has to get close to its customers and learn their various business needs firsthand. The company's carefully chosen and highly trained sales force plays a major part in this by constantly apprising H-P of needs and problems it encounters in the marketplace. What its customers see as problems, H-P sees as opportunities.

In addition, H-P's post-sale services are industry leaders. In 1987, the company again achieved a number-one position in customer support satisfaction, according to results that H-P compiled from a survey by Datapro International, a leading market-research organization. H-P offers a single, integrated set of support services to its customers, and the same team that puts a customer solution together remains responsible for supporting it after the sale.

Modern information technology has made the world smaller, and H-P must sell in an international marketplace as well. At present, just under half its business is generated outside the U.S. Enhancing its ability to compete in the highly competitive domestic and world markets is a management philosophy that spurs creativity while carefully monitoring costs, which helps explain H-P's impressive increase in earnings in 1987. It also now boasts the strongest product portfolio in its history, a good omen for the future.

H-P, like other companies in the high-tech information processing field, looks for new reps who are college graduates with backgrounds in computers and business and who have selling experience. Training includes two to five weeks of classroom work, depending on product line, and then on-the-job work with an experienced rep lasting from one to three months. The formal training concentrates on product knowledge (computers, information systems, measuring instruments, and so on) and on professional selling skills, preparing the trainee for the position of customer representative (as sales reps at H-P are called). There are five different sales forces, so no individual rep presents the company's whole line.

In 1987, H-P began a policy of equipping all its customer reps with portable PCs and printers, using its own equipment to increase the sales force's effectiveness and productivity. The salespeople have instant access to specific information on products, competition, ordering, and so on, and they can generate quick, accurate price and delivery quotes right on the customer's premises. The PC offers reps additional advantages, too. It is a big help with paperwork (the bane of all field reps), it makes communications with the home office easier via electronic mail, and it boosts reps' motivation as well as their actual selling time with customers. Moreover, H-P reps find that using the lap-top PC in the presence of customers differentiates them markedly from sales reps of competing companies.

H-P reps sell to large corporations, hospitals, medical offices, wholesale distributors, major retailers or dealers, and original equipment manufacturers (OEMs), which are other computer companies needing components. Territories vary in size, ranging from part of a large city to several states. Reps generally work alone, but, as noted, they enjoy strong backup from technical people and support teams who help in preparing a sale site, in installing a major H-P system or equipment, and in providing preventive maintenance and repair service. Reps also are supported by H-P's extensive, sophisticated media ad and promotion materials.

Salaries for trainees average about $25,000, with senior salespeople averaging about $50,000; a bonus kicks in when a rep sells 110% of quota. The company guarantees 80% of the target quota (consisting of 50% base salary and 50% commissions); thus, successful reps can be very successful indeed, earning over $100,000. There is no cap, and super-successful reps can go to $200,000. Also, H-P rewards those reps who service existing accounts that are not expected to buy expensive new equipment or systems but that must be called on anyway.

Other benefits include: medical, dental, and life insurance; disability and retirement plans; profit sharing and stock purchase plans; a 401K plan; a savings plan; tuition assistance (100%, if job related); flex-time scheduling; and a company car.

H-P is decentralized, informal, conducive to innovative problem solving, and open. At the same time it is goal-oriented, competitive, and hard driving. Opportunities for reps are good, with promotions up through sales and then, if appropriate, into product development and management. It offers a fine present and a promising future.

HONEYWELL, INC.

VITAL STATISTICS

Entry Level Salary for Sales: **$26,000**
Senior Level Salary for Sales: **$40,000–$50,000**

Benefits

medical/dental: **Yes**	child care: **No**
life insurance: **Yes**	retirement plan: **Yes**
disability: **Yes**	savings investment plan: **N/A**
travel allowance: **Yes**	tuition assistance: **Yes**
company car: **Yes**	relocation assistance: **Yes**
profit sharing plan: **No**	memberships: **No**
stock purchase plan: **Yes**	

Corporate Culture Index (1 = lowest, 10 = highest)

training:	**7**	security:	**8**
support:	**8**	mobility:	**8**
benefits:	**9**	intangibles:	**9**

Address: Honeywell Plaza, Minneapolis, MN 55408
Contact: Staffing; telephone 612/870-5614

Honeywell, Inc., ranks 63rd on the Fortune 500 list. In 1987 it posted sales of $6.7 billion, an increase of 24% over 1986. Part of this growth came from the acquisition of Sperry Aerospace; still, the company's other business units grew at a 9% clip in 1987.

Honeywell, Inc. is the world's largest control technology company. It all began with a Honeywell invention—the thermostat. Today, Honeywell designs, manufactures, and sells high-technology control systems—systems that help consumers, businesses, and government to control their environment.

Honeywell's worldwide operations center on four business units: Home and Building Automation Control; Industrial Automation and Control, which produces industrial control systems and advanced sensors; Space and Aviation Systems, the leading supplier of systems and controls for commercial aviation and an important contributor to military avionics and space applications; and Defense and Marine Systems, a supplier of marine and conventional weapons defense systems to the U.S. and its allies. Honeywell's goals for the immediate future are to increase sales moderately while increasing earnings substantially.

Long-term growth is projected to be above average as Honeywell exploits its six strategies for future development: (1) to concentrate heavily on the fastest growing segments of its present markets; (2) to expand into adjacent markets by taking advantage of its superior products, technology, distribution, and reputation; (3) to increase international penetration by concentrating on those geographical areas with the fastest growth; (4) to develop new product lines with continued investment in research and development; (5) to expand its profitable low-investment service businesses; and (6) to market products and services more aggressively in all areas, perhaps teaming up with other industry leaders.

With this emphasis on aggressive marketing, it is no surprise that Honeywell has a strong commitment to the training and development of its personnel. For instance, it maintains an extensive videotape library with over a hundred ongoing technical courses to be used by its technical staff. Its sales reps also benefit from an intensive training program, comprising six to seven weeks of formal classroom study followed by six to seven months of supervised on-the-job training at the branch where the trainee will work. The classroom work orients trainees to the company, teaches them product information, and helps to develop selling skills. On-the-job training takes the new reps out on sales calls with experienced sales reps; here the new reps are judged on how well they can transfer the newly acquired selling skills to the actual marketplace. In addition, sales reps continue to be trained on new product information throughout their careers.

Because the company feels that its sales reps *are* Honeywell, representing the entire company, it looks for new hires who are personable and professional. Although there is no hard-and-fast rule about educational requirements, a college degree is the norm, preferably in business or marketing. Prior selling experience is *very* helpful, even if it involved only a summer job. Technical knowledge is also helpful, but is necessary only in the more high-tech selling divisions. To determine whether a sales rep candidate and the company are suited to each other—and to find the best slot for successful candidates—Honeywell administers a battery of 18 validated interest tests to determine abstract and verbal aptitude and personality, and to gather biographical information.

Honeywell sales reps market major control systems. They sell mainly to large corporations with office buildings and manufacturing plants, to major real estate developers, to refineries and other original equipment manufacturers (OEMs), to major industries, and to the U.S. government. Reps have relatively small territories, generally requiring no more than a day's drive, so few overnight trips are needed. Reps work alone or in teams, depending on what an account demands. Normally, sales reps do not install or demonstrate the company's control systems, but they do teach the customers how the systems work and what they will accomplish. Product knowledge is essential, but when special technical assistance is necessary, it is available. Other support includes up-to-date advertising, sales promotion, and new product information materials; assistance with administrative/clerical chores where possible; and, especially, the research and development of new products.

To help salespeople learn more about their products and markets, they are provided with a Honeywell Sales Professionals Club, a setting in which reps from all divisions can sharpen their selling skills and get to know one another. They meet during off hours generally once a month, except during the summer, in 15 key cities across the country.

Sales reps at Honeywell work on a salary-plus-incentive program. After six months on the base salary, the new hire is eligible for the incentive bonus, which runs from 4% to 6% of the base salary. Thus, a recent graduate after six months (spent in the training program most probably) might earn around $26,000 ($24,500 base plus $1500 incentive). The compensation for senior sales personnel ranges from $40,000 to $50,000—but it must be noted that a small number of reps (1% to 2%) earn up to $100,000 in the Commercial Building Materials and Services division (preventive maintenance).

Other benefits include: medical/dental insurance, life insurance, disability and retirement plans, profit sharing, a stock purchase plan, tuition assistance, a travel allowance, paid moving expenses, and a company car. Moreover, Honeywell sales reps are on a good path to top management. Honeywell has instituted an aggressive leadership development process designed to identify promising and qualified executives in the sales corps who will be able to fill key positions in the future.

Honeywell is an informal, first-name type of company that insists on a professional, conservative demeanor (there is a dress code). It is a solid, high-status company where employees tend to stay for a long time. It is market-driven, but it is personal, too.

INTERNATIONAL BUSINESS MACHINES (IBM)

VITAL STATISTICS

Entry Level Salary for Sales: **Highly competitive**
Senior Level Salary for Sales: **Highly competitive**

Benefits

medical/dental: **Yes**		child care: **Referral service**	
life insurance: **Yes**		retirement plan: **Yes**	
disability: **Yes**		savings investment plan: **N/A**	
travel allowance: **N/A**		tuition assistance: **Yes**	
company car: **N/A**		relocation assistance: **Yes, plus spouse placement for transferred personnel**	
profit sharing plan: **N/A**			
stock purchase plan: **Yes**		memberships: **Wellness programs**	

Corporate Culture Index   (1 = lowest, 10 = highest)

training: **10**		security: **9**	
support: **10**		mobility: **9**	
benefits: **10**		intangibles: **10**	

Address: Armonk, NY 10504
Contact: Personnel; telephone 914/765-1900

IBM ranks 4th on the Fortune 500 list. In 1987 it posted worldwide sales of over $54 billion, an increase of almost 6% from 1986. Profits, at $5.2 billion, were up almost 10% from 1986.

IBM, the "Big Blue" giant of the industry, found itself pressed in the 1980s to take a hard look at its place in the market and to *think* about the way it does business. Part of the soul-searching came as a result of the intense competition IBM faced (and still faces) on all fronts of the computer market—huge Japanese companies challenged its dominance of the main-frame market, and domestic and foreign companies provided highly competitive products in the minicomputer, PC, software, and systems integration markets. As Edward E. Lucente, IBM vice president in charge of U.S. marketing, said, "It's not an all-blue world anymore."

Another part of the problem that caused declining sales and loss of market penetration during the early 1980s lay in the very success that IBM had enjoyed for so many years. The company became overly bureaucratic; it simply took too long for new products to get through the development cycle. The sales force became product-oriented, concentrating more on moving IBM equipment and software than on the problems that customers wanted solved. To meet these challenges, IBM undertook what *Fortune* described as probably the most massive redeployment by a company in decades. What's more, IBM accomplished this without firing anyone. A new and leaner IBM, one whose employees are trained (and retrained) to meet the challenges ahead, is now in place, and ready to get on with the 1990s.

The redeployment fixed on two main goals: to stimulate design and development of new product (machines and software) and to beef up the already first-class sales force to ensure future growth. Also, using an early-retirement plan, normal attrition, and other incentives, the company trimmed personnel and costs—a third major target of the revamping. Tackling the product-lag problem, the company formed five autonomous product groups, whose managers (in mainframes, mid-range, PC, and communications systems) are to act like entrepreneurs in their areas in order to cut bureaucracy and speed up production. A fifth group will concentrate on providing state-of-the-art equipment components like memory chips.

In the sales end of the operation, one major aim was simply to get more muscle into the field. Thousands of IBM employees were moved from manufacturing and administration, where they were redundant, to marketing and selling, where IBM needs to make gains. In two years, the company increased its marketing force by 20%. Moreover, the new reps were in many cases seasoned IBM employees with valuable technical experience as plant workers, lab technicians, and managers.

Turning these people into successful reps was a challenge, but IBM, with expenditures of more than $1 billion a year, deploys a budget larger than Harvard University's for educating its work force and customers. The marketing training program itself is a combination of on-the-job training and classroom instruction that lasts for a year or more. In addition, IBM has a self-study program that allows trainees to use an interactive computer setup to practice sales calls on a "manager" in an industry of their choice. Formal training takes place in centers in Atlanta and Dallas, and the work is intense. There is a great deal of role-playing as trainees act out sales calls with the teacher, a device that causes stress even in veteran employees. There's a real sense of camaraderie, though, and that keeps morale up and lays the basis for future teamwork.

Although product knowledge and a technical understanding of IBM systems are an important part of the training, the final weeks are spent on industry specialization. Trainees, with the help of their branch managers, select an industry in which to specialize. Then the training program explores the kinds of problems managers in that industry face in operations, personnel, distribution, and so on, giving the new rep insight into the areas of concern of a specific class of IBM's customers. This is in keeping with IBM's emphasis on the consulting aspect of selling rather than simply moving the product off the shelf.

Information handling, the real business of IBM, draws a sales rep more deeply into a customer's business than almost any other kind of product or service does. For instance, IBM reps and marketing account teams provide customers with a wide range of services (planning, education, training, consulting, system configuration, hardware and software installation, and maintenance), involving the most sensitive aspects of the customer's operations (finances, design, and fulfillment). To do this effectively, reps must determine their customers' specific needs and tailor their recommendations to fit them precisely. That's what IBM training is all about in today's competitive marketplace.

Sales trainees need to have a college degree, but IBM is interested in trainees with a variety of technical and liberal arts backgrounds. In the past, the company primarily recruited top athletes because it looked for those with leadership, determination, and a positive outlook. Now the company is putting more of a premium on experience and is moving to recruit more field reps from a variety of fields.

Salaries for marketing reps at IBM are competitive with those offered by other companies in the same field. Salaries, bonuses, and commissions, of course, will vary with the product line and operating group. Support in training and advertising is first-rate. Promotion opportunities are excellent for qualified reps—IBM's present CEO, John F. Akers, began his career in sales. Other benefits are goldplated: medical, dental, and life insurance; a relocation plan with spouse placement; employee assistance programs; work arrangement programs (leave of absence, individual work schedules, and so on); and many others.

IBM has a very corporate, drive-to-succeed atmosphere. It's at the top of its industry, and it looks for people who are tops in what they do. Those who qualify can make excellent careers for themselves.

NCR CORPORATION

VITAL STATISTICS

Entry Level Salary for Sales: **$25,000**
Senior Level Salary for Sales: **$55,000**

Benefits

medical/dental: **Yes**
life insurance: **Yes**
disability: **Yes**
travel allowance: **Yes**
company car: **No**
profit sharing plan: **Yes**
stock purchase plan: **Yes**

child care: **Yes, referral system**
retirement plan: **Yes**
savings investment plan: **Yes**
tuition assistance: **Yes**
relocation assistance: **Yes**
memberships: **No**

Corporate Culture Index: (1 = lowest, 10 = highest)

training: **8**
support: **8**
benefits: **9**

security: **8**
mobility: **8**
intangibles: **9**

Address: 1700 South Patterson Boulevard, Dayton, OH 45479
Contact: Personnel; telephone 513/445-5098

NCR Corporation ranks 74th on the Fortune 500 list. In 1987 it posted sales of more than $5.5 billion, up 16% from 1986. Profits, at $419 million, increased 25% from 1986.

NCR Corporation develops, manufactures, markets, installs, and services business data processing systems for worldwide markets. NCR champions open systems and industry, meaning that it works to foster standardization among the products offered by different manufacturers of data processing equipment. The aim is to make it possible for the components of different manufacturers to work together ("interoperability," as it's called) to form a unified data processing network. NCR's own equipment is designed so that it can serve as the base for many products; for instance, an NCR financial workstation uses the same basic structure as an NCR personal computer.

This approach to manufacturing hardware and software has its analog in the company's marketing approach. NCR's basic selling strategy, what it calls its "directional strategy," is to sell the largest volume of products to all customers who could use those products. This contrasts with other companies' strategies that call for developing many products for use in a few specific fields.

NCR equipment and systems are manufactured with the ability to interface easily with other systems. NCR also has the advanced communications capabilities to link its systems with already existing systems—even ones containing products that NCR did not manufacture. The company thus can upgrade a customer's existing data processing system simply by adding to it, instead of starting over from square one every time.

To ensure that its products are indeed suitable for a wide range of potential customers, NCR has divided them into six major families: (1) industry-specific workstations, (2) general-purpose workstations, (3) multiuser computer systems, (4) large computer systems, (5) communications processors, and (6) synergistic products and services. In pursuing its marketing strategy, NCR believes that its customers' needs have become so complex that no one manufacturer can hope to offer all things to all clients. Thus, it takes a different tack and offers interoperable products that are capable of reaching out to many markets and serving the business system needs of a wide range of customers.

NCR's most important systems include transaction processing systems and office information systems. Transaction processing systems are online systems that monitor transactions as they occur, processing them, and updating databases as required. Electronic checkout counters at supermarkets are an obvious example. Office processing systems deal with sharing and transferring files within and between work groups in a business firm or corporation. These systems have enormous market potential.

NCR uses five basic strategies to sell its systems: account management, sales force specialization, software alliances, multiple sales channels, and customer services. For every current or potential account, NCR has an account manager, a person who is fully responsible for the account. NCR sales reps have specialized knowledge; that is, they are trained to know the kinds of systems required by customers in specific businesses. NCR also maintains close alliances with independent software developers. This allows it to provide its customers with the widest range of applications software possible. NCR also markets its systems through multiple channels so that it can reach the maximum number of prospects. Direct sales is the primary channel, but the company also uses resellers and wholesale distributors. Finally, NCR services its customers by offering them support that includes education and training, maintenance, consulting, systems integration, and network support.

Training for NCR reps takes about six months and consists of alternating sessions of classroom work and on-the-job training. The program takes place at headquarters in Dayton and in the field. Reps acquire product knowledge and selling skills, and they learn the information processing needs of the business industries to which they will be selling. NCR looks for college graduates with degrees in business, computers, engineering, or finance. Sales experience is not necessary, but it is a definite plus. Reps must explain NCR products to customers and be able to demonstrate and install them, too. They may work alone or in teams, depending on the situation. Territory size and time on the road will also vary accordingly.

Salaries for trainees are competitive, ranging from about $25,000 on up; senior salespeople earn about $55,000 and up. Commissions and incentives can add to a rep's salary, as well, and they also depend on the product line. Other benefits include: medical, dental, and life insurance; disability and retirement plans; profit sharing and stock purchase plans; a car allowance; a travel allowance; paid relocation expenses; tuition assistance; and a referral system for child care.

The climate at NCR is aggressive and dynamic, as one might expect in this very competitive market. NCR products are known and respected throughout the business community, especially in the large wholesale and retail industries, and the company is working hard to keep it that way.

PITNEY BOWES, INC.

VITAL STATISTICS

Entry Level Salary for Sales: **$20,400**
Senior Level Salary for Sales: **$33,109**

Benefits

medical/dental: **Yes**
life insurance: **Yes, basic and supplementary**
disability: **Yes, short and long term**
travel allowance: **Yes**
company car: **No**
profit sharing plan: **Yes**
stock purchase plan: **Yes**

child care: **N/A**
retirement plan: **Yes**
savings investment plan: **Yes**
tuition assistance: **Yes**
relocation assistance: **N/A**
memberships: **N/A**

Corporate Culture Index (1 = lowest, 10 = highest)

training: **9**
support: **10**
benefits: **9**

security: **10**
mobility: **9**
intangibles: **9**

Address: Walter H. Wheeler, Jr. Drive, Stamford, CT 06926
Contact: Human Resources; telephone 203/356-5000

Pitney Bowes ranks 175th on the Fortune 500 list. In 1987 it enjoyed sales of $2.5 billion, up 13% from 1986. Pitney Bowes is a major manufacturer of office machines and mail- and paper-handling systems.

Pitney Bowes today is much more than the "mailing machine company" familiar to so many office and mailroom workers. It now offers a full line of copiers, shipping and weighing systems, and production mailing systems that are designed to answer the paper-handling needs of just about any company. With a client base of over one million, the company has plenty of experience in meeting the needs of a diverse range of customers.

PB has always been known for its commitment to its customers and to its employees. When PB saw that it would have to modernize its equipment from electromechanical to electronic devices, it refused to lay off a single production worker. Instead, it set about retraining its employees in the new technologies, proving that PB values quality—not only in its products and services, but in employee relations as well.

Pitney Bowes has several major business units that are heavily involved in selling (Dictaphone and PB Business Supplies), but we will concentrate here on the company's major unit—Pitney Bowes Business Systems. The PB Business Systems sales reps call on current customers and also scout for businesses that are not yet aware of the benefits of PB equipment. The reps are trained to help these businesses improve their productivity by offering solutions to their office production and mailing problems.

The impressive sales training program is as broad as it is detailed. It accommodates experienced sales professionals as well as inexperienced recent college graduates. It begins on the first day of hire and continues for three months in house and in the field. There are specific programs designed to support new hires in any of the various career paths the company offers, including selling the company's more sophisticated product lines.

The first two weeks of training take place at the local district level. During the third week, trainees attend a four-day session on selling skills and time management at a regional location. They also explore critical customer-care issues and learn how to penetrate certain markets. For the next four months, new hires spend one day a week training with the local manager, learning about both products and applications. At that point, the new hire is sent to the Pitney Bowes National Training Center in Atlanta, Georgia, for five days. There the trainee participates in an extensive program that polishes selling skills, product knowledge, and program applications.

After this initial formal instruction, additional training on products and on selling skills is provided throughout a sales professional's career. The entire sales training program is supported by an extensive library of state-of-the-art materials designed exclusively for Pitney Bowes. Management training, on an ongoing basis, is also available to qualified candidates.

PB reps sell directly to individual professionals, business firms, and major corporations in industry; they also sell to federal, state, and local governments and government agencies. At present, PB Business Systems has a sales force of about 3700, including field sales management. All are responsible for selling PB products and for satisfying customers' product and service needs, following up on installation, and ensuring that the PB systems perform as they should.

In support of its reps, PB offers good, qualified leads through many sources, such as telemarketing on local and national levels, and highly polished sales tools (brochures, visualizers, magazine ads, proposal kits, and so on). Each administrative section also helps reps with the typing of proposals, collections, and support service actions. In the field, customer service offers an automated service dispatch system that ensures timely repair of equipment.

Some PB reps work on a fixed-salary-plus-commission basis, and others work on straight commission. The fixed salary is $20,400. Commissions are based on a percentage of total sales, of course, but are awarded only if those sales come to 60% or more of the quota the rep is assigned to meet. Reps may also have a bonus of about $15,000 added to their salaries if they meet their sales targets. Bonuses for managers are computed on a quarterly basis at a fixed rate and depend on the managers' success at achieving a certain percentage of their sales quota. Given these variables, reps can expect to earn anywhere from $24,000 at the low end to $100,000 at the high end, but they average about $33,000. Salespeople in more senior positions average about $50,000 annually.

Benefits at PB are excellent. All reps' transportation and insurance expenses are reimbursed (there is no company car). There are group medical, dental, and life insurance plans; profit sharing and stock purchase plans; educational assistance programs; a retirement plan; a credit union; and other benefits. For its benefit program, PB has been cited on several occasions as one of the leaders in the industry.

As one might expect from PB's commitment to its employees, promotion opportunities are very good. Virtually all promotions are from within, and there are more than ten different professional sales positions that a rep can go into after training. Sales can also lead into management and, with experience, into home office product management and marketing positions.

PB looks for new hires who have an ability to learn, initiative, motivation, good communication skills, persistence, resilience, and impact. A college degree is required and technical or computer training is a big plus (qualifications will vary at different divisions). Many regional offices at present coordinate internships and cooperative programs with local colleges. Though a major corporation, Pitney Bowes offers the sense of working for a small company with a group of dedicated colleagues. It is informal by corporate standards, but it looks for, encourages, and rewards talent.

UNISYS CORPORATION

VITAL STATISTICS

Entry Level Salary for Sales: **$28,000–$32,000**
Senior Level Salary for Sales: **$50,000–$75,000+**

Benefits

medical/dental: **Yes**
life insurance: **Yes**
disability: **Yes**
travel allowance: **Yes**
company car: **No**
profit sharing plan: **Yes**
stock purchase plan: **Yes**

child care: **No**
retirement plan: **Yes**
savings investment plan: **Yes**
tuition assistance: **Yes**
relocation assistance: **Yes**
memberships: **Smokenders**
Weight Watchers
Wellness program
On-site fitness program

Corporate Culture Index   (1 = lowest, 10 = highest)

training: **10**
support: **9**
benefits: **10**

security: **9**
mobility: **9**
intangibles: **10**

Address: P.O. Box 418, Detroit, MI 48232
Contact: Personnel; telephone 215/542-4211

Unisys is one of the largest computer makers in the U.S., ranked 36th on the Fortune 500 list. 1987 sales nearly hit the $10 billion mark, a whopping 31% jump from 1986, while profits rose to $578 million, level with the previous year.

In the summer of 1986, two well-established old-line computer companies, Burroughs and Sperry-Rand, combined to form a new hybrid firm: Unisys ("The Power of Two"). By mid 1988, with a leaner workforce (down by some 25,000 employees), a sharply reduced debt burden, and strong earnings growth, the company had become what market analysts like to call "lean and mean."

With mainframe computer sales worldwide growing only 8% per year, mainframe makers are looking for new ways to stay profitable. Unisys's solution has been to emphasize "open systems," permitting computers made by different firms to communicate easily with each other. "Full connectivity" is the goal in these new "multivendor" environments. That means, for example, that Hong Kong Bank's new $50 million worth of Unisys computers can talk to IBM mainframes at half the cost, with double the power.

The company's sales force of 7500+ worldwide has been quite successful at retaining old Sperry and Burroughs accounts while wooing new customers away from main rivals DEC and IBM. Unisys markets mainly to financial, industrial, and communications companies, airlines, the federal government, and defense contractors. Subaru of America, for example, distributes more than 18,000 imported cars every year using Unisys information systems; Sunshine Biscuits tracks more than 44 billion cookies and crackers a year using one Unisys A10 mainframe.

Reps' territories vary in size according to client density from small urban sections to large rural stretches. Reps occasionally work in teams, but most travel alone on expense account. Some 3000 reps work the roads for Unisys, so the country is pretty well covered without much overnight travel. The turnover rate of between 10% and 15% is low.

Sales questions are handled by the district sales manager or by tech support, if the problem is technical. Advertising and promotional materials, administrative support (including research), and product instruction are well coordinated by branch and local sales offices. To some degree, reps train customers in the use of specialized products, particularly when selling to large corporate accounts. More commonly, however, reps install and demonstrate products as a way of promoting the benefits of Unisys equipment over rival products.

This company is looking for a few good salesmen and women, who must be articulate, presentable, and confident, and who have a college degree and a strong interest in sales. Training begins with a 16-week program in Valley Forge, Pennsylvania, combining classes in computers, selling skills, FAB (Features, Advantages, Benefits) and COS (Customer Oriented Selling) with intensive instruction in product knowledge.

Trainees climb an unusually defined promotional ladder from field sales rep to staff positions, back to sales management, and then on up to staff jobs at a higher level. A first-year sales trainee earns between $28,000 and $32,000; an average senior sales executive makes between $50,000 and $75,000. Bonuses and commissions are carefully calculated according to predefined sales goals and quotas.

Benefits include: medical and dental insurance, tuition assistance (100%), a car allowance (except in New York City), group life and disability insurance, a retirement and pension plan, a profit sharing and 401K savings plan, dependent care plan, relocation expenses, membership in Smokenders, Weight Watchers, a wellness program, and use of an on-site fitness center.

The atmosphere at Unisys is corporate and aggressive, as befits a major high-tech corporation. The excitement of the job lies mainly in demonstrating the superiority of Unisys products over rivals IBM and DEC in tackling specific data processing applications. This is a new company competing in a field long dominated by a tiny handful of household names, and CEO Michael Blumenthal, for one, believes in the energy generated by the creation of a new company out of two old ones.

Citing economist Joseph Schumpeter describing the strength of "creative destruction," Blumenthal says: "The people of Unisys have found that a big merger contains the power to shatter old conventions and to release new ideas and the confidence to bet on them."

WANG LABORATORIES, INC.

VITAL STATISTICS

Entry Level Salary for Sales: **$25,000**
Senior Level Salary for Sales: **$60,000–$65,000**

Benefits

medical/dental: **Yes**	child care: **Yes**
life insurance: **Yes**	retirement plan: **Yes**
disability: **Yes**	savings investment plan: **No**
travel allowance: **Yes**	tuition assistance: **Yes**
company car: **No**	relocation assistance: **N/A**
profit sharing plan: **Yes**	memberships: **Country club**
stock purchase plan: **Yes**	**memberships in Lowell, Mass.**

Corporate Culture Index   (1 = lowest, 10 = highest)

training:	**9**	security:	**9**
support:	**10**	mobility:	**9**
benefits:	**10**	intangibles:	**10**

Address: One Industrial Avenue, Lowell, MA 01851
Contact: Human Resources; telephone 508/656-6777

Wang Laboratories, Inc., ranks 146th on the Fortune 500 list. In 1987, it posted more than $2.8 billion in sales, up 7% from 1986. The company suffered losses in the first half of 1986, ending up fiscal 1987 with an overall loss of $70.7 million.

Wang Laboratories, Inc., designs, manufactures, and markets computer and communications systems, and provides related products and services. Its products are geared mostly to data and text processing, but the company offers image and voice processing products as well. Wang's products and services are designed to provide customers with solutions and systems that allow them to manage their operations and to communicate information more effectively.

Wang took a large blow to its earnings in the first half of 1987 (more than $100 million). Second half earnings reduced the loss, to the $70.7 million figure, and the company is looking to turn operations around in 1988. This was due to several factors: a loss of momentum in U.S. operations in a very difficult domestic market, problems in consolidating its major manufacturing operations, expenses based on higher revenues than were received, lower-than-planned shipments of key high-end systems, and losses from certain investments in subsidiary operations.

By mid 1987, however, the company had already moved to stem the losses. It strengthened its management team, decentralized some operations, kept up an active pace of new product introductions, reduced costs, and developed a more realistic long-term strategic plan for the company's future. These and other steps brought about a steady improvement in sales and earnings for the second half of 1987.

The company has buckled down to work and set itself a series of ambitious—and reachable—long-term goals. It intends to become number one in customer satisfaction in its field in three to five years and to hold an unchallenged place as one of the top three computer/communications companies throughout the 1990s. Wang is also determined to increase its market share by 20% a year over the next three to five years. Achieving these goals in a highly competitive industry will mean hard work all around, but especially in marketing and sales.

Wang fields a sales force of 1500 to 2000 reps. About 80% of all new hires come primarily from the competition, with the rest from college campuses. Prior sales experience and technical training are required, as is graduation from a good college with good grades—in a technical subject. Reps hired from the competition must survive five interviews and receive five approvals before they are accepted.

New hires are carefully trained in one of two programs. Reps hired from the competition receive a two-week cram course that concentrates on product knowledge (Wang equipment, systems, and services) and, to a lesser degree, on professional selling skills. Trainees who are recent graduates take a longer course of six to nine months, again concentrating on product knowledge and selling skills, but in much more detail. The training takes place at headquarters in Lowell, Massachusetts, and in the field in alternating segments of two to three weeks each. Only when the new hire is judged to be up to speed is he or she assigned a territory.

The reps sell to one of Wang's seven vertical markets: finance, legal, manufacturing, state and local governments, the federal government, professional services (for example, accounting), and a general category that includes construction, publishing, and others. Some reps' territories are based only on geography; others are based on selling to one of the vertical markets, no matter where it is situated. In a rep's early years, the territory normally will be on the small side (for instance, the financial district of Chicago) and will require few overnights. Later, when a rep is assigned to a major account, he or she may travel wherever that account has offices—even overseas. For the most part, reps work alone, but there is a first-rate sales support staff for technical questions. Reps have ready access to anyone in the company they feel can give them an answer to a question.

Reps demonstrate the capabilities of Wang equipment and show how the products will benefit the customer's business. They need to know their products thoroughly, and they must also know the needs of the market segment they serve. Keeping up to date on this information is part of their responsibility, and a big factor in forging a successful career at Wang. Field reps start as associate marketing reps (AMRs) and move through five levels before becoming a district manager. From there, a number of staff positions are possible next steps, and the company prefers to promote from within.

Salaries for trainees average about $25,000, with senior salespeople averaging about $60,000 to $65,000 total. Compensation includes both commission and bonus payments, which in turn depend on making quotas. The quotas are based on territory productivity and vary from rep to rep. Exceeding quotas can make bonus and commission payments very substantial (six-figure incomes are enjoyed by 1% or 2% of the sales force). Other benefits include: medical, dental, and life insurance; disability and retirement plans; profit sharing and stock purchase plans; a 401K plan; tuition assistance; a child care program (full flex-time program); and a home mortgage program.

Wang is a dynamic and aggressive company, eager to firmly establish its place in the top ranks of the industry. Coming off a disappointing several years, it is enthusiastic about recapturing its momentum and moving into new high-tech areas (its new Wang Integrated Image System, for example). It offers real, professional challenges along with splendid opportunities for career growth to those reps with the right mix of technical savvy, customer rapport (a major concern in this customer-driven company), and aggressive salesmanship.

XEROX CORPORATION

VITAL STATISTICS

Entry Level Salary for Sales: **$25,000+**
Senior Level Salary for Sales: **$100,000+**

Benefits

medical/dental: **Yes**	child care: **Yes**
life insurance: **Yes**	retirement plan: **Yes**
disability: **Yes, short and long term**	savings investment plan: **Yes**
travel allowance: **N/A**	tuition assistance: **Yes**
company car: **N/A**	relocation assistance: **Yes**
profit sharing plan: **Yes**	memberships: **Smokenders**
stock purchase plan: **Yes**	**Weight Watchers**
	Wellness program

Corporate Culture Index   (1 = lowest, 10 = highest)

training: **10**		security: **9**
support: **10**		mobility: **9**
benefits: **10**		intangibles: **10**

Address: P.O. Box 1600, 800 Long Ridge Road, Stamford, CT 06904
Contact: Personnel; telephone 203/968-3421

Xerox Corporation ranks 34th on the Fortune 500 list. In 1987 it had sales of more than $10 billion, an increase of 11% from 1986. Profits at $578 million were up 24% from 1986. These figures do not include sales and earnings from Xerox's Financial Services unit.

Xerox Corporation is a multinational office information systems giant so widely known that its trademark has come into our language as a verb meaning "to photocopy" (though the company campaigns against this usage). Yet Xerox is not alone, and faces stiff competition, domestic and foreign. To meet these challenges and to maintain its premier position in the office information products and systems market, in 1985 Xerox went through a restructuring that continued through 1987.

One of the main segments of Xerox slated for change was its direct sales force of 4000+. The professionalism and expertise of Xerox's sales reps are well known throughout the industry, but the company decided to try to make a good thing better. The strategy was to reorganize the sales force and target more clearly the different segments in its Business Products and Systems market. Xerox's sales force was then realigned to fit each segment.

The Business Products and Systems operation develops, manufactures, markets, and services Xerox's whole range of document processing equipment and systems. This includes Xerox duplicators, electronic printers and typewriters, workstations, network systems and other related products, software, and supplies.

Xerox has identified four basic segments in its business products market: custom systems, some 1000 major commercial accounts, standard commercial accounts (made up of medium-sized businesses), and small business accounts. To service these customers even more effectively, Xerox reorganized its U.S. Marketing Group sales force, converting most of its former product specialists into reps presenting the full line of products. The sales force now comprises marketing representatives, who service the low-end, small business accounts; account managers and account representatives, who service the middle and high-end commercial accounts; and national account managers (250 of them), who service the largest accounts.

In 1987, the company further formed two dedicated sales forces to meet the needs of two distinct customer groups. The Special Markets Group (100–150 reps) addresses low-end, entry-level, and specialized markets; it sells to them principally through third-party channels such as agents, dealers, distributors, original equipment manufacturers, and certain resellers, and also through telemarketing. The new Custom Service Division addresses the very special needs of the company's largest customers, such as the federal government, who need new and better ways to process billions of documents. The Custom Service Division produces and integrates custom systems for such accounts, using products and technologies from Xerox and from other sources. "We are making it as easy as possible for our customers to do business with Xerox," explains Paul A. Allaire, president of Xerox Corporation.

Xerox looks for sales rep candidates who have a college degree (any major) and who are aggressive and personable, and demonstrate a willingness to put in long hours, work hard, and improve themselves. A good academic record is important because it shows dedication to excellence. Experience with computers or other technical disciplines (math, science, information systems) is also helpful. Prior experience in sales or retailing is a definite plus, but it is not necessary.

Xerox provides a first-rate training program for its new reps. Training is for one of three product lines: copiers, document systems (network of workstations), or laser printers. Training takes place in a classroom—first at the district level, then at the training center near Leesburg, Virginia.

Classroom training runs in cycles, alternating with periods of on-the-job training in the field with an experienced sales manager. The classroom work totals about six weeks spread out over a year. At first, emphasis is on customer satisfaction and selling skills, then on product knowledge. Trainees videotape themselves and keep the tape to check on how they have improved after training. Self-study and improvement (for example, reading trade journals) is encouraged.

Territories vary in size; one rep, for instance, works only *two floors* of the World Trade Center in New York City. Reps generally work within 50 miles of their homes and there is little overnight travel. Typically, reps sell in teams of a sales rep, service rep, and maybe a sales manager. Emphasis is on close customer contact, and Xerox reps get to know their customers' businesses in detail and then meet their needs with Xerox products. Reps sell to anyone who needs a copier: businesses large and small, professionals' offices, hospitals, *anyone.*

Salaries for sales trainees average about $25,000 plus commissions; senior salespeople can go to $100,000 plus commissions; there is *no limit* on total income. Xerox promotes "targeted compensation," whereby reps who make their sales quota can earn 150% of their base salary. There is no set formula; some reps have a 40/60 split between salary and commissions, others 30/70. Other benefits include: medical, dental, and life insurance; disability and retirement plans; profit sharing and stock purchase plans, a 401K plan; tuition assistance; child care; and paid relocation expenses.

The climate at Xerox is strictly corporate. Reps "dress for success," and the pace is very up-tempo, with a sense of excitement, energy, and drive to please the customer. Promotion opportunities are good (the present CEO, David T. Kearns, was a sales rep), but many reps prefer just selling. There is a great deal of pressure to succeed, and yet many Xerox reps thrive in such a situation.

CONSTRUCTION
MATERIALS AND GLASS

This industry presents an interesting picture. The nationwide decline in construction has hurt the materials business, and, frankly, the balance sheets show it. But at the same time, new and profitable areas are on the horizon, and the companies that seize those opportunities will, so to speak, have laid down solid foundations.

Construction materials are a $38-billion-a-year business. Traditionally, the biggest profit center is home building, especially single-family homes, which concentrate large amounts of materials in small areas. Since fewer and fewer people are building their own homes, those profits have declined. However, even though fewer people are building, more are renovating. Today's strongest construction markets are in renovation, and companies that can compete there, such as Owens-Corning Fiberglas, for example, are doing better than ever.

A number of different products go under the heading of "construction materials." One segment is fabricated structural metal—columns and joints that become the frameworks for bridges, office towers, and transmission lines. The high cost of transporting these metals means that most plants will have a market radius of not much more than 200 miles. Another is concrete, which, because it is so vital to roads and railways, could take an upturn in the next few years if the government puts more effort into rebuilding America's crumbling infrastructure. In addition, bricks are one area where American companies have narrowed the trade deficit. They now export bricks to the tune of $88.5 million a year.

One sector of the industry that's doing particularly well is prefabricated metal buildings. Most are commercial and industrial, and the rest are mainly agricultural and "community," in other words, public buildings. The prefab industry's sales grew by 5% in 1987 and are at the highest levels seen since the 1970s, accounting for nearly $3 billion in sales. Most of the customers for prefab buildings are in the service industries—fast food, auto dealerships, or health care, to name a few—which are among the fastest growing sectors of the economy.

And then there's glass. "Flat glass" includes window glass, cathedral glass, antique glass, insulating glass, picture glass, windshield glass, and tempered glass—nearly $2 billion worth. Profits in flat glass have fallen somewhat in recent years, but that's largely a result of the unprecedented high sales that accompanied the office construction boom of the early 1980s. Analysts predict a rebound in office construction in the 1990s that ought to put glass on top. New products, like electrochromic glass, which makes it possible to set and adjust the amount of light coming through the windows almost at will, are sure to make the glass industry's future something worth looking into!

TRADE ASSOCIATIONS

Flat Glass Marketing Association 913/266-7013
National Building Material Distributors Association 312/724-6900
National Glass Dealers Association 703/442-4890
National Lumber and Building Material Dealers Association 202/547-2230

PERIODICALS

Building Supply Home Centers
Construction Equipment
Glass Digest
Glass Magazine

CERTAINTEED CORPORATION

VITAL STATISTICS

Entry Level Salary for Sales: **$25,000**
Senior Level Salary for Sales: **$49,000**

Benefits

medical/dental: **Yes**
life insurance: **Yes**
disability: **No**
travel allowance: **Yes**
company car: **Yes**
profit sharing plan: **Yes**
stock purchase plan: **Yes**

child care: **No**
retirement plan: **Yes**
savings investment plan: **N/A**
tuition assistance: **Yes**
relocation assistance: **Yes**
memberships: **Yes**

Corporate Culture Index   (1 = lowest, 10 = highest)

training: **8**
support: **8**
benefits: **7**

security: **8**
mobility: **8**
intangibles: **7**

Address: P.O. Box 860, Valley Forge, PA 19482
Contact: Personnel; telephone 215/341-7000

CertainTeed Corporation ranks 294th on the Fortune 500 list. It posted sales of more than $1 billion in 1987, up 4% from 1986; net profits for 1987 were more than $61 million, up 7% from 1986.

CertainTeed Corporation is a major manufacturer of construction materials for home and commercial buildings. Its product lines can be categorized into three industry segments: fiber glass products, building materials, and piping products. Fiber glass products include insulation for homes and commercial buildings and for use in other industrial and automotive applications. CertainTeed also makes fiber glass reinforcements that add light-weight strength to a variety of products, and the company offers a range of engineered materials for the construction and fiber-reinforced industries.

CertainTeed's building materials segment manufactures roofing, solid vinyl siding and windows, soffit and ridge vents, and aluminum doors and windows. The company is also a major wholesale distributor of building materials used in residential and commercial construction. The piping products segment manufactures A/C and PVC pipe and fittings and PVC products for electrical applications as well. CertainTeed is also a wholesale distributor of pipe system components for the utility industry.

The construction industry is an especially volatile one. So many factors, a number of them not under the control of those in the industry, play a significant role in the amount of construction planned, begun, and finished. World events, such as the depression of oil prices in the mid 1980s, for example, can lead to a downturn in construction. The stock market crash of late 1987 clouded the short-term outlook for home and commercial construction, as well. Nevertheless, CertainTeed feels its prospects are secure for continued growth as it concentrates on finding new business and improving its product lines. The company—and its sales reps—are particularly sensitive to changes in customer preferences, and used to responding to them quickly.

Sales training for such a volatile and competitive industry is naturally a high priority for CertainTeed. The formal training program is remarkably condensed, lasting only a month. The trainee is first exposed to the company's products and to the market situation, learning construction statistics and other information on the present state of both residential and commercial building markets. Along with this, trainees go through the professional selling skills program, a program for teaching basic selling skills.

Trainees then go on plant tours, familiarizing themselves with the way CertainTeed products are manufactured, and also study product literature the company has developed. Finally, the new hires experience job-site training, where they observe how company products are demonstrated, sold, and used in different types of construction. The month-long program takes place at the company's headquarters in Valley Forge, Pennsylvania, and at selected job sites and plants. After being evaluated on insulation installation and basic selling skills, the successful trainee goes into the field for more supervised on-the-job training.

CertainTeed reps work alone and generally maintain home offices. Their territories vary in size, running from one to six states, depending on population density. Reps average about two nights a week on the road, but this also depends on the territory size. Reps are given considerable independence, but they are expected to manage their territories effectively and to open new accounts; and they are rewarded on the basis of how well they perform these functions. They must demonstrate CertainTeed products and instruct customers on how best to use and install them. For the most part their customers are construction contractors and wholesale distributors of construction materials; reps don't have much contact with end users. The company's sales force is made up of 110 reps in residential sales and 60 in industrial sales.

CertainTeed reps receive a salary plus commission. The average salary for a trainee is around $25,000. Senior salespeople's salaries average around $49,000. Commission is paid quarterly if the company's sales are at least 80% of what was estimated for that quarter. If sales are running ahead, the commission is higher. Reps receive additional kinds of support, too. Administrative/clerical help is provided where possible, and promotion materials and research are forthcoming on special sales and incentive programs. Reps are expected to follow developments in their territories on their own, however.

Other benefits include: group medical and life insurance, a retirement plan, profit sharing and stock purchase plans, a travel allowance, tuition assistance, paid moving expenses, and a company car. The company offers refresher training programs on an ongoing basis. It also maintains a work-study internship program with some local colleges.

CertainTeed looks for new hires who are assertive but personable. A college degree is required, with a business or technical major preferred. The rep must be articulate and highly self-motivated, able to search out and find new markets independently. Promotion opportunities are good at CertainTeed. Reps can pursue a career path from sales rep to sales manager to district manager, or go into marketing as a product or marketing manager. Company policy is to reward good performance and to promote from within.

As befits the construction industry, the climate at CertainTeed is aggressive and dynamic. The company itself is reaching out to make acquisitions in the construction materials field that will ensure its long-term growth and its place in the forefront of the industry. It expects its reps to do the same in seeking out new markets and new accounts. The rewards for both will be substantial.

CORNING GLASS WORKS

VITAL STATISTICS

Entry Level Salary for Sales: **$30,000**
Senior Level Salary for Sales: **$47,000–$65,000**

Benefits

medical/dental: **Yes**	child care: **Yes**
life insurance: **Yes**	retirement plan: **401K**
disability: **Yes**	savings investment plan: **N/A**
travel allowance: **Yes**	tuition assistance: **Yes, and for**
company car: **Yes**	**children of**
profit sharing plan: **Yes**	**employees**
stock purchase plan: **Yes**	relocation assistance: **Yes**
	memberships: **Yes, at local YMCA**

Corporate Culture Index   (1 = lowest, 10 = highest)

training:	**9**	security:	**9**
support:	**8**	mobility:	**8**
benefits:	**10**	intangibles:	**10**

Address: Corning, NY 14831
Contact: Personnel; telephone 607/974-9000

Corning Glass Works ranks 186th on the Fortune 500 list. In 1987 it enjoyed more than $2 billion in sales, up 7% from 1986. Net profits were more than $200 million, an increase of 14% from 1986.

Corning Glass Works develops, manufactures, and sells high-tech products to industrial, consumer, and scientific markets. Its Industrial Operations Division deals with products for communications (optical fibers, video display screens/molded optics, and other glass products) and specialty materials (aerodynamic headlamps and emission-control products for the automotive industry, new ceramic technologies) and silicon-based products from Dow Corning, a joint venture of Corning and Dow Chemical.

Corning's Consumer Operations Division produces the popular Corning Ware and Corelle dinnerware lines and new products like Visions (top-of-the-range cookware), Pyrex Clear Advantage (new glass bakeware with a nonstick surface) and Storage Plus (a line of glass storage containers designed to go from refrigerator to microwave for convenient reheating of food).

In the science and health areas, Corning Glass is a leading supplier of laboratory equipment, supplies, and disposables (over 4000 items in all). It also is a worldwide leader in the production of glass-lens materials for prescription eyewear and sunglasses. Corning has also acquired Met-path, Inc., a leading clinical-testing company, and Hazleton Laboratories Corporation, a supplier of products and services for biological and chemical research.

Corning, basing its actions on 1987 sales and on its confidence in its key markets, is planning to expand its manufacturing facilities for consumer housewares, emission-control products, television glass, and scientific glassware. Sales of optical fibers for long-distance use were lower in 1987, so Corning is now turning its attention to the use of fiber in short distance applications (homes and businesses). In addition, the company is continuing to streamline and reorganize with an eye to reducing costs, increasing its focus on manufacturing and technology, and concentrating its resources on new market opportunities in each of its operating segments.

Training sales reps to work in these different and often highly competitive markets is a complex task, and Corning Glass is in the process of revising its training program to make it more comprehensive and effective. Right now, it begins by pairing the new hire with a Corning retiree for two or three days of on-the-job field work. This gives the new hire a chance to assimilate the old pro's experience, learn about the company's climate, hear "war" stories, and the like, resulting in a real, down-home company orientation session.

This is followed by several weeks of classroom work, concentrating on product knowledge. This training is decentralized and specifically keyed to the product group in which the new hire is going to work. It is held in Corning, New York, and is followed by field work visiting customers in the relevant product category. As would be expected with such a wide range of products and customers, new hires are exposed to a variety of accounts in their training. Follow-up training is also available, particularly in new product information.

Corning reps do not normally deal with the end users of the company's products. They sell to wholesale distributors in the consumer products and scientific areas and to major companies and original equipment manufacturers in the communications and industrial areas. In the consumer products area, however, Corning is making special efforts to increase distribution by aggressively expanding its houseware line into department stores, food stores, chain stores, and other such outlets. It has also mounted national advertising campaigns in television and print media for its consumer housewares line, introducing its new products and reinvigorating interest in its long-known and accepted ones.

Territories vary in size, according to population density, but reps should count on spending 30% to 50% of their time on overnights (there are 40 territories, each with its own rep). Corning reps work alone and generally do not install or demonstrate their products. With a new product, however, a rep may have to teach customers what it's for and how it's used.

Corning offers other kinds of sales support in major R&D programs, quick answers to any technical problems reps may have, good advertising and sales promotion materials, and clerical/administrative help when possible. Corning looks for new reps who have a college degree (BA or BS) with a science major. They want reps who are comfortable with and are able to handle technical materials, concepts, and products. Technical knowledge is very helpful and so, too, is prior sales experience.

A sales trainee's average beginning salary is around $30,000. The salaries of senior sales executives range from $47,000 to $65,000. A bonus is also available for reps in technical and consumer sales. This bonus, however, is not automatic; it is based on performance. The company, moreover, is committed to promotion from within. Other benefits include: a full medical/dental insurance plan, group life insurance, disability and retirement plans, a profit sharing plan, a 401K savings plan, full tuition assistance *and* educational assistance for employees' children, parental leave, a company car, and paid moving expenses.

Corning Glass Works is a high-tech company in outlook and in product base. On a personal basis, however, it is warm and close-knit, retaining a degree of paternalism from its earlier days.

OWENS-CORNING FIBERGLAS CORPORATION

VITAL STATISTICS

Entry Level Salary for Sales: **$28,000**
Senior Level Salary for Sales: **$45,000–$50,000**

Benefits

medical/dental: **Yes**
life insurance: **Yes**
disability: **Yes**
travel allowance: **Yes**
company car: **Yes**
profit sharing plan: **No**
stock purchase plan: **Yes**

child care: **No**
retirement plan: **Yes**
savings investment plan: **Yes**
tuition assistance: **Yes**
relocation assistance: **Yes**
memberships: **Smokenders**

Corporate Culture Index (1 = lowest, 10 = highest)

training: **9**
support: **8**
benefits: **9**

security: **9**
mobility: **9**
intangibles: **9**

Address: Fiberglas Tower, Toledo, OH 43659
Contact: Corporate Employment Department; telephone 419/248-8000

Owens-Corning Fiberglas Corporation ranks 144th on the Fortune 500 list. In 1987 it had sales of $2.9 billion, down 21% from 1986. The sales dip resulted from a major restructuring completed in 1987.

Owens-Corning Fiberglas undertook a major restructuring of its operations and its financing in the mid 1980s. Its lower sales revenue in 1987 resulted from the sale of some of the company's components and the withdrawal of some of its product lines. Owens-Corning's net profit in 1987, however, soared to $200 million, reflecting the company's successful turnaround in containing costs and divesting itself of underperforming components. The company is now considerably stronger, financially and competitively, and expects to meet future challenges from a much improved posture.

Founded in 1938 as a joint venture of Owens-Illinois, a glass products manufacturer, and Corning Glass Works, Owens-Corning became a publicly owned company in 1952, and today is the world's leading manufacturer of fiber glass materials (many of which are marketed under the trademark "Fiberglas") and a major producer of polyester resins. Owens-Corning operates in three business units: the Construction Products Group, the Industrial Materials Operating Division, and an International unit.

The Construction Products unit is a market leader in thermal and mechanical insulation and in roofing products, including fiber glass roofing insulation for the new housing (commercial and residential), remodeling, and repair markets. Perhaps this unit's most widely known product is its Pink Panther insulation. The Industrial Materials unit manufactures fiber glass–reinforced plastics and yarns and polyester resins, which it sells to the original equipment manufacturers of automobiles, boats, electronic equipment, plumbing components, appliances, fuel storage tanks, oil field pipes, and defense items (tanks, ballistic armor, and aerospace materials). The International unit supervises the company's manufacturing and marketing interests in 20 countries throughout the world.

Although the construction unit accounts for more than half the company's sales, the company's other two units are increasing in importance, improving Owens-Corning's product mix. This is good because the construction industry is notoriously volatile. In addition, the Industrial unit was able to gain a significant increase in net profit simply by operating more efficiently. This, combined with a strong overseas showing in 1987, makes the future prospects of Owens-Corning particularly bright.

To fill the sales reps spots in its construction and industrial units, Owens-Corning first draws up a job analysis with the job's specifications and then hires according to it. The company puts heavy emphasis on the following: planning and organization, easy rapport, tenacity, high work standards, persuasive ability, analytical ability, and tolerance of stress. The company interviews new hires with these particular qualities in mind.

A college degree or professional experience is required, and sales experience is a definite plus. No special technical knowledge is necessary. The training program lasts approximately five and one-half weeks and takes place at the Toledo headquarters and in the field. The program covers selling and writing skills, product knowledge, problem solving, and career planning. It also includes a plant tour and a visit to the research department. Training is continuous as reps move up the corporate ladder, but its emphasis switches from product knowledge and technical expertise to the broader areas of management skills, business operations, complex problem solving, and decision making.

Reps in the construction unit sell to distributors, general contractors, builders, and architects, but not to end users. In the industrial unit, reps sell to manufacturers and the government. Reps may carry small samples with them for demonstration purposes, but they are more likely to invite a distributor's buyer or general manager to visit a test site where the product's specific properties can be best demonstrated. Reps generally work on their own; their territories are relatively compact (within a radius of about 50 miles of their home), and overnights are few. It is a common practice, however, for Owens-Corning to relocate new hires during their first few years with the company.

The average salary for trainees is about $28,000, with senior salespeople earning from about $45,000 to $50,000. Incentives can raise these figures, but those incentives depend on performance. Other rep support includes: substantial ad and promotion materials (in all media), administrative/clerical help, new product research, and continued training as the rep's career advances. The career development program helps employees realize their goals and achieve job satisfaction.

The rest of the benefits package is substantial. It includes: medical, dental, and life insurance (with post-retirement medical and life insurance for employees and their dependents); a disability plan; a 401K pension plan; a stock purchase plan; paid moving expenses; a tuition assistance plan that reimburses 100% of costs; and a company car.

The climate at Owens-Corning is open, not to say laid-back, but sales reps must assume a great deal of responsibility. They are expected to manage their territories as if they were their own businesses, and this means being alert and heads up all the time. Tolerance of stress is a very handy trait to have when working the Owens-Corning markets. Even so, the turnover rate among sales reps is low, the job is rewarding if demanding, and the advancement prospects are excellent.

PPG INDUSTRIES, INC.

VITAL STATISTICS

Entry Level Salary for Sales: *$22,000–$25,000 with liberal arts background*
$32,000–$36,000 with technical background
Senior Level Salary for Sales: *$50,000–$65,000*

Benefits

medical/dental: **Yes**
life insurance: **Yes**
disability: **Yes**
travel allowance: **Yes**
company car: **Yes**
profit sharing plan: **No**
stock purchase plan: **No**

child care: **Yes**
retirement plan: **Yes**
savings investment plan: **No**
tuition assistance: **Yes**
relocation assistance: **Yes**
memberships: **No**

Corporate Culture Index   (1 = lowest, 10 = highest)

training: **8**
support: **8**
benefits: **9**

security: **9**
mobility: **9**
intangibles: **9**

Address: One PPG Place, Pittsburgh, PA 15272
Contact: Human Resources; telephone 412/434-3131

PPG Industries, Inc., ranks 78th on the Fortune 500 list. In 1987 it posted sales of more than $5 billion, up 11% from 1986. PPG is the world's leading supplier of automotive and industrial finishes.

PPG Industries, Inc., a major, diversified manufacturer of industrial products, was founded in 1883. Today, it concentrates on three major businesses: glass, coatings and resins, and chemicals. The products of these operations serve a variety of industries around the world, including manufacturing, building, processing, and services. The company runs 75 major manufacturing sites in the U.S. and abroad, and it maintains 11 research and development facilities.

PPG Glass manufactures glass products for construction, automotive, and industrial uses. Its products include flat and fabricated glass, environmental and coated glass, continuous-strand and chopped-strand fiber glass, Adzel fiber glass, and resin composites. PPG glass is used in automobiles, commercial and residential construction, aircraft, and various industrial markets. Its fiber glass is used in transportation, construction, electronics, and various recreational and industrial markets.

PPG Coatings and Resins (C&R) produces automotive and industrial coatings, trade paint, metal pretreatment chemicals, adhesives, sealants, and printing inks. It is the leading supplier of coatings to the automotive industry and its after-markets. Its products are also used in commercial and residential construction and maintenance, and in appliance, container, and other industrial finish markets.

PPG Chemicals is the world's fourth largest producer of chlorine and caustic soda. It also produces chlorine derivatives, phosgene and derivatives, optical resins, sulfur chemicals, silica products, swimming pool chemicals, and other specialty chemicals. These products are used in chemical manufacturing and synthesis, in soaps and detergents, in pulp and paper making, in water treatment, in personal care products, and in various industrial markets.

PPG sees a promising future as it pursues a policy of changing its product mix to include more high-value and fewer commodity-type products. It plans to continue its expansion into the $3-billion medical electronics field, while at the same time enhancing its presence in the Far East, Europe, and South America. Overall, it will continue streamlining its operations in order to make them more efficient and cost-effective.

To recruit and train sales reps for its various companies and operating divisions, PPG relies on the managers of its 80 branches throughout the country. PPG management relates to its branches the way baseball's major leagues relate to their farm clubs. Sales reps usually start in the branches and then, if they demonstrate real talent and turn in top performances, they are sent up to the majors of the company's management team.

Although training may vary from branch to branch, there are general guidelines throughout the company. The training program for new reps lasts from three to four weeks, and it comprises both classroom work and on-the-job training. The program concentrates on developing selling skills, product knowledge, and the understanding of that particular branch's market. Because PPG's markets differ so widely, sales reps—even in the same business area—may find themselves calling on quite different customers with quite different needs. For instance, sales reps in the glass unit may be selling to window and door manufacturers in construction, automobile fabricators who make windshields, or wholesale distributors handling mirrors for residential or industrial use. A rep may call on three of these groups or perhaps service only a handful of *large* customers in one or more of the groups, or even work with just *one* customer, if the account is large and complex enough to require such intensive management. As a rule of thumb, a rep's "territory" covers accounts totaling from $20 million to $50 million in annual sales.

PPG reps act as professional and technical consultants to their customers. They need to learn as much about the businesses of their accounts as they do about PPG's business in order to solve a customer's problems with the right PPG products and services. For example, to help its auto refinish customers, the C&R group recently installed training facilities in a number of its refinish warehouses. Reps must match these products and services with the needs of their accounts.

Understandably, the requirements for sales reps at PPG vary greatly depending on the local branch or business area in question. Generally, a college degree is strongly preferred, but it is not absolutely necessary. The same is true for prior sales experience and for technical knowledge. Salaries, however, do reflect educational levels. PPG is a straight-salary company, and beginning salaries for reps with liberal arts degrees range from $22,000 to $25,000. For those with technical degrees, especially if they did well in college, the beginning salary range is $32,000 to $36,000. Senior sales executives' salaries range from $50,000 to $65,000. And sales reps who distinguish themselves are very likely to move up in the company.

PPG supports its salespeople with good promotional and advertising materials, especially new product information. It also provides clerical/administrative help and extensive R&D into new product development. Other benefits include: medical and dental insurance plans, group life insurance, disability and retirement plans, a savings plan, child care, tuition assistance, a travel allowance, paid moving expenses, and a company car.

PPG today (the company's old name was Pittsburgh Plate Glass) is a high-tech company with a generally corporate atmosphere. In recent years, it has consolidated its operations to make them more cost-effective and competitive. This has resulted in a more dynamic, aggressive, go-get-'em climate, and sales reps who fit the bill are likely to do well with the company.

USG CORPORATION

VITAL STATISTICS

Entry Level Salary for Sales: **$25,000–$26,500**
Senior Level Salary for Sales: **$40,000**

Benefits (Flexible benefits program)

medical/dental: **Yes**
life insurance: **Yes**
disability: **Yes**
travel allowance: **Yes**
company car: **Yes**
profit sharing plan: **Yes**
stock purchase plan: **Yes**

child care: **No**
retirement plan: **Yes**
savings investment plan: **N/A**
tuition assistance: **Yes, 80% undergraduate, 100% graduate**
relocation assistance: **Yes**
memberships: **Park, lakes, golf Wellness program**

Corporate Culture Index   (1 = lowest, 10 = highest)

training: **10**
support: **9**
benefits: **10**

security: **9**
mobility: **10**
intangibles: **10**

Address: 101 South Wacker Drive, Chicago, IL 60606-4385
Contact: Employment Resources; telephone 312/606-4000 ext. 4394

USG Corporation ranks 142nd on the Fortune 500 list. In 1987 it enjoyed sales of more than $3 billion, a 6% increase from 1986. Net profits, however, at $204 million, were 9% below 1986.

USG Corporation was established in 1985 as a management holding company for United States Gypsum Company and several other subsidiary companies. Today, USG manages a largely decentralized group of four core businesses concentrated in the building products industry. This concentration is deliberate, and it constitutes the first element of the corporation's long-term strategies. As recently as 1985, only 79% of USG's business was in the building industry, while today that figure is approximately 90%, a reflection of the corporation's determination to focus its efforts in the one area it knows best. The four core businesses are: U.S. Gypsum Company, L & W Supply Corporation, Masonite Corporation, and USG Interiors, Inc.

U.S. Gypsum Company is the largest manufacturer in the world of gypsum products for the building and industrial markets. Its gypsum board, joint treatment, plaster, and industrial gypsum products are all number one in the U.S. market. L & W Supply Corporation operates 140 distribution centers in the U.S., supplying gypsum board and other products. It distributes 11% of the wallboard in this country. Masonite Corporation is the leading U.S. producer of hardboard siding, roofing, paneling, and molded door products. USG Interiors, Inc. is the largest integrated company serving the growing, multibillion-dollar commercial interiors market.

Other strategies pursued by USG to establish it as one of the nation's leading construction materials producers include: improving the performance of all its profit centers, using research and development to create major new products, increasing emphasis on both the repair and remodeling markets, and acquiring businesses with great growth potential in the building field. To implement this last strategy, USG is divesting itself of those subsidiaries and product lines that fail to meet its profitability goals or fit in with its overall concentration on the building industry. USG has already scored considerable success in implementing these strategies and is intent on pursuing them vigorously in the future. As with all construction-related firms, though, USG's performance is directly affected by swings in the national economy.

To be a successful USG rep, you must know the corporation's products *and* the construction business. USG reps must feel comfortable with the entire construction cycle. They must be able to talk to architects to ensure that USG products are specified in the building plans. They need to know about and be comfortable with the various building trades, how much roofing a building will need, for example, or how much sheetrock an added bedroom will take. Finally, they must deal with the subcontractor on the job site itself. Since all USG components sell materials that are used at the site, reps must know how and when the material is to be used—and delivered; it must not arrive late and hold the job up, or arrive too early and get in the way or cause storage problems. USG reps spend a lot of time in hard hats, jeans, and boots on the job site keeping track of how it all goes on and smoothing over any last-minute glitches.

Because USG's management style is decentralized, it relies on its district managers to hire sales reps according to their needs. In all cases, technical knowledge of construction is required, and if the new hire doesn't have it, USG teaches it. Candidates for the rep position must have a BA at least; about half of all USG reps have degrees in engineering or architecture, and half have degrees in business or liberal arts.

USG's training program is extensive, taking place on and off over a two-year period. It utilizes a series of self-study courses designed especially by USG and includes an 11-day classroom session, which covers the professional selling skills, product knowledge, and some physics. The reps monitor their own progress throughout the training with a self-development guide, and their performances are evaluated after every segment in discussions with their district managers.

Territories vary in size, and how much time a rep spends on the road depends on the type of assignment and product line. Reps may be selling acoustical ceilings and wall panels, or suspended ceilings, or office interiors, or drywall for new homes. The work is never routine, however, and each job presents its own problems and challenges. The company offers all kinds of support: promotion materials, clerical/administrative help, new product development, and on-site technical support teams. There is also a summer internship program, when conditions permit.

Salaries for trainees average from about $25,000 to $26,500, and senior salespeople earn about $40,000. There are bonuses, too, averaging about 5% of salary. Other quite extensive benefits include: medical, dental, and life insurance; disability and 401K plans (including certain post-retirement health care and life insurance benefits); a travel allowance; a stock purchase plan; tuition assistance of 100% for graduates and 80% for undergraduates, up to a $3500 maximum; paid relocation expenses and a relocation bonus; and a company car.

Advancement opportunities are excellent at USG. All senior officers of the corporation started out as sales reps, and company policy is to promote from within. USG looks for management potential in its sales force of over 950 reps, which may in part account for the company's relatively low turnover rate among reps.

USG reps work alone for the most part and take on a great deal of responsibility. The corporate climate is warm and friendly; it is especially hospitable to career-oriented people who are free-spirited, eager to work independently, and willing to get their clothes a little dirty on the job site.

CONSUMER PRODUCTS

There is a lot more to this business than "Avon ladies" at the front door. Some of the nation's largest corporations and most prominent financiers are to be found here. Soaps and detergents make our lives hygienic and livable. Cosmetics and perfumes intoxicate us with allure and romance. And all add up to some very big bucks.

The colossus Procter & Gamble, maker of diapers, toothpaste, soaps and detergents, had the distinction of being the largest single advertiser in the country, putting more than $1 billion of its $17 billion in sales into advertising alone in 1987. Soaps and detergents (Ivory, Tide, Head & Shoulders, Cascade) accounted for a little under a third of that total. Procter & Gamble ran neck and neck with rival Lever Brothers in detergents and lost out in bar soaps.

Industry sales overall rose by 2% last year, to $10 billion. The greatest growth has been in liquid detergents, which have dramatically risen in recent years and may eventually capture half the market.

Because the demand for soap and detergent products is generally no greater than the annual increase in population, aggressive sales and marketing are a prime ingredient of success. New and more effective chemicals, and new delivery systems, like dissolving packets of detergent, play a crucial role in spurring sales on.

Cosmetics, perfumes, and skin-care products may be dealing only with appearances, but in the industry, the competition and the sales are very real. Perfumes are a $3-billion-a-year industry. In 1987, cosmetics sales came to nearly $5 billion and skincare to more than $2 billion.

Products for sensitive skin have been especially profitable in the past few years as consumers become more and more interested in mixing good health with high fashion. Interestingly, the most money is to be made in the more expensive product lines, like Estee Lauder, and in the less expensive, drugstore lines, like Noxell's Cover Girl. The products in the middle range tend to get squeezed out of the profit margins.

Fortunes in cosmetics are not etched in stone. Revlon, for example, drained its profits from beauty products for its health-care lines and went from being an unchallenged number one in every outlet to an also-ran in the downscale drugstore market in a decade. Now, under new high-powered management, it is trying to make a comeback by buying Max Factor's Halston lines and Yves Saint Laurent's fragrances (and, rumor has it, by working on a fragrance to be promoted by Vanna White).

As you may have guessed, there are a lot of airs in this industry. But if you're aggressive and make a good sell to a drugstore chain or a high-class cosmetics counter, it won't be long before you catch the sweet smell of success on the wind.

TRADE ASSOCIATIONS

Consumers Union of United States (CU) 914/667-9400
Cosmetics, Toiletries and Fragrances Association 202/331-1770
National Housewares Manufacturers Association 312/644-3333
Soap and Detergent Association 212/725-1262

PERIODICALS

Consumer Reports
Housewares
Product Marketing

ALBERTO CULVER COMPANY

VITAL STATISTICS

Entry Level Salary for Sales: **$23,000–$25,000**
Senior Level Salary for Sales: **$35,000–$38,000**

Benefits

medical/dental: **Yes**
life insurance: **Yes**
disability: **Yes**
travel allowance: **Yes**
company car: **Yes**
profit sharing plan: **Yes**
stock purchase plan: **Yes**

child care: **No**
retirement plan: **No**
savings investment plan: **N/A**
tuition assistance: **Yes, 75%**
relocation assistance: **Yes**
memberships: **No**

Corporate Culture Index   (1 = lowest, 10 = highest)

training: **9**
support: **9**
benefits: **9**

security: **8**
mobility: **9**
intangibles: **10**

Address: 2525 Armitage Avenue, Melrose Park, IL 60160
Contact: Personnel; telephone 312/450-3000

Alberto Culver Company ranks 472nd on the Fortune 500 list. In 1987 it had record sales of more than $500 million, up 18% from 1986. Its earnings in that period were $18.1 million, a 37% increase from 1986.

Alberto Culver is a leader in the toiletries industry. It has developed a full line of high-quality hair-care products in its own laboratories. It manufactures and markets these products through four of its six operating divisions: Domestic Toiletries, International, Professional, and Sally Beauty Company. The company's other major marketing area, foods, is handled by its two remaining operating divisions: Household/Grocery and Milani Food Service.

The Domestic Toiletries Division markets the Alberto VO5 line of shampoos, hair sprays, conditioners, and other hair-care products. It also markets Alberto styling products, FDS Feminine Deodorant Spray, and other toiletry items sold at retail. The company expects that the return to classic, more structured hair styles will benefit its hair spray products, and it looks forward to increased sales in this market in the future.

The International Division markets the company's product line worldwide, operating in more than 100 countries. It is particularly excited about its new partnership with the Hattori-Seiko Company in Japan, since it feels it will be able to gain a significant share of the Japanese hair-care market.

The Professional Division produces and distributes a wide range of hair-care products to beauty salons, barber shops, and retailers in the beauty industry. The division also produces educational and cultural programs for users of those products at both the professional and retail levels. For instance, in 1987 it produced a training film for cosmeticians that explained the special requirements in caring for black hair, the first educational support of its kind available at the retail level.

The Sally Beauty Company operates 600 stores, domestically and internationally, that serve the beauty salon and barber trade. It is the market leader in beauty supply business, meeting the needs of professional hair stylists and cosmetologists with cash-and-carry convenience. The stores, which are located throughout the U.S. in shopping centers, appeal as well to the retail customer, who uses them to buy just the right products between visits to beauty salons.

The Household/Grocery and Milani Food Service divisions constitute Alberto's presence in the food market. The Household/Grocery division offers a line of products to the retail market, primarily supermarkets and mass merchandisers. The products include the Mrs. Dash line of low-sodium products; Molly McButter, a low-sodium, low-cholesterol butter substitute; SugarTwin, an artificial sweetener; Baker's Joy, a flour and oil baking spray; and others. Milani Food Service produces and distributes more than 400 food items to hotels, restaurants, health-care facilities, and schools.

Alberto is confident about future growth. Its markets are relatively recession-resistant, and it is working on aggressive marketing and new product development to spur increased sales. In 1987 Domestic Toiletries added cable TV to its advertising mix, finding it an excellent medium for reaching the young, style-conscious consumer. Sally Beauty Company has new stores planned. And Milani Food Service has established a National Accounts Department to facilitate its handling of special larger accounts with multiple outlets and a Special Markets group to take care of business obtained from state and federal government contracts.

Alberto is looking for potential sales reps who know what they want to do, not people who tried something else and then decided to sell as a last resort. It wants college graduates who demonstrate an independent, entrepreneurial spirit; self-starters with a desire to succeed will be the ones most likely to get a job with the company. Prior sales experience is not necessary, but it is a big plus. Training in the Toiletries Division is informal and takes place mostly in the field. New reps spend four to five weeks with their district sales manager learning the accounts and the product lines. Training then continues on an informal basis with an emphasis on merchandising, pricing, placing ads, displaying the products in the best way possible, and so on.

Alberto Toiletries reps sell to all outlets that carry this kind of product—chain stores, department stores, drugstores, grocery stores, and distributors. The territories are generally small, usually covering metropolitan areas (rural and out-of-the-way areas are handled by brokers). Reps work alone, making calls, setting up displays, checking pricing, rotating stock, and coordinating store specials with media advertising, which Alberto uses extensively.

Salaries for trainees range from $23,000 to $24,000; senior salespeople earn $35,000 to $38,000. Bonuses are also offered, and for reps to win a full bonus they must not only hit their quotas but also meet their MBO (management by objectives) goals, which are established in negotiation with their district sales managers. They receive excellent support from the company in major advertising, help with administrative/clerical chores, and R&D. Alberto is also committed to promotion from within, and the various divisions present many selling opportunities. Other benefits include: medical, dental, and life insurance; a disability plan; profit sharing and stock purchase plans; tuition assistance (75% of costs, up to $1750 per year); paid relocation expenses; a travel allowance; and a company car.

Alberto offers a good stable opportunity for those who like selling and like working on their own. Reps find the job fast-paced and demanding, but they also have the products, the authority, and the support to succeed.

CHESEBROUGH-POND'S, INC.

VITAL STATISTICS

Entry Level Salary for Sales: **$24,000**
Senior Level Salary for Sales: **$54,000**

Benefits

medical/dental: **Yes**	child care: **No**
life insurance: **Yes**	retirement plan: **Yes**
disability: **Yes, short and long term**	savings investment plan: **N/A**
travel allowance: **Yes**	tuition assistance: **Yes**
company car: **No**	relocation assistance: **Yes**
profit sharing plan: **No**	memberships: **No**
stock purchase plan: **No**	

Corporate Culture Index   (1 = lowest, 10 = highest)

training:	**8**	security:	**9**
support:	**9**	mobility:	**9**
benefits:	**8**	intangibles:	**10**

Address: 33 Benedict Place, Greenwich, CT 06836-6000
Contact: Personnel; telephone 203/661-2000

Chesebrough-Pond's ranks 304th on the Fortune 500 list. In 1987, the first year after its merger with Unilever, it had sales of over $1 billion, up 8% from 1986.

In 1986 Unilever acquired Chesebrough-Pond's, Inc. With the acquisition, Chesebrough became a division of Unilever and underwent a restructuring, divesting itself of some product lines and companies and taking on some others, so that now it is concentrated on the areas in which it has traditionally scored its greatest successes—personal-care products, packaged foods, and cosmetics and fragrances.

In this restructuring, Chesebrough's international businesses were integrated into Unilever's worldwide operations while Unilever's personal care products businesses were merged with Chesebrough's. This created one of the largest personal products companies in the U.S. Chesebrough's operations comprise three main divisions: the Health and Beauty Products

Division, the Prince Matchabelli Division, and the Packaged Foods Division.

The Health and Beauty Products Division markets such well-known brands as Aim, Close-up, and Pepsodent toothpastes; Signal mouthwash; Vaseline Intensive Care Lotion and Q-Tips; and Rave hair spray. The Prince Matchabelli Division markets a line of fragrances including the very successful Elizabeth Taylor's Passion, Aviance, Night Musk, Cachet, Vervé, and Windsong. Also among this division's products are Aziza products and the Cutex line of nail-care products. Added to this was Impulse body spray for women from Unilever. The Packaged Foods Division markets the popular Ragú line of sauces and the Ragú Foodservice, a business comprising tomato products and quality sausage sold to restaurants, schools, institutions, pizza chains, and other customers.

Purchasing, manufacturing, engineering, and product development were divisionalized to give the operating units more independence and also to deliver their support to each division more economically and efficiently. The merger with Unilever also gives Chesebrough access to that company's extensive research capabilities; Unilever devotes in excess of $600 million a year to R&D in order to develop new products and to improve existing ones. Taking advantage of this capacity, along with its own strengthened product development activities, will allow Chesebrough to maintain and expand its superior line of products in its core businesses in the future. The research will also involve devising new marketing and sales strategies to improve Chesebrough's position in the business it has pursued for over 100 years—consumer products for the whole family.

In Chesebrough's market, selling is what counts. The company looks for potential reps who show a capacity for hard work, who are able to work alone, and who actually *like* selling. Reps must enjoy working with people and with products that people use personally—health-care and beauty aids, fragrances, and cosmetics. Selling these products doesn't take a great deal of technical knowledge or business acumen; it does take enthusiasm and real concern for the end users of the products, even if they are not the ones Chesebrough reps sell to directly.

Chesebrough reps are college graduates, with majors in liberal arts or business. Interestingly enough, the company has had better experience recruiting from Midwestern colleges and the Big Ten schools rather than from the high-prestige Ivy League schools of the Northeast. Prior sales experience is not necessary; it is more important for potential reps to show that they are innovative, good at problem solving, and self-motivated. On the road, where reps spend most of their time, they will be on their own, with little supervision or prodding from their district sales managers.

Typically, new Chesebrough reps begin by selling Matchabelli Division's cosmetics and fragrances. Successful reps may then move on to merchandising the beauty and health-care line or go on to the Ragú food division. As reps move up the corporate ladder, they assume progressively more responsibility, going from sales reps responsible for retail accounts in one territory to key account managers who handle more important wholesale accounts in larger, more productive territories. The ladder can lead right up to a corporate vice presidency of sales. The company does promote from within, and it gives employees as much responsibility as they feel they can handle. A number of the reps, however, do stay in the field because they enjoy the selling.

Sales training generally lasts about eight weeks and is the responsibility of the manager of the division or unit doing the hiring. Training takes place both at headquarters in Greenwich, Connecticut, and in the field. Because no prior experience is required, the company strongly stresses selling techniques and product knowledge. It also relies a great deal on on-the-job training to acquaint the new hires with their territories and their customers. For the most part, reps sell to major drugstores, department stores, chain stores, and, in the case of the Ragú line, to food brokers. The selling is competitive, and reps often must explain and demonstrate certain products, especially in the health and beauty lines. Territories vary in size, but reps may be on overnights most Mondays through Thursdays.

The average salary for a trainee is $24,000; senior salespeople can earn $54,000. A 15% commission is also added to salary. Other benefits include: medical, dental, and life insurance; disability and retirement plans; 100% tuition assistance; paid relocation expenses; and a company car.

There is real camaraderie to be found at Chesebrough, and a good career, too, for those who really love selling.

ECOLAB, INC.

VITAL STATISTICS

Entry Level Salary for Sales: **$19,000–$22,000**
Senior Level Salary for Sales: **$50,000+**

Benefits

medical/dental: **Yes; choice of coverage**	child care: **No**
	retirement plan: **Yes**
life insurance: **Yes**	savings investment plan: **N/A**
disability: **Yes**	tuition assistance: **Yes**
travel allowance: **N/A**	relocation assistance: **Yes**
company car: **Yes, for managers**	memberships: **No**
profit sharing plan: **No**	
stock purchase plan: **No**	

Corporate Culture Index (1 = lowest, 10 = highest)

training:	**10**	security:	**8**
support:	**9**	mobility:	**8**
benefits:	**8**	intangibles:	**9**

Address: Ecolab Center, St. Paul, MN 55102
Contact: Human Resources; telephone 612/293-2233

The leading worldwide developer and marketer of "premium institutional and residential services," Ecolab ranks 331st on the Fortune 500 list, with sales in 1987 topping $1 billion, up a hefty 65% from 1986.

Who ever heard of Ecolab? The company employs about 13,000 people worldwide, providing some rather unusual services, such as "warewashing"—the process of cleaning the plates, glasses, utensils, and kitchen equipment used in food preparation and serving—and a 1400-member direct sales and service organization (the industry's largest) just to push Ecolab's "Solids Team" of detergent systems for on-premises laundries.

Ecolab's far-flung enterprises include the Institutional Division, which offers warewashing, laundry, and specialty products to hotels, hospitals, schools, prisons, and restaurants. This division also includes a Textile Care Division, a Pest Division, a Janitorial Division, and Klenzade, which markets "the first lubricant for beverage plant conveyers using solid product technology."

It also recently acquired Chemlawn, the leading supplier of lawn-care services to residential customers in North America, staffed by more than 3500 "professional specialists" providing lawn care for 1.7 million residential customers.

Perhaps only an Ecolab sales rep can truly understand all of Ecolab's unusually amorphous products and services. But Ecolab reps are not reps in the usual sense, but individual entrepreneurs who, after a full year of training, buy their territory from the parent company, along with the chemicals necessary, and begin operations as independent "specialists" in their respective service fields.

Ecolab seeks out prospective reps with mechanical aptitude and the ability to install and repair equipment ranging from lawn-care to hospital-service and rug-cleaning equipment. An entrepreneurial attitude tops their list of requirements, with educational background—"high school, some college"—trailing behind. Prior sales experience is helpful, as is technical knowledge, but not necessary.

The sales training program is unusually thorough, focusing on professional selling skills and orientation toward such arcane procedures as the ubiquitous warewashing. The program combines classroom work with on-the-job training at one of two centers in New Jersey and California. This year-long "apprenticeship" (during which the average trainee makes only $19,000 to $22,000) is a prelude to intensive testing and evaluation of the rep in the field by the district sales manager.

Once a rep in the Institutional Division buys into a territory from the company, it is clearly an advantage to build up a client base and stick things out until profits build. This reduces a rep's inducement to try to move up to top management, since that $300,000 to $400,000 investment cannot be recouped. A senior sales executive at Ecolab tends to pull in $50,000 plus bonus and commission.

Reps live in their territories, making overnight stays a rarity, as unusual as selling in a team. As independent entrepreneurs, reps are not entitled to expense accounts, though they are free to phone the district manager and headquarters in St. Paul for sales support.

In the Institutional Division, all 3500 reps report to their district managers, who are responsible for providing whatever support might be necessary by way of advertising and promotional materials, typing, filing, computers, and research into new products.

Reps are constantly on call to teach customers how to operate new machines and new products, processes, and procedures. Reps also frequently demonstrate new Ecolab products and services at restaurants and trade shows, where corporate attire is called for. Still, the atmosphere at the company is described as "laid-back"—not too surprising, when you get right down to it, for a company specializing in nitty-gritty, down-to-earth stuff such as pest control, lawn care, and dishwashing.

Benefits include medical and dental insurance, tuition assistance, a company car (for managers only), life and disability insurance, child care, a retirement plan, and paid relocation expenses. Profit sharing and stock purchase plans are reserved for management at senior levels and are not open to reps.

The services provided by Ecolab might seem a bit strange, but the U.S. lawn-care business (to take just one example) has now hit the $1 billion mark in sales and is growing as fast as crabgrass. Dishes will always need to be washed, lawns taken care of, and chemicals developed to kill pesky bugs. So who cares if Ecolab is not exactly a household name? They seem to be doing just fine without the brand name publicity.

THE GILLETTE COMPANY

VITAL STATISTICS

Entry Level Salary for Sales: **$25,000**
Senior Level Salary for Sales: **$40,000+**

Benefits

medical/dental: **Yes**
life insurance: **Yes**
disability: **Yes**
travel allowance: **N/A**
company car: **Yes**
profit sharing plan: **Yes**
stock purchase plan: **Yes**

child care: **No**
retirement plan: **Yes**
savings investment plan: **No**
tuition assistance: **Yes**
relocation assistance: **Yes**
memberships: **Weight Watchers On-site fitness center**

Corporate Culture Index   (1 = lowest, 10 = highest)

training: **9**
support: **9**
benefits: **9**

security: **9**
mobility: **9**
intangibles: **9**

Address: Prudential Tower Building, Boston, MA 02199
Contact: Personnel; telephone 617/421-7700

The Gillette Company ranks 135th on the Fortune 500 list. In 1987 it had total sales of more than $3 billion, up 12% from 1986. At the same time it enjoyed net earnings of $230 million, an increase of 27% from 1986.

The Gillette Company, founded in 1901, develops, manufactures, and sells a wide range of products for personal care. Its principal product lines include: razors and razor blades, toiletries and cosmetics, writing instruments and office products, Braun electric shavers and other small appliances, and Oral-B products. In 1987, the company paid a cash dividend on its common stock for the 82nd consecutive year.

The company's most important business lies in its line of blades and razors, which accounted for about 33% of Gillette's 1987 sales. Sales are international, and in most major markets consumers continue to buy more Gillette blades and razors than those of all its competitors combined. The company attributes its success to its extensive worldwide distribution of quality shaving products, its continued technical innovation, and its highly effective marketing and promotion campaigns—all of which provide Gillette with a sound basis for sustaining its leadership in its principal line of business.

Gillette's sales of toiletries and cosmetics resulted in markedly higher profits in 1987, owing mainly to higher sales and margins in its foreign operations. U.S. sales in 1987 were flat and profits were up slightly. The main products in this division are: deodorants/anti-perspirants (Right Guard, Soft & Dri), shaving creams (Foamy), and hair sprays (White Rain). Other lines include: hair products (shampoos, conditioners, home permanents, and styling aids) and skincare and bath products.

Gillette's Writing Instruments and Office Products Division is a world leader in the sale of writing instruments and correction fluids. Its principal lines are: Paper Mate, Flair, Waterman, and other established brands. Correction fluids are marketed primarily under the Liquid Paper brand name. In 1987 the sales of writing instruments and office products were slightly higher than during the preceding year, but profits were substantially higher.

Braun is a German manufacturer of electric shavers and small appliances and has a line of personal-care and oral-care appliances, too. It is strong in Europe and in other world markets, including the U.S. Oral-B Laboratories is a leading oral-care-products company that Gillette acquired in 1984. Its introduction of a line of premium-quality toothbrushes and a children's toothpaste in 1987 contributed to the division's improved performance for that year.

Much of Gillette's success in 1987 must be credited to its sales force (sales *forces*, really, as there are separate groups for the razor business, the personal-care business, and the writing instrument business). *Sales & Marketing Management* magazine ranked the company's sales force as number one in the metal companies category (despite the Razor Division cut-back on full-time salespeople). It restructured itself, reducing the number of its territories and concentrating the bulk of its sales efforts on its key accounts. In the Razor Division, the field salespeople were encouraged to focus more on talking to buyers for major accounts about pricing, display, distribution, and promotion than on just trying to move product. At the same time, the company relied more on part-time merchandisers to monitor operations at the point of sale. Thus Gillette not only selects and trains its reps with care, but it also deploys them in the most effective manner possible.

The Personal Care Division (toiletries and cosmetics), which is the Gillette segment treated here, does not normally recruit from college campuses. Instead it uses ads, agencies, and, of course, the competition. The division looks for graduates with a business background who have successful sales experience in the same or related fields. Training takes place mainly in the first two years of hire in four stages. First there is a basic orientation (including product knowledge, markets, and accounts) that lasts from six to nine months. During the remaining time, reps go through advanced selling skills, negotiation, and management training. The course is heavily weighted in favor of practical experience; only 25% of it takes place in the classroom in the division's headquarters in Boston, while 75% takes place in the field.

Most sales are made to large chain operations (grocery, discount, and variety stores). Beginning reps visit the retailers and set up displays, work for shelf space, and so on. More advanced reps sell to the headquarters of the same chains. Management training and promo-tracking are built into the training so that reps do not get stuck at the lowest levels. A definite career path leads from rep to key account rep ($5 to $12 million responsibility) to management training in Boston to regional training supervisor to district manager. There is a constant dialogue between the company and the rep concerning career progress, where the rep wants to go, how he or she can get there.

Salaries for trainees average about $25,000; senior salespeople average about $40,000 plus a bonus to equal an average of $55,000. If a rep meets 100% of quota, the bonus can come to 30% of base salary. Other benefits include: medical, dental, and life insurance; disability and retirement plans; profit sharing and stock purchasing plans; a 401K plan; tuition assistance (100% if job related); paid relocation expenses; and a company car.

The atmosphere at Gillette is corporate but friendly. It is an old-line New England company that values hard work and integrity. A stable company with a good fix on its markets and the determination to see that they are well served, Gillette is very active outside the U.S., and for years it has run domestic high-impact, high-visibility media ad campaigns. With its solidity and fine advancement program, Gillette offers sales-oriented people an excellent opportunity.

KIMBERLY-CLARK CORPORATION

VITAL STATISTICS

Entry Level Salary for Sales: **$18,000–$22,000**
Senior Level Salary for Sales: **$40,000**

Benefits

medical/dental: **Yes**	child care: **N/A**
life insurance: **Yes**	retirement plan: **Yes**
disability: **Yes**	savings investment plan: **Yes**
travel allowance: **Yes**	tuition assistance: **$650 per year**
company car: **Yes**	relocation assistance: **Yes**
profit sharing plan: **No**	memberships: **No**
stock purchase plan: **Yes**	

Corporate Culture Index   (1 = lowest, 10 = highest)

training:	**9**	security:	**10**
support:	**9**	mobility:	**9**
benefits:	**9**	intangibles:	**9**

Address: Neenah Operations Headquarters, 401 North Lake Street, Neenah, WI 54956
Contact: U.S. Consumer Sales; telephone 414/721-2000

Kimberly-Clark Corporation ranks 85th on the Fortune 500 list. In 1987 it had sales of $4.8 billion, up 14% from 1986. It has paid a quarterly dividend on its stock for over 50 years.

Kimberly-Clark was founded in 1872 as a manufacturer of newsprint. Today it is a worldwide manufacturer of forest products employing advanced technologies in absorbancy, fiber-forming, and other areas. The company produces and markets a wide range of personal care, health care, and other consumer products. These include such famous trademarks as: Kleenex, Huggies, Kotex, New Freedom, Hi-Dri, Depend, and others.

While K-C's Consumer Division is the company's unquestioned leader in sales, its products are also found far afield from the supermarket and drugstore. K-C produces traditional types of paper for newspaper and book publishing as well as specialized papers to answer other communications needs. Hospitals use K-C disposable gowns in their operating rooms, and their medical instruments are often shipped to them in K-C–produced sterile wrap. And hospital beds are very likely to be fitted with comfortable cushioning pads produced by a K-C subsidiary.

Much of the long-term growth the company expects to enjoy is predicated on its strong technological base. The Corporate Science and Technology unit is responsible for basic research and the development of new technologies, and this commitment to continuing innovation and development makes the company a good bet for the long haul. In addition, its great diversity and its many subsidiaries and allied businesses give salespeople a wide range of career paths. K-C offers sales opportunities selling consumer products to traditional outlets, merchandising paper for publishing and other specialized needs, or selling health-care products to hospitals. The firm also has other diverse holdings, including a commercial airline, a maintenance center for the servicing of corporate-type aircraft, a trucking company, and an insurance company.

Most new sales rep positions at Kimberly-Clark open up in the Consumer division, the company's top revenue producer. Training at K-C is intensive but it is more job-oriented than classroom-oriented. The training period for new hires lasts about 18 months, but is not continuous. The new hire begins by spending three to nine months in the field, with a district manager or regional trainer, in on-the-job training. Supplementing this are training materials that have been carefully adapted to K-C's products and company style.

Next, the trainee goes to headquarters in Neenah, Wisconsin, for two weeks of classroom instruction and intense sessions on product knowledge and "win-win" sales procedures. Because of the great diversity of products manufactured by K-C, training encompasses a wide range of different accounts.

Other support offered by K-C includes heavy advertising and promotional materials, administrative/clerical assistance, and, most importantly, research and development of new products. In turn, Kimberly-Clark is looking for candidates who have had some sales experience (many of K-C's reps, for instance, have been referred to the company by customers or by other sales reps). A college degree is preferred (85% of new sales hires have one), but not necessary.

Selling in K-C's Consumer Division is done at the retail and wholesale levels, not at the end-user level. During the 1980s, K-C refined its sales organization, so that today it has separate forces for handling grocery store, mass drugstore merchandising, and military PX sales. A telephone sales force has also been added. K-C reps do not have to instruct their customers or demonstrate their products; for the most part the customers know what they want. The reps must see to service and delivery, however, and work on promotion and marketing plans that will help their customers run their businesses more efficiently and profitably.

Beginning salaries for sales trainees range from $18,000 to $24,000, plus a bonus. Average senior sales executive salaries run from $40,000 up, plus a bonus. Bonuses are determined by each unit's profitability; if the entire unit is doing well, the reps receive a substantial bonus (as much as 35% of base salary). This arrangement encourages a sense of teamwork, which, along with product knowledge and aggressiveness, is a hallmark of the K-C sales staff. It is also a trait fostered by K-C management in its ambitious effort to radically improve the company's profit picture.

In addition, there is plenty of room to grow at K-C. A new hire can grow from being a sales rep to senior rep to account manager to district manager. Training is offered all along the way (in the form of annual evaluations and regular testing at seminars), and each step up brings the employee more responsibility and increased compensation.

Other benefits include: a medical/dental insurance plan, group life insurance, disability and retirement plans, a company car and travel allowance, a matching stock purchasing plan and optional investment/savings plan, and tuition assistance of up to $650 per year per employee.

The company's superior products are backed by aggressive, relentless marketing efforts. Employees constantly seek—and find—better ways to promote, sell, and distribute K-C's products, and to improve their own individual performances. Although large, the firm has a "small company" atmosphere—reps and management are on an informal, first-name basis. Reps receive all the support they need. Most importantly, they are all encouraged to pursue outstanding customer service, which accounts for K-C's success in gaining its share and more of the coveted shelf space in retail stores.

LEVER BROTHERS COMPANY

VITAL STATISTICS

Entry Level Salary for Sales: **$30,000+**
Senior Level Salary for Sales: **$50,000–$60,000+**

Benefits

medical/dental: **Yes**
life insurance: **Yes**
disability: **Yes**
travel allowance: **N/A**
company car: **Yes**
profit sharing plan: **Yes**
stock purchase plan: **No**

child care: **No**
retirement plan: **Yes**
savings investment plan: **Yes**
tuition assistance: **Yes**
relocation assistance: **Yes**
memberships: **Smokenders**

Corporate Culture Index   (1 = lowest, 10 = highest)

training: **7**
support: **8**
benefits: **8**

security: **8**
mobility: **9**
intangibles: **8**

Address: 390 Park Avenue, New York, NY 10022
Contact: Personnel; telephone 212/688-6000

Lever Brothers Company ranks 145th on the Fortune 500 list. In 1987 it posted sales of more than $2.8 billion, up 15% from 1986, and profits of $7 million. Lever Brothers is part of the holding company Unilever PLC/NV, which also acquired Chesebrough-Pond's in 1986.

Lever Brothers is a major manufacturer and marketer of high-quality household and food products. Until 1986, it was also in the personal-care products business, but, with the Chesebrough acquisition, Lever's unprofitable Personal Products line was merged with that company's more successful Health and Beauty Products Division. The move helped Lever, which now concentrates on its two core operating units: Household Products and Lever Foods/Shedd's. Both these divisions achieved all-time market share highs in 1987.

The Household Products Division is the larger of the two Lever units, accounting for about $2 billion of the company's almost $3 billion revenue in 1987. Over the past decade, the division has launched a major new brand in each of the household categories in which it competes. Familiar Lever names are: Surf (laundry detergent) and Sunlight (automatic dishwashing liquid); and the favorite standard bearers Wisk (laundry detergent), Dove (beauty bar soap), Caress (body bar soap), and Snuggle and Final Touch (liquid/dryer fabric softeners). And, of course, the company also produces the long-time favorite—Lifebuoy.

The Lever Foods/Shedd's Division is a double winner—topping both the branded and the foodservice margarine markets. Its noted brand-name products include: Promise (positioned as the "heart smart" spread), Imperial margarine, Shedd's Spread Country Crock (a dominant low-fat spread), and I Can't Believe It's Not Butter! (a no-cholesterol) spread. Other brand-name products are Mrs. Butterworth's syrup and pancake mix. The division is also the nation's largest supplier of margarine products to the foodservice industry—to commercial food-servers (restaurants, hotels, and fast food outlets) and to those that are noncommercial (hospitals, schools, and airlines). In addition, Lever's Special Markets unit sells its products to the military and to Alaska, Hawaii, and Puerto Rico, which are considered separate territories. It grew impressively in 1987, and at year's end, Chesebrough's special markets business was transferred to the Lever unit.

Lever Brothers looks for new reps who are college graduates with a marketing or management background; prior sales experience is not necessary. Sales rep candidates should also show that they have leadership capabilities and that they can assume responsibility. The parent company, Unilever, takes a committed stance on training, seeking to instill a sense of responsibility and involvement in all of the employees in its far-flung empire. This, it believes, is the best way to create a lean and highly competitive business enterprise. Given the intensely competitive markets that subsidiaries such as Lever sell to, an efficient, market-driven organization is essential. Only quality products innovatively and aggressively sold succeed here.

Lever's training program, at least in the household division featured here, is field-oriented with heavy emphasis on getting to know the company's customers and their businesses. It involves a week of training, a week in the field supervised by a unit manager, and then another week of training. Training is held all over the country in hotels and conference centers and it stresses professional selling skills, product knowledge, making good presentations, territory management, and the like. After six months, an advanced seminar prepares reps for more responsibility and hones their selling and marketing skills.

The latter is very important, given the high level of company spending on media advertising. Reps receive copies of Lever's print ads and lists of

TV shows the company sponsors so that they can develop ways of using the promotions to gain maximum sales from their customers. When a new product comes on the market, reps receive "launch books" to help them plan their selling strategies and introduce the new product as effectively as possible. A rep's performance is reviewed regularly, beginning in the second month of employment, and these reviews are crucial to promotion. Company policy encourages promoting from within, and reps can move up through several ranks in the sales and marketing areas.

Lever Brothers' 8000 reps work mostly alone, calling on retailers (chain stores, supermarkets, drugstores, and wholesale distributors). The reps don't demonstrate products; rather, they try to show customers how the widely known, fast-moving, and heavily advertised Lever products will increase their business and help bring more traffic into the client's store. The territories vary in size according to density of accounts. If the territory is a rural one with accounts widely separated geographically, the rep will spend most of the time on the road. A metropolitan territory, on the other hand, will involve much less travel.

Salaries for sales trainees average about $30,000, with senior salespeople averaging from about $50,000 to $60,000. Included here are both bonuses and commissions, which are dependent on performance and making company quotas and goals. Other benefits include: medical, dental and life insurance; disability and retirement plans; a profit sharing plan; a matching savings plan; tuition assistance (100%); paid relocation costs; and a company car.

Lever Brothers operates in a hard-driving, competitive, big-numbers market. All its products have high recognition and acceptance by the public, and its advertising and promotion campaigns employ all media and are thoroughly professional in execution. Household products and foods do not require much high-tech savvy, but they do need a strong selling attitude and the ability to play the heavy media advertising card for all it's worth. Advancement opportunities are good, the line is not really vulnerable to business cycles, and, for smart, aggressive reps who enjoy selling, the rewards can be substantial.

PREMARK INTERNATIONAL, INC.

VITAL STATISTICS

Entry Level Salary for Sales: **$25,000**
Senior Level Salary for Sales: **$50,000+**

Benefits

medical/dental: **Yes**	child care: **No**
life insurance: **Yes**	retirement plan: **Yes**
disability: **Yes**	savings investment plan: **Yes**
travel allowance: **Yes**	tuition assistance: **Yes**
company car: **Yes**	relocation assistance: **Yes**
profit sharing plan: **No**	memberships: **Smokenders**
stock purchase plan: **Yes**	**Weight Watchers**

Corporate Culture Index   (1 = lowest, 10 = highest)

training:	**8**	security:	**9**
support:	**9**	mobility:	**9**
benefits:	**9**	intangibles:	**10**

Address: 1717 Deerfield Road, Deerfield, IL 60015
Contact: Personnel; telephone 312/405-6000

Premark International, Inc. ranks 178th on the Fortune 500 list. In 1987 it enjoyed sales of over $2 billion, up 12% from 1986. Profits for 1987 were $72 million, up sharply from 1986, a year for which profits were significantly depressed by one-time charges.

Premark International is a manufacturer and marketer of consumer and commercial products, including the brand names Tupperware, Wilsonart, Hobart, West Bend, Vulcan, and Precor. The company's operations are global in scale, with 38% of its total 1987 sales coming from outside the U.S. Premark's business is divided into three main segments: Tupperware, the Food Equipment Group, and Consumer and Decorative Products.

Tupperware outsells by a two-to-one margin all U.S. competitors combined. It is the world's largest manufacturer of high-quality plastic food-storage and serving containers. Tupperware accounted for 41% of Premark's 1987 sales. The Food Equipment Group manufactures and markets equipment used commercially. About 70% of its sales comes from the foodservice market, fast-food chains, restaurants, and institutions; the balance comes from supermarkets, convenience stores, bakeries, and butchers. This group accounted for 37% of Premark's 1987 sales. Consumer and Decorative Products manufactures and markets decorative laminates used in the furniture and the building and remodeling markets, and it is a leader in the marketing of small electric kitchen appliances. It also includes the Precor line of high-quality fitness equipment. This group accounted for 22% of Premark's 1987 sales.

Premark believes the future holds great promise for its products, if it continues to change with the times. All of Premark's businesses—including its commercial ones—depend directly on the consumer for their future growth. Consequently, Premark's management monitors demographics and changing lifestyles very closely. Its products will sell or not depending on how well they fit with the way people live in the 1990s and beyond.

As Premark sees it, the U.S. population is aging. The median age will be 36 in the year 2000 (up from 30 in 1980), and by 1995 over 60% of adult women will be in the work force. This last figure is already making an impact on the way the company markets its Tupperware line. Other trends noted by Premark include a renewed emphasis on the home, when the busy working adults find some time to spend there, which is good news for its line of decorator products. People also will be eating out more, without much time left over for big, formal family dinners, which means that the Food Equipment Group should find an expanding future market. Changes in consumer lifestyles are reinforcing this trend, too, with people eating smaller meals—"grazing"—and showing a more adventurous approach toward trying new types of foods, such as Japanese, Mexican, Thai, and so on. All this will mean more business for restaurants and fast-food suppliers—and the need for different equipment to prepare the new foods—which also helps Premark's prospects.

Selling at Premark is more than the classic American Tupperware party, which has followed the Fuller Brush man into American folklore. Premark's other business segments employ a more standard type of selling, similar to that of other companies operating in consumer-driven markets. The Food Equipment Group will be discussed in detail here, particularly the Hobart line of food equipment used by major food service providers.

Hobart manufactures big ovens, deep friers, scales, food cutters and slicers, refrigerators, and machines for washing dishes and cutlery—all of the size used by professional food retailers and servers (supermarkets, fast-food hamburger and pizza chains, and so on). Items used in the food *retail* business (slicers, scales, and refrigerated cabinets) are sold directly to supermarkets. Items that are sold to the food *service* business (large deep friers, cooking ovens, and food storage lockers) are sold to dealers, who in turn sell to the delis, chains, and restaurants).

Hobart looks for new reps with some background in the food equipment or restaurant business. A college degree is preferred, but the company is not inflexible about it; experience in some part of the industry counts for a lot. Prior selling experience is also helpful, but not required. Training lasts about six months, rotating back and forth from class to field work. The program uses a good deal of hands-on training; new reps try out the large-scale equipment, make meals, and test the scales. They must learn, firsthand, how the equipment is used, cleaned, and maintained. Because the equipment is large, reps do not take it with them or demonstrate it on the customer's premises. Rather, a rep will take a prospective customer to a nearby existing customer using the piece and demonstrate it there. Reps usually work alone, but Hobart services all its equipment with its own technicians. This technical service provides great support for the rep in the field. Reps spend all their time calling on clients, but their territories can vary in size from a zip code area to a state.

Salaries for trainees average about $25,000; senior salespeople average about $50,000 plus. There is a commission and also an incentive payment that kicks in when quotas are met. A rep can make $100,000 in salary and incentive in a banner year—but not every year is a banner one. Other benefits include: medical, dental, and life insurance; disability and retirement plans; a stock purchase plan; a 401K plan; a savings plan; tuition assistance, paid relocation expenses; a credit union; and a company car. Reps at Hobart—and at Premark—have good advancement opportunities; the company maintains a policy of promoting from within.

Premark offers salespeople a remarkably wide range of selling techniques, from the Tupperware party to the more standard wholesale and retail selling of its other divisions. In any case, the company keeps close tabs on its markets and is prepared to be flexible in meeting future challenges. Salespeople with food business experience can find good careers here.

THE PROCTER & GAMBLE COMPANY

VITAL STATISTICS

Entry Level Salary for Sales: **Highly competitive**
Senior Level Salary for Sales: **Highly competitive**

Benefits (Flexible Benefit Plan)

medical/dental: **Yes**
life insurance: **Yes**
disability: **Yes**
travel allowance: **Yes**
company car: **Yes**
profit sharing plan: **Yes, providing retirement benefits**
stock purchase plan: **Yes**

child care: **Yes**
retirement plan: **Yes**
savings investment plan: **N/A**
tuition assistance: **Yes**
relocation assistance: **Yes**
memberships: **On-site health club**

Corporate Culture Index   (1 = lowest, 10 = highest)

training: **10**
support: **10**
benefits: **10**

security: **8**
mobility: **9**
intangibles: **9**

Address: P.O. Box 599, Cincinnati, OH 45202
Contact: Personnel; telephone 513/562-1100

Procter & Gamble ranks 17th on the Fortune 500 list. In 1987 it posted sales of $17 billion, a 10% increase from 1986. The company is the country's leading package-goods marketer.

Procter & Gamble was founded in 1837 in Cincinnati, Ohio, as a candle- and soapmaking company. Since then it has grown to a giant concern with at least one of its products in 95 out of 100 homes in the U.S.—"a penetration unequaled by any other manufacturer of anything," according to *Fortune* magazine.

Today, P&G products are household names in over 100 countries worldwide. The company is one of the leading U.S. advertisers and a major supporter of basic research and product development, and, in the marketing area, P&G is considered the founder of the modern brand-management system. Indeed, the whole management of modern consumer package goods—from product research and development, to advertising and promotion, to delivery and display—seems to have been pioneered by P&G, the "house that Ivory built."

P&G's list of familiar products includes: Ivory soap, Tide laundry detergent, Head & Shoulders shampoo, Cascade dishwashing detergent, Crisco shortening, Duncan Hines cake mixes, Folger's coffee, Crest toothpaste, and Pampers disposable diapers. P&G also produces paper products, soft drinks, orange juice, and pharmaceuticals.

P&G is as selective in its personnel as it is in its brands. It looks for the best, trains them intensively, and rewards them well. For instance, P&G selects its new hires from recent graduates, not from other companies. It does this because it is serious about promoting from within, feeling that this is a great motivator for its personnel. It also wants the opportunity to train talented young people exclusively in the ways and procedures of P&G.

There is no one kind of individual that P&G is looking for; it hires an extremely diverse group as sales reps. It needs many different talents and many different personality types, which is understandable considering the variety of products, brands, and markets that the company deals with. In general, only college graduates are considered, but this is not always the case. An undergraduate or someone else without a degree who persuades the company that he or she belongs in retail selling can be hired. Even with graduates or MBAs, P&G does not concentrate on academic excellence alone. The company is interested in people who show leadership, initiative, and drive. It's a company that asks not so much, "What do you know?" as, "What have you accomplished?" Doers and achievers are the ones who get job offers from P&G. In the words of a P&G recruiting brochure, the company wants employees with "strong motivation to achieve, an outstanding record of leadership, strong oral and written communication skills, a high level of intelligence, and creative flair." Quite a lot, but then the company offers a lot as well.

P&G sales training begins on the job, with a day or two of orientation in the rep's district to acquaint the rep with the company and with the brands and accounts he or she will be handling. The rep then makes sales calls with a manager or another trainer who demonstrates how the selling is done and the accounts are managed. More formal training follows at headquarters in Cincinnati, with visits to P&G laboratories and manufacturing plants. More importantly, since career development plays such a major role at P&G, training and upgrading of skills is continuous throughout a rep's employment with the company.

P&G reps deal primarily with retail stores and wholesale distributors

—anyone who sells a consumer product. Reps are expected to handle their products in the store, seeing that the stocks are rotated properly, that shelf space is maintained or enlarged, that displays and other promotional plans are implemented, and so on. The reps are also expected to sell concepts as well as products. They explain to their retail or wholesale customers that the more P&G products they move off the shelves, the better it is for both of them. They use the tremendous marketing and advertising clout of P&G to help their accounts bring customers into the store and sell merchandise. Although reps may demonstrate a new product to an account, their main purpose is to help store managers and distributors find new ways to increase demand for P&G products.

Salaries at P&G are very competitive. The company has the reputation of demanding the best—and generally getting it. Offers to trainees vary depending on product line, but starting salaries will probably be in the mid twenties, with excellent advancement prospects. If the company wants a candidate, it can be very flexible in what it will offer. For instance, it will help the trainee find housing in Cincinnati and can be sensitive to the problems of two-career couples. P&G will go the extra mile to meet the legitimate needs of the candidates it is interested in hiring.

Benefits are excellent. They include: full medical and dental insurance, group life insurance, a disability plan, a retirement/profit sharing plan, a stock purchase plan, child care, a cafeteria, paid moving expenses, tuition assistance, and a company car. In addition, P&G offers child-care leave, organ transplant insurance, adoption assistance ($2000 per adoption), an on-site health club, and many other perks.

P&G values risk-taking, innovation, integrity, and creativity. It looks for a dedication to excellence over a long period of time, which may be why it favors student athletes and those who have served in the military. Paper qualifications are all very well, but P&G wants to know what a candidate has *done*, and what a prospect is likely to *do* for the company. It presents a very intense, very exciting, and very demanding place to work. It is a remarkably successful company, and it wants its reps to be, too.

REVLON

VITAL STATISTICS

Entry Level Salary for Sales: **$32,000–$33,000**
Senior Level Salary for Sales: **$48,000**

Benefits

medical/dental: **Yes**	child care: **No**
life insurance: **Yes**	retirement plan: **Yes**
disability: **Yes**	savings investment plan: **Yes**
travel allowance: **Yes**	tuition assistance: **Yes**
company car: **Yes**	relocation assistance: **Yes**
profit sharing plan: **No**	memberships: **No**
stock purchase plan: **No**	

Corporate Culture Index   (1 = lowest, 10 = highest)

training:	**8**	security:	**9**
support:	**8**	mobility:	**9**
benefits:	**8**	intangibles:	**9**

Address: 625 Madison Avenue, New York, NY 10022
Contact: Personnel; telephone 212/527-4942

A privately held company owned by financier Ronald Perelman, Revlon does not release sales or profit figures. According to *Fortune*, it ranks 5th in the soap and cosmetics industry, and 167th on its 500 list.

When Perelman, Revlon's chairman, took the famous "Fire and Ice" company private in July 1987, he announced plans to return what *Fortune* called "this famous but fading beauty" to its heyday as the number-one purveyor of cosmetics in the world.

From its former peak as leader of the cosmetic pack under founder and cosmetics genius Charles Revson, Revlon today trails behind Noxell and Maybelline in discount stores, while it consistently lags behind rival Estee Lauder in the trendier, more upscale boutiques.

But this dowager is not about to quit yet and has a good deal of fiery life left in her. Revlon has been dramatically boosting sales by two means:

acquisitions (Max Factor, including Halston and Almay, and the cosmetics and fragrance lines of Yves Saint Laurent, including Charles of the Ritz) and the repackaging of Revlon products in more elegant containers (half the game in this business) to appeal to the more upscale buyer.

The legendary sales skills of Perelman himself have been widely credited for reversing Revlon's sales slide, doubling the number of major Revlon department store accounts to 2000 by paying personal visits to the stores' senior management.

But the heart of any sales effort still comes down to sales reps, and how well they do selling to the buyers that count—major department store and drugstore chains. Revlon favors new recruits with prior sales experience or aptitude, and an upbeat, optimistic sense of themselves. College degrees are all very well, but not necessary; technical knowledge is utterly beside the point.

The sales training program balances on-the-job training with classroom work in selling skills, along with regular meetings with regional sales managers. Revlon senior sales management also has an amazingly effective secret weapon: a massive 3-inch-thick sales manual painstakingly researched and compiled for the benefit of new hires. Revlon claims that this hefty tome contains the right answers to all the best questions even the most curious new rep might have. Emphasis is also placed on the frequency of face-to-face contact with regional sales managers, who are responsible for keeping the reps revved up for Revlon.

A rep's territory might consist of three New York City blocks, or all of some rural state; but, wherever they are, reps typically spend nearly all their time on the road, working alone, on expense account, salary, and a bonus plus commission.

The average trainee receives $33,000 in compensation, while senior sales execs clear $50,000 plus a bonus and commissions. At Revlon, the more you sell, the more you earn. Benefits include medical and dental insurance, tuition assistance (100% if job related), life insurance, disability (long and short), a retirement plan, and relocation expenses. At 10%, Revlon considers its rep turnover rate "acceptable" and roughly standard for the industry.

Reps install displays and demonstrate products, perform stock rotation, and do whatever it takes—everything but dance a jig—to persuade major account buyers that Revlon products are once again the best around. The 500 reps in Revlon's Fragrance Division, as well as those in other divisions, all receive extensive sales support in the form of advertising and promotional materials (including the "unforgettable" Richard Avedon ads featuring "the most unforgettable women in the world"). The corporate atmosphere, as befits a world-famous cosmetics and fragrance giant, is stylish, sales-driven, and fast-paced.

When it comes to training, support, benefits, and security, Revlon ranks right at the top of its industry. Its lipstick-bright future looks rosy indeed.

ELECTRONICS

Whoever told Benjamin Franklin to go fly a kite probably had no idea that he had set in motion a chain of discoveries that would revolutionize life on this planet. And after Thomas Edison got hold of Franklin's discovery, light, sound, and energy were never the same.

This section examines the two major sectors of the electronics industry: electronic components, which are the basic building blocks of commercial and military equipment, and consumer electronics, including TVs, calculators, CDs, VCRs, and other "necessities of life."

The $45 billion electronic components industry has shown healthy growth in recent years, and sales are expected to increase by 10% annually over the next four years. The most significant challenge facing the industry is Japanese competition. The good news there is America's lead in semiconductors. Sales of semiconductors grew in 1987 by 13% to $18 billion. Semiconductor companies have found it more profitable to merge and share the high costs of manufacture as well as research, which eats up nearly 15% of sales revenues.

The other element of the components industry is electron tubes, which are essential to television picture tubes and microwaves. Microwave tubes don't just go into space-age ovens. They find their way into TV broadcasting and communications equipment and radar. (As a matter of fact, 75% of the electron tubes manufactured in the United States are bought and used by the military.)

Consumer electronics products fall into four broad categories: video, audio, home information, and personal electronics. Last year, $41 billion worth of retail goods were sold. Sales of consumer electronics have, astonishingly, tripled since 1980!

The video industry includes television, video-cassette recorders (VCRs), camcorders, and satellite earth stations. TV factory sales came to 20 million units, or $6.2 billion, in 1987. Now that more than half of America's homes have a VCR, it's hard to believe that they didn't exist until a few years ago. Even so, in 1987 VCR sales amounted to more than $5 billion. Satellite earth stations are expensive, with just 1.5 million in use, though they account for $625 million worth of sales.

The audio industry includes compact disc players (CDs), stereo systems, tape decks, and car radios. Audio components are a $1.5 billion a year industry, in which effective distribution has been the key to success. The virtue of components is that consumers can mix and match speakers, tuners, headphones, or what have you to meet their own precise needs. Keeping this whole array of products available to a wide variety of retailers is a real challenge and pays real rewards.

The backbone of the home information industry, personal computers, is discussed elsewhere, but there's more to it than that. Personal copiers are growing at a phenomenal rate, and industry analysts predict that they will grow by 15% a year for several years to come. Retail sales of telephones, while not explosive, are steady. Answering machine sales grew by nearly a million units just in 1987 and mobile telephones are becoming more and more popular with businesspeople. Personal electronics covers a wide array of products—electronic watches, home security systems, calculators, healthcare products like electronic thermometers and blood pressure gauges, video games, appliances, and musical instruments.

There's lots of work to be done and many sales to be made. The idea of harnessing a rep's energy with electricity is really electrifying!

TRADE ASSOCIATIONS

American Electronics Association 408/987-4200
Electronic Industries Association 202/457-4900
National Electronic Distributors Association 312/298-9747

PERIODICALS

Electronic Business
Electronic News
Electronics Week

GENERAL ELECTRIC COMPANY

VITAL STATISTICS

Entry Level Salary for Sales: **$30,000**
Senior Level Salary for Sales: **$90,000**

Benefits

medical/dental: **Yes**	child care: **No**
life insurance: **Yes**	retirement plan: **Yes**
disability: **Yes**	savings investment plan: **Yes, with**
travel allowance: **N/A**	**stock**
company car: **Yes**	**purchase**
profit sharing plan: **No**	**plan**
stock purchase option: **Yes**	tuition assistance: **Yes**
	relocation assistance: **Yes**
	memberships: **Smokenders**
	Weight Watchers
	On-site fitness
	program

Corporate Culture Index   (1 = lowest, 10 = highest)

training:	**8**	security:	**9**
support:	**9**	mobility:	**8**
benefits:	**8**	intangibles:	**9**

Address: 3135 Easton Turnpike, Fairfield, CT 06431
Contact: GE Applicant Referral Center, Building 36-1, Schenectady, NY 12345; telephone 518/385-2504

General Electric Company ranks 6th on the Fortune 500 list. In 1987 it had total sales of more than $39 billion, up 12% from 1986. At the same time, record profits of $2.9 billion were up 17% from 1986.

General Electric Company has been on a long march of its own since 1981 when its present CEO, John F. Welch, Jr., took office. It has pared down by reducing its work force to 100,000, and beefed up by purchasing such major—and disparate—businesses as Kidder Peabody & Company, RCA Corporation, and NBC. In a time when diversified companies are narrowing their scope and focusing their operations, GE is moving ahead on all fronts. And it has plenty of fronts, too many to list *in toto* here.

GE's operations are divided into three large segments that encompass 14 major units. The segments are: technology businesses, services businesses, and core manufacturing businesses. The technology segment emphasizes using the latest technologies to create solutions to its customers' problems rather than concentrating on selling a lot of products. This approach has made GE a world leader in aircraft engines, aerospace, plastics, medical systems, and factory automation.

The services segment emphasizes providing its customers with added value, that "extra something" that makes the difference in the services sector of the economy. In this area, GE is a leader in financial services (three major companies), television (NBC), and communications services (six diverse operating units). The *core manufacturing* segment emphasizes creating high-quality, low-cost products even in today's ever tighter, tougher, more competitive markets. This strategy makes GE a leader in appliances, lighting, industrial and power systems, electrical distribution and control, motors, and transportation systems.

To manage this vast array of businesses, GE has opted for trimming its corporate staff and pushing decision-making down the line to operating heads. It believes that this allows the individual units to respond to changing conditions and markets faster and more innovatively than working through layers of bureaucracy. The pressure to perform well, though, is still very much there. The new GE "vision" of itself is "being number one or two in the market position" in each of its business units. To GE, this means *world* market position as well, because GE sees the world's economies and financial markets as inextricably linked. Units that do not show this kind of strength are prime candidates for divestiture—as are managers and other employees of underperforming units.

The heat is very definitely on at GE, and no one feels it more than the dozen or more sales staffs at the various operating units. Just about every kind of selling imaginable can be found under the GE umbrella: customers include industry, consumers, and government, and the products range from light bulbs to aircraft engines to TV shows. But the one constant at GE is the pressure. Generally, candidates for sales jobs should have at least a bachelor's degree, preferably in electrical, mechanical, or industrial engineering, but this is not true of all divisions. At GE Lighting, the company featured here, a degree is preferred but not necessary. Moreover, at GE Electrical Distribution and Control, the sales division is turning to two-year colleges for a supply of new salespeople. They've found that many of the top engineering school graduates stay only for a couple of years and then go off to get an MBA and pursue a career other than selling. They hope that using "co-op" students who have worked for the company while studying will give them a more stable and dedicated sales force.

Training depends on the unit. It involves mostly a mix of classroom and on-the-job training spread out over 18 months. The classroom work at GE Lighting consists of three modules—product applications, business skills, and marketing strategies—each lasting about a week to ten days. The classes are given at the company's Cleveland headquarters, but most reps also attend courses in sales and marketing at GE's Management Development Institute at Croton-on-Hudson, called Crotonville. This is particularly true of reps who will be working with major accounts such as the aerospace and auto industries. GE is looking to train reps who are self-starting and who can "take on responsibility for their own productivity."

At GE Lighting, reps call on contractors and large distributors and work with a dizzying array of specifications and quantities. In order to make a sale, the rep must bid on the business, and reps have good backup from their district managers on complex sales. Additional support comes from excellent ad and promotional materials and from top-grade R&D that provides a constant stream of new and improved products. Reps generally work alone and in territories that require no more than two or three overnights a month. Team selling is used on the key accounts—more so now after the major sales coup of being selected as sole supplier of state-of-the-art electronics for GM's new Saturn auto plant.

Salaries for trainees average $30,000, with senior salespeople earning about $90,000. A hefty incentive payment plan allows reps to make *more* in incentive pay than in salary. GE may be a pressure company to work for, but it also rewards performers very well. Other benefits include: medical, dental, and life insurance; disability and retirement plans; a 401K plan; a savings plan that includes stock purchase options; tuition assistance for career-related or individual development programs; paid relocation expenses; and a company car.

In the words of GE's CEO, "I can think of no place in the world with such an exciting array of businesses." Exciting, yes, and hard-driving too. GE is for achievers, and for them it's a good place.

MOTOROLA, INC.

VITAL STATISTICS

Entry Level Salary for Sales: **$24,000–$27,000**
Senior Level Salary for Sales: **$40,000–$60,000**

Benefits

medical/dental: **Yes**	child care: **No**
life insurance: **Yes**	retirement plan: **Yes**
disability: **Yes**	savings investment plan: **Yes**
travel allowance: **Yes**	tuition assistance: **Yes**
company car: **Yes**	relocation assistance: **Yes**
profit sharing plan: **Yes**	memberships: **Wellness program**
stock purchase plan: **Yes**	**Discount at certain health clubs**

Corporate Culture Index   (1 = lowest, 10 = highest)

training:	**7**	security:	**8**
support:	**8**	mobility:	**8**
benefits:	**10**	intangibles:	**9**

Address: Motorola Center, 1303 East Algonquin Road, Schaumburg, IL 60196
Contact: Staffing; telephone 312/397-5000

Motorola, Inc., ranks 62nd on the Fortune 500 list. In 1987 it posted sales of more than $6 billion, up 14% from 1986. At the same time it had profits of $308 million, up 59% from 1986.

Motorola, Inc., is a leading manufacturer and marketer of electronic equipment, systems, and components in both the U.S. and international markets. It is one of the few end-equipment manufacturers able to draw on expertise in both semiconductor technology and government electronics.

Motorola's business is divided into the following seven operating areas. The Communications Sector designs and manufactures two-way radios, pagers, and other forms of electronic communications systems that have many commercial and industrial applications. The Semiconductor Products Sector designs and produces a wide range of discrete semiconductors and integrated circuits for use in the computer, consumer, commercial, and industrial markets. The Information Systems Group provides all the elements needed for distributed data systems.

The Government Electronics Group researches and develops advanced electronics systems for defense and other governmental agencies, as well as for the commercial and international markets. The Systems Group designs and manufactures cellular radiotelephone systems, mobile radiotelephones, and other such equipment. The Automotive and Industrial Electronics Group produces a variety of electronic modules for use in the motor vehicle, industrial equipment, and major appliance industries. The New Enterprises organization manages Motorola's entry into emerging new businesses in the high-growth, high-technology areas.

Motorola sees the future in very positive terms; it is confident that its core businesses are sound and will grow not only in absolute terms, but in market share as well. To support its operating groups, the company plans to intensify its R&D efforts, continue its investment in capital equipment, improve its product quality and manufacturing efficiency, and strengthen its commitment to "total customer satisfaction."

In the early and mid 1980s, Motorola was troubled by the uneven quality of its products and by the time it took to develop and deliver them. The company has regained ground it lost then by addressing its problems not with massive layoffs and restructuring, but by educating its labor force, from top executives right on down. Today, Motorola annually spends about 2.4% of its payroll (roughly $44 million) on training its employees, double the average percentage that companies spend on training. The Motorola Training and Education Center (MTEC) in Schaumburg, Illinois, runs a series of ongoing classes and seminars for trainees, plant workers, engineers, professionals, and executives. Many of the courses are mandatory, and they are all designed to provide Motorola employees with the skills and knowledge they need to succeed in fiercely competitive domestic and world markets.

Sales training for new Motorola reps is intensive but largely decentralized. For instance, product training and company orientation are the responsibility of the operating business sector or group. The length of such training will vary with the complexity of the product line. All the reps, in addition, take a course on professional selling skills, which includes an early development segment, an experienced segment, and a managerial segment. In any case, classes will be mixed with on-the-job training, with reps working at first under supervision of a line manager or a district sales manager, for instance.

In keeping with the decentralized nature of the company, reps tend to stay in product areas, with little movement to other groups/sectors. In truth, a semiconductor rep may not even know what a two-way communications rep sells. Some reps will work only a single type of account such as hospitals or government agencies; other reps work with retailers, wholesalers, and consumers; still others sell to manufacturers who "add value" to the product and resell it. There is a lot of different selling at Motorola —different product lines and different markets. Territories vary, too. Some encompass one city, some two states; and traveling can range from no overnights a month to several. Also, reps work their accounts alone.

The sales force itself is large and diverse, numbering about 4200 and composed of reps with many different backgrounds. Generally, Motorola looks for college graduates with degrees in technical subjects, a BSEE, for instance, or a major in computer science. Prior sales experience is helpful, but not necessary. There is a career ladder for sales reps leading through advanced selling and account management to marketing and to corporate management, if that seems warranted. Many reps, though, prefer to stay in the field selling, and there is room enough and reward enough for both approaches.

Salaries for beginning reps range from $24,000 to $27,000; senior salespeople average about $40,000 to $60,000. Salaries and commissions will vary with product line, with semiconductors and two-way communications (cellular phones) the highest paying at present (compensation in these lines can run to six figures in certain cases). Commissions can run as high as 50% of base salary. Motorola offers good support, too, in quality ad and promotion materials, administrative/clerical help, and R&D on new products.

Other benefits include: medical, dental, and life insurance; disability and retirement plans; profit sharing and stock purchase plans; a 401K plan and a savings plan; tuition assistance (100%); paid relocation expenses; and a company car.

Motorola is a company that respects people—its customers and its employees. It is also a company in a competitive, high-tech, international world. It is completely committed to "total customer satisfaction," and no matter how hectic the pace of business becomes, it doesn't forget that. Reps who can operate well with such a commitment will find Motorola a dynamic and rewarding place to be.

TEXAS INSTRUMENTS

VITAL STATISTICS

Entry Level Salary for Sales: **$28,000**
Senior Level Salary for Sales: **$55,000–$75,000**

Benefits

medical/dental: **Yes**	child care: **No**
life insurance: **Yes**	retirement plan: **Yes**
disability: **Yes, short and long term**	savings investment plan: **Yes**
travel allowance: **Yes**	tuition assistance: **Yes**
company car: **Yes**	relocation assistance: **Yes**
profit sharing plan: **Yes**	memberships: **Smokenders**
stock purchase plan: **Yes**	**Weight Watchers**
	Wellness program
	On-site fitness center

Corporate Culture Index   (1 = lowest, 10 = highest)

training:	**10**	security:	**7**
support:	**9**	mobility:	**8**
benefits:	**10**	intangibles:	**10**

Address: 13500 North Central Expressway, P.O. Box 655474, Dallas, TX 75265
Contact: Personnel; telephone 214/995-2011

Texas Instruments ranks 75th on the Fortune 500 list. In 1987 it had sales of more than $5.5 billion, up 12% from 1986. Profits, at $309 million, were up an astonishing 950% from 1986, when the company showed profits of only $29 million.

Texas Instruments, quite obviously, turned a corner in 1987. Its net earnings performance in 1987 showed a remarkable gain, helped by significantly improved profitability in its components segment and reduced losses in its service segment. TI began a strategic review process in 1985 to better position its businesses in those areas that represent solid, long-term opportunities, and clearly the strategies it developed are now taking hold.

TI develops, manufactures, and markets a variety of products in the electrical and electronics fields for industrial, government, and consumer use. Basically, the company operates five core business segments: components, defense electronics, digital products, metallurgical materials, and services.

The products in the corporate segment include semiconductors (such as integrated circuits, discrete devices, and subassemblies) and electric and electronic control devices. The semiconductor market grew strongly in 1987, reflecting the strength of the electronic end-equipment markets. The electronic portion of the segment was up moderately on the strength of the appliance, heating, ventilation, and air-conditioning markets, more than offsetting the soft automotive and military aircraft markets.

The defense electronics segment products include radar, infrared surveillance systems, missile guidance and control systems, and electronic warfare systems. This segment achieved net record sales for 1987, but its profitability was unchanged from that of 1986. TI's digital products segment provides such items as minicomputers, professional personal computers, symbolic processing computer systems, electronic data terminals and printers, industrial control systems, electronic calculators, and learning aids. This segment operated at a loss in 1987 because of lower volume, the bankruptcy of a major customer, and continuing investment in new products. Much smaller in impact on TI's revenue picture are the metallurgical materials segment (clad materials, precision engineered parts, and electronic connectors) and the services segment (primarily collecting and processing seismic data in connection with petroleum exploration). Sales in the services segment were down moderately, but losses were significantly contained by extensive cost-reduction measures.

TI is a leading high-tech company on the comeback trail after some bad times in the mid 1980s. It is particularly careful with the hiring and training of its sales force because of the nature of its products and competitiveness of its markets. It hires only electrical engineers (BSEEs) and puts them through a training program that lasts anywhere from 12 to 18 months. Candidates for sales rep jobs should have good grades (at least a 3.0 GPA) from a good engineering school. The training program is held at the company's Dallas or Houston plants, and it consists of regular classes, study, individual presentations to the class twice a month (on which trainees are graded), and assignments in design engineering or product engineering. There is also on-the-job training, practice in presentation skills, and intensive product knowledge sessions, all closely monitored and evaluated.

Upon successful completion of the training, the new hire, known as a technical sales associate, becomes a technical sales representative and is assigned a sales territory in one of the 52 field offices. Throughout the company, the emphasis is on the idea that *engineers sell to engineers*. In the components segment, which is featured here, technical expertise is particularly relevant as TI is shifting its product mix from low-margin commodity chips to more lucrative customized specialty products. Knowledgeable reps are essential to this kind of selling.

Components reps sell mostly to major corporations (original equipment manufacturers such as IBM or Ford), who design the TI chip or component into their products. Reps may be assigned to many accounts or to only a few key accounts. In any case, the distribution of the 52 field offices and the number of reps (500) make overnight travel rare. Reps work in teams a great deal, and alone or as a team they have access to all the company's expertise to answer any problems—TI is not a stickler for following the chain of command in such situations. Reps enjoy excellent worldwide sales support via PC and satellite.

Salaries vary with the business segment, but trainees average $28,000 or more, and senior salespeople average from about $55,000 to $75,000, depending on productivity. There is a definite path of promotion from rep to national accounts rep to district sales manager and so on. Promotions are generally within sales, not to general management, but even here a good field rep may have to take a pay cut in order to go to the home office. Field selling at TI is good business. Other benefits include: medical, dental, and life insurance; disability and retirement plans; profit sharing and stock purchase plans; a 401K plan; a savings plan; tuition assistance; a car allowance; and paid relocation expenses.

TI is a major player in the high-glamour, high-tech game. It is a get-things-done company in a tough, demanding market, which is why it likes to see evidence of initiative and hard work in its sales rep candidates (for example, summer jobs, student activities, and elected offices). To succeed here, reps need drive as well as smarts. The company in turn supports its sales and marketing people with good career opportunities, high-quality products, and total customer commitment.

WESTINGHOUSE ELECTRIC CORPORATION

VITAL STATISTICS

Entry Level Salary for Sales: **$30,000**
Senior Level Salary for Sales: **$65,000**

Benefits

medical/dental: **Yes**
life insurance: **Yes**
disability: **Yes**
travel allowance: **N/A**
company car: **Yes**
profit sharing plan: **No**
stock purchase plan: **Yes**

child care: **No**
retirement plan: **Yes**
savings investment plan: **Yes**
tuition assistance: **100%**
relocation assistance: **Yes**
memberships: **Smokenders**
Weight Watchers
Wellness program
On-site fitness center
Employee assistance program

Corporate Culture Index (1 = lowest, 10 = highest)

training: **10**
support: **9**
benefits: **9**

security: **9**
mobility: **10**
intangibles: **10**

Address: Westinghouse Building, Gateway Center, Pittsburgh, PA 15222
Contact: Personnel Manager; telephone 412/244-2000

Westinghouse Electric Corporation is America's third-largest electronics company. It ranks 33rd on the Fortune 500 list. With more than $10 billion in sales in 1987 (flat from the year before), profits still climbed a respectable 10% to $740 million.

Everyone has heard of Westinghouse, but hardly anyone (not even on Wall Street) quite understands what it does anymore. These days, the century-old company that built a famous name in refrigerators, washers, dryers, and stoves is up to its ears in defense electronics, power generation, financial services, broadcasting, and soda-bottling, to name just a few of its highly diversified and highly profitable activities.

A market leader in a business with no market (nuclear power plants) and a major player in some rather rapidly shrinking markets (nuclear fuel fabrication), Westinghouse has nevertheless managed to pull off one of the major corporate comebacks of the decade, a turnaround management expert Robert Waterman favorably compares to Ford's as "an optimistic message about corporate America's ability to renew itself."

Generous growth rates have been sustained without unduly damaging the company's venerable "techie" tradition, a domination from top to bottom by "relentless engineering types with as much flash as a drawer of slide rules," says *Forbes* magazine, albeit admiringly.

Sales training is, not surprisingly, very technical, with sales responsibility largely in the hands of the kind of people who are perfectly comfortable talking about transformers and circuit-breakers, switching systems and power cogeneration. Which is, of course, how it should be.

The company likes candidates to have strong college backgrounds, preferably in electrical engineering. But physics, business, math, and accounting will do, so long as graduates rank in the top third in their class and are familiar with computer systems.

Training is intensive and extensive, lasting from one and a half to two years, with no formal "graduation" other than a "transfer to a permanent position in the field," that is, a territorial assignment. Early on, the new rep is assigned field responsibility, closely supervised by a district sales manager. But ongoing classroom and video instruction and self-study programs continue, in tandem with on-the-job training.

Trainees learn about different accounts, from both the technical and the business points of view. Typical customers include original equipment manufacturers, utilities, distributors, general contractors, and the U.S. military.

Reps spend a lot of time on the road, at least 40% overnight. Territories might cover an industry or a state, or some highly specialized product subcategory. Reps work alone, on expense account, reporting directly to district sales managers. A turnover rate of 5% confirms the Westinghouse tradition of successful, informed selling of products conceived by engineers for engineers, with rarely a nontechnical type in the procurement chain to clog the works.

Sales reps hardly ever install or demonstrate products—their role is more that of problem solver. The sales force of 2000+ is well supported by advertising and sales materials, ongoing product development, and administrative/clerical aid.

The average salary for a sales trainee is $30,000, if the trainee is a trained electrical engineer, while a senior sales executive earns $65,000 plus "incentive compensation"—usually 10% of base salary. Benefits include:

medical and dental insurance, tuition assistance (100%), a company car (with no allowance), a group life insurance and disability plan, as well as a retirement/pension plan, a 401K plan, and an employee assistance program.

Westinghouse is a career-minded company with a corporate atmosphere, one which considers itself "almost paternalistic," as befits one of only 22 firms to appear on both the 1917 and 1987 list of *Forbes'* 100 largest American corporations. With a work force cut back from its 1974 high of 200,000, and productivity gaining 6% per year, Westinghouse is still very much an engineer's dream home: built to last.

FOOD, FOODSERVICES, AND TOBACCO

It's hard to imagine anything more basic to life than food. Of all the different industries surveyed in this book, none has been around or promises to stay around longer than the food industry. Since the dawn of time, people have raised and produced food.

The tobacco industry is closely related to the food industry. For example, Philip Morris, the cigarette company, owns both General Foods and Kraft. Both are highly diversified and complex industries that continually grow and develop over time as the economy and consumer trends change and shift. Both go through a long and complicated process of distributing products from vast farms to factories to warehouses to distributors to consumers.

The food industry is by no means simple, encompassing edibles as diverse as ice cream, canned peas, corn flakes, and dog food. In 1987, total food industry sales were nearly $322 billion. This represented a little less than 2% growth over the previous year. Most food industry sales reps deal directly with retail grocers and spend a lot of their time consulting with customers on product lines and service management.

Health consciousness has affected sales in recent years, as poultry has grown steadily while red meat has declined (though it still accounts for 80% of America's meat products business).

Most sectors of the food industry grow slowly and steadily, basically keeping pace with the growth rate of the population. Sales, in other words, increase as more and more families have new mouths to feed. For example, processed and canned fruits and vegetables, breakfast cereals, and confectionery products (what we mortals call candy) all grew by roughly 2%–3% over 1987.

One exception to the rule of slow, steady growth has been ice cream. From 1982 to 1987, ice cream and frozen dessert sales increased by more than 20%. Health conscious or not, Americans eat more than 18 pounds of ice cream each year. And not just kids. Gourmet ice creams, like Häagen-Dazs and Dove Bars, have turned grownups into ice cream enthusiasts. Success doesn't come much sweeter than that.

At the tobacco end of the industry, profits are higher than ever, largely as a result of high retail prices and increased exports. Also, the manufacturers have, by switching to automation, slashed their costs, leaving more room for profits. Yet, the industry faces stiff challenges because of the health issues concerning tobacco. Sales have been slipping as 41 states and more than 80 cities and counties have placed heavy restrictions on smoking in public. Recently, cigar, snuff, and chewing tobacco consumption have dropped 5% a year. A jury even decided recently that a cigarette company could be held liable for a smoker's lung cancer. Market shifts are thus being closely watched and followed.

A growing sector of the industry nowadays is the "price/value" segment, which sells cigarettes for less than regular prices by straight discount or by putting more cigarettes in each pack—an especially valuable marketing tool because most cigarette smokers come from lower income brackets. National media advertising has been supplemented with new marketing strategies such as direct mail and intensive promotional efforts.

The food and tobacco industries have greatly consolidated in the past few years through a number of mergers and acquisitions. This has left the existing companies in a very strong position for the future.

FOOD AND FOODSERVICES INDUSTRY

TRADE ASSOCIATIONS

National Food Brokers Association 202/789-2844

PERIODICALS

Food Engineering
Progressive Grocer

TOBACCO INDUSTRY

TRADE ASSOCIATIONS

Tobacco Association of the United States 919/782-5151
Tobacco Institute 202/457-4800

PERIODICALS

Tobacco International
TR (Tobacco Reporter)

CONAGRA

VITAL STATISTICS

Entry Level Salary for Sales: **$27,000**
Senior Level Salary for Sales: **$47,000+**

Benefits

medical/dental: **Yes**	child care: **No**
life insurance: **Yes**	retirement plan: **Yes**
disability: **Yes**	savings investment plan: **Yes**
travel allowance: **Yes**	tuition assistance: **Yes, 75%**
company car: **Yes**	relocation assistance: **N/A**
profit sharing plan: **Yes**	memberships: **Wellness program**
stock purchase plan: **Yes**	**On-site fitness program**
	Aerobics

Corporate Culture Index   (1 = lowest, 10 = highest)

training:	**7**	security:	**9**
support:	**8**	mobility:	**8**
benefits:	**9**	intangibles:	**8**

Address: ConAgra Center, One Central Park Plaza, Omaha, NE 68102
Contact: Human Resources; telephone 402/978-4000

ConAgra is a highly diversified family of companies operating in three basic segments of the food chain: Agriculture, Processing, and Prepared Foods. In 1987, the company's operating profits reached $149 million on total sales, up 41% from $9 billion in 1986. ConAgra ranks 4th in the food industry on the Fortune 500 list, and 41st overall.

When Charlie Harper left his post at Pillsbury to help revive an ailing company called Nebraska Consolidated Mills back in 1974, few food industry watchers could ever have predicted that, by 1986, the newly restructured ConAgra would have experienced a twelvefold increase in sales over ten years, to a total of more than $6 billion.

ConAgra now enjoys $10 billion in annual sales from such widely dispersed holdings as Armour meat products, Banquet frozen foods, Country Pride and Country Skillet poultry products, and Singleton seafoods.

Today, the company ranks first in lamb sales nationwide, second in chicken and pork, second in beef, and a resounding first in overall domestic meat sales. Even acts of God (such as major droughts) can't seem to stunt ConAgra's growth: tight supply conditions tend to work in favor of food processors, even if the farmers themselves get hurt.

ConAgra Food Service Company markets Award, Armour, Banquet, Morton, Patio, and Chun King frozen foods to a wide variety of institutional customers such as schools, colleges, prisons, and government facilities. In 1987, the company introduced more than 20 new products, including a new line of upscale Oriental entrees and Award's "Tastes of America" regional-theme finger food appetizers.

Reps spend all their time on the road, covering territories ranging in size from half a state to one or two states. Reps work alone, on expense account, reporting directly to the district sales manager. They rarely train customers, but they do assist their clients' institutional managers in all phases of menu planning.

For sales positions, ConAgra says it favors candidates who display "personality, common sense, and aggressiveness." A college degree is preferred, but not required. The same goes for prior sales experience.

Training is managed at the local level by the district sales manager, who is responsible for recruiting and hiring new reps, sending them out for an extended 16-month period of on-the-job training, and overseeing one day of more formal training every other month.

Classroom work features programs by video training producer Stephen Covey ("Seven Basic Habits") and classes in sales motivation and product knowledge. No individual evaluation follows training, but with the low employee/trainee ratio of 5:1, plenty of individual counselling is available, when needed.

The average salary for a sales trainee is around $27,000, while a senior sales executive earns around $47,000 plus commission. Benefits include: medical and dental insurance, tuition assistance (75% with a passing grade), a company car (with car allowance), a group life and disability insurance plan, a retirement/pension plan, a credit union, and free aerobics classes at the on-site fitness center.

Promotion possibilities are well defined by a career ladder running from sales rep to a "key account" to district sales manager to divisional sales manager, and on up. The top job would be a home office sales job managing budgets and promoting new products, that is, if the prestige of working out of the imposing Omaha headquarters were worth the significant cut in pay. Many reps prefer to remain reps and make a lot more.

ConAgra is so highly diversified that selling for this company is the equivalent of bringing America's produce to market. "Getting the right product to the right customer at the right time . . . is the common marketing thread in all ConAgra companies," says Jim Kennedy, vice president of marketing. From chemical fertilizer to meat packing to frozen food to catfish, ConAgra is there. "Whether the product is corn, beans or soybean meal," ConAgra insists, "our systems are in place to move big volumes quickly from areas of surplus to areas of need, almost anywhere in the world."

GENERAL FOODS CORPORATION

VITAL STATISTICS

Entry Level Salary for Sales: **$25,000+**
Senior Level Salary for Sales: **$45,000+**

Benefits

medical/dental: **Yes**	child care: **No**
life insurance: **Yes**	retirement plan: **Yes**
disability: **Yes**	savings investment plan: **Yes**
travel allowance: **Yes**	tuition assistance: **Yes**
company car: **Yes**	relocation assistance: **Yes**
profit sharing plan: **No**	memberships: **Fitness center**
stock purchase plan: **No**	**Credit union**

Corporate Culture Index   (1 = lowest, 10 = highest)

training:	**8**	security:	**8**
support:	**9**	mobility:	**9**
benefits:	**8**	intangibles:	**10**

Address: 250 North Street, White Plains, NY 10625
Contact: Sales Management Careers; telephone 914/335-2500

General Foods Corporation is a division of Philip Morris Companies, Inc. In 1987, it had sales of $9.9 billion, up 2.9% from 1986, and listed operations income of $722 million, down 2.7% from 1986. This decrease, however, reflects restructuring costs of $117 million. General Foods Corporation, the world's largest diversified food company, became a division of Philip Morris in 1985.

In 1987 General Foods reorganized itself into three operating companies: General Foods USA, General Foods Worldwide Coffee and International, and Oscar Mayer Foods. In the restructuring, a substantial number of staff positions were eliminated, and decision-making was pushed down the line to bring it closer to the employees serving the various marketplaces. Some manufacturing facilities were also reorganized to improve efficiency and save money, while additional savings were realized through changes in other overhead functions.

General Foods USA, in 1987, increased its unit sales by 2.3%. The company has a line of very well-known products and accounts for a great deal of shelf space in everyone's local grocery store. Its established products did well in 1987, generally increasing their market share. These included cereals such as Post Grape Nuts, Natural Raisin Bran, Super Golden Crisp, and Pebbles. During that year, GF also introduced an innovation in cereal packaging—the resealable Zip-Pak. Other brands that performed well were Jell-O, which reversed a decline, Kool-Aid, Crystal Light, and Country Time, which increased their share of the powdered beverages market to 77.4%. GF's bakery business also had a good year; Entenmann's successfully expanded into the Pacific Northwest, and the company completed its acquisition of the Charles Freihofer Baking Company, a major regional baker in the Northeast. Finally, GF introduced new products in all menu areas, including bakery goods, Kool-Aid and Jell-O products, and convenience foods from Culinova, Impromptu, Ronzoni, and Bird's Eye.

General Foods Worldwide Coffee and International's unit volume increased 3.5% in 1987. However, the gain was all in international operations, and was more than offset by a decline in GF's domestic coffee business, which includes such major products as Maxwell House and Sanka. However, Oscar Mayer Foods continued its leadership in sliced luncheon meats, bacon, and hot dogs in 1987, increasing its unit volume 3.6% from 1986. This division also introduced Zappetites, a line of snack foods made especially for the microwave oven, and the Lunchables line of convenient light meals comprising meat, cheese, and crackers.

GF sales reps are the ones responsible for getting the company's products and displays into stores; for checking pricing, rotating stocks, and working out merchandising with the store management; and for meeting certain unit and personal goals, quotas, and targets. The selling is very competitive. Reps are constantly installing and checking food displays and arranging for special sales and co-op ads for promoting selected items. They must be thoroughly knowledgeable not only about their products, but also about their customers' businesses and the grocery market in general. They are called on to make decisions on the spot, and one of their main tasks is to increase GF's share of the most desirable shelf space in order to improve sales.

GF looks for new sales rep candidates who have a college degree and who are self-starters with a real desire to sell. Prior sales experience is very helpful but not necessary. To underline its emphasis on selling, GF has candidates undergo a 12-week session of on-the-job training in the field making calls *before* taking formal training classes. This is to ensure that those who go on to the formal series of five-day training programs are the top prospects for becoming successful GF sales reps. The training program itself is made up of a series of ongoing seminars, each lasting five days, and primarily consisting of a professional selling segment. Completion of the seminars qualifies reps for advancement, and later on the training includes such topics as account management, supervisory skills, and management development.

Territory size varies with population density, namely, the number of grocery stores, supermarkets, and so on, to be serviced. In heavily urbanized areas such as New Jersey, for instance, there would be no overnight travel, whereas in more sparsely populated Wyoming, a rep should expect to be on the road a lot. Reps work alone, but they do have excellent backup in the form of heavy, highly professional ad and promotion materials, administrative/clerical help when possible, and development of new products in the various menu areas. GF's reputation and widely recognized line of brand-name products is also a big help in selling store managers and in persuading them to give more and better shelf space to the company's products.

The average salary for a sales trainee is about $25,000, with senior salespeople's salaries averaging about $45,000. In addition, GF offers a salary incentive plan (SIP), which can total from 5% to 10% of base salary. The percentage is based on salary level, which, in turn, is dependent on how long and how successfully the rep has been selling for the company. Advancement prospects are excellent, with many routes to the top and constant training all the way.

Other benefits include: medical, dental, and life insurance; disability and retirement plans; a savings plan; tuition assistance up to 100% and an allowance of $50 for books; a credit union; paid relocation expenses; and a company car and travel allowance.

General Foods has a warm and friendly atmosphere, even though it is a giant in the industry, hectic, fast-paced, and highly competitive. The company offers a solid future with many paths and opportunities to advance.

GEO. A. HORMEL &
COMPANY

VITAL STATISTICS

Entry Level Salary for Sales: **$25,000**
Senior Level Salary for Sales: **$50,000**

Benefits

medical/dental: **Yes**	child care: **No**
life insurance: **Yes**	retirement plan: **Yes**
disability: **Yes**	savings investment plan: **No**
travel allowance: **N/A**	tuition assistance: **Yes**
company car: **Yes**	relocation assistance: **Yes**
profit sharing plan: **Yes**	memberships: **No**
stock purchase plan: **Yes**	

Corporate Culture Index   (1 = lowest, 10 = highest)

training:	**8**	security:	**9**
support:	**8**	mobility:	**7**
benefits:	**9**	intangibles:	**8**

Address: 501 16th Avenue N.E., P.O. Box 800, Austin, MN 55912
Contact: Human Resources; telephone 507/437-5611

Geo. A. Hormel & Company produces and markets processed and packaged foods to retail grocers, and foodservice and industrial customers. In 1987, the company ranked 172nd on the Fortune 500 list and 20th on the list of largest foodservice companies. 1987 sales topped $2 billion, an 18% jump from the year before, with profits at $46 million, also up 18% from 1986.

When you hear the name "Hormel," you probably think "Spam." The world-famous luncheon meat celebrated its fiftieth anniversary (to worldwide acclaim) in 1987. Hormel's other major meat product, Cure 81 ham, celebrated its twenty-fifth birthday in 1988.

Hormel's principal products are processed red meats, which it sells fresh, frozen, cured, smoked, cooked, or canned. Hormel is also a leading producer of whole and processed turkey products, and a leader in selling "farm raised, grain-fed catfish." Customers are mainly retailers and wholesale distributors working for independent grocery stores or national food-service chains. Reps rarely, if ever, demonstrate products (the Hormel name is usually sufficient guarantee).

Hormel is interested in trainees who exhibit all the basic personality traits that make a good sales rep: "good communication skills, good discipline, and skill at details"—preferably in economics and/or accounting. A college degree is required, either in marketing or business. Prior sales experience is also helpful, though not a formal requirement.

The training program gives more emphasis to on-the-job training than to formal instruction. Trainees spend about 80% of their time in the field. Training is conducted at district sales offices located in most larger U.S. cities. The program lasts from three months up to a year, and features a plant tour, a general corporate orientation, a review of corporate policies, and generalized instruction in selling skills and practices.

Individual evaluation is handled by the district sales manager, who also assigns reps to territories tending toward compact dimensions: either a small city or part of a state—too small, in most cases, to require many overnight stays. Turnover is relatively low (10%–12%), considering the extremely fierce competitiveness of the foodservice field.

The sales force of 375+ is well supported when it comes to advertising and sales promotional materials. Administrative support and clerical assistance are also generously provided. The company will not divulge exact salaries, but describes them as "competitive" with the industry, indicating a training range in the mid twenties and senior sales salaries running up to $50,000, plus commissions.

According to the company itself, the corporate atmosphere is "warm, family-like" and "dynamic," with a "damned positive!" attitude. Benefits include: medical and dental insurance, tuition assistance, a company car (no allowance), disability and group life insurance, a retirement/pension plan, and a stock purchase and 401K plan.

Relocation expenses are provided, if and when reps climb the somewhat limited promotional ladder from smaller, poorer territories to more lucrative, senior accounts.

After nearly a century of profitably filling the carnivorous mouths of America, Hormel continues to turn old-fashioned raw materials into "new traditions"—like the New Traditions frozen cheeseburger that prompted a *Wall Street Journal* reporter to exclaim: "It's a simple idea that excites me."

This is not a job for a committed vegetarian. But if you don't mind meat (or maybe even like Spam!), it is well worth noting that Hormel is keeping pace with a notoriously fast-paced industry.

KRAFT, INC.

VITAL STATISTICS

Entry Level Salary for Sales: **$21,000**
Senior Level Salary for Sales: **$45,000**

Benefits

medical/dental: **Yes**	child care: **No**
life insurance: **Yes**	retirement plan: **Yes**
disability: **Yes, short and long term**	savings investment plan: **Yes**
travel allowance: **Yes**	tuition assistance: **Yes**
company car: **Yes**	relocation assistance: **Yes**
profit sharing plan: **Yes**	memberships: **Smokenders**
stock purchase plan: **Yes**	**Weight Watchers**
	Wellness program
	On-site fitness center

Corporate Culture Index (1 = lowest, 10 = highest)

training:	**9**	security:	**9**
support:	**8**	mobility:	**8**
benefits:	**10**	intangibles:	**9**

Address: Kraft Court, Glenview, IL 60025
Contact: Human Resources; telephone 312/998-2000

Kraft ranked 2nd in the food industry in 1988 nationwide, and was added to the Philip Morris empire the same year. Net sales for 1987 increased 27% from 1986 to nearly $10 billion, while net income increased 18.5% to $489 million. Kraft ranked 31st on the Fortune 500 list in 1987.

Kraft is a company that knows what it likes: food. And what its customers like: "Good food and good food ideas." "Food is where we want to be," proclaims a recent annual report. As a result, Kraft has been divesting itself of all nonfoodservice business, most notably its $2 billion sell-off of its Duracell battery division in early 1988.

Now, Kraft once again means food, and food only. It produces all kinds of food (more than 1000 brands), including such number-one national household names as Philadelphia Brand cream cheese, Miracle Whip salad dressing, Parkay and Chiffon margarine, Breyer's and Frusen Gladje ice creams, Lender's bagels, and Light & Lively and Sealtest dairy products.

"We're returning to our roots," Kraft chairman John Richman gleefully announced to the *Wall Street Journal* following the Duracell sale. "We've got a 100% food focus for the first time in ten years." This means that the job of Kraft's 2100+ sales reps (more than one quarter of whom are women) is to see that levels of the company's products are maintained, or strengthened, in grocery stores and supermarkets around the country.

Kraft likes leadership qualities in its reps, as well as "initiative and aggressiveness combined with a high sociability factor, good communication skills, experience in or facility for gathering and analyzing data, and indications of being a team player." A BA in marketing or business wouldn't hurt either, or even an MBA if you cherish ambitions of becoming one of Kraft's richly rewarded marketing "fast trackers" assigned to key "Headquarters Accounts."

Sales training includes eight weeks of basic training in the new hire's sales district, conducted by a district supervisor assisted by experienced salespeople. The basic course covers product knowledge, selling skills, retailing, and territory management, and it involves a combination of classroom and on-the-job coaching. After this, all new hires begin "Comprehensive Selling," a 24-section self-study program complete with case studies to be evaluated by the supervisor. Evaluation consists of a questionnaire filled out by the trainee to determine his or her comprehension level, and specialized training in such arcana as PC usage and data analysis.

The line of promotion runs from sales rep to HQ account manager to sales supervisor to manager of HQ accounts. Kraft's six sales regions are divided into 60 districts. A promotion-from-within system ensures a low turnover rate of 9%. Skills, performance, and potential are all measured for promotion, and about 20% of the total sales force is promoted every year on all levels.

Reps work alone, with access to top management through a call to the district supervisor. Though most sales are to grocery retailers, warehouses and other wholesale distributors are also frequent sales targets. Reps are assigned to some 40 accounts, which they visit on a weekly or biweekly basis, without much overnight travel. Advertising and sales promotional support includes printed materials, typing, filing, and computer support, although responsibility for computerization has been gradually shifting into the field as reps receive hand-held and lap-top computers.

The starting salary for an entry-level sales rep is a total of $24,000 ($21,000 salary plus $3000 bonus), while senior sales execs draw a $45,000 salary and approximately $7000 bonus for a grand total of $52,000.

Benefits include: full medical and dental insurance, tuition assistance

(100%), company car (no allowance), group life insurance, short- and long-term disability, retirement/pension, profit sharing, stock purchase, 401K, savings, memberships in Smokenders and Weight Watchers, a wellness program, an on-site fitness center, and relocation expenses. Other incentives include a points-for-merchandise program with a large national department store, contests, trips, and district party funds.

What more can you say about a company that in 1987 reported "record tonnage" in shipments of Cheez Whiz?

PHILIP MORRIS COMPANIES, INC.

VITAL STATISTICS

Entry Level Salary for Sales: **$22,000–$24,000**
Senior Level Salary for Sales: **$50,000**

Benefits

medical/dental: **Yes**	child care: **No**
life insurance: **Yes**	retirement plan: **Yes**
disability: **Yes, short and long term**	savings investment plan: **N/A**
travel allowance: **Yes**	tuition assistance: **Yes**
company car: **Yes**	relocation assistance: **Yes**
profit sharing plan: **Yes**	memberships: **No**
stock purchase plan: **No**	

Corporate Culture Index   (1 = lowest, 10 = highest)

training:	**7**	security:	**7**
support:	**8**	mobility:	**8**
benefits:	**9**	intangibles:	**6**

Address: 120 Park Avenue, New York, NY 10017
Contact: Personnel; telephone 212/880-5000

Philip Morris, the world's largest food company *and* the nation's largest cigarette manufacturer, ranked 7th on the Fortune 500 list, has 37.8% of the domestic market share. In 1987 net earnings were $1.8 billion, up 25% from 1986. Operating revenues rose 9% to $27.7 billion.

Philip Morris is more than the nation's top cigarette manufacturer. Owner of General Foods, Kraft, Miller Brewing, and Oscar Mayer, Philip Morris also offers financial and real-estate services through Philip Morris Credit Corporation and Mission Viejo Realty Group.

The total domestic market for cigarettes is declining at present by 2% per year (down to 28% of American adults from 30% in 1985). But tobacco revenues and profits have never been higher. This paradox has been pulled off with sharply higher prices, lower costs, and vastly increased exports (100 billion cigarettes last year alone).

As things stand now, predictions of future core business contraction are being offset by this growing company's strong work ethic. The company's 3300-member sales force is selling fast and hard and keeping up with changing popular tastes. The corporate atmosphere is sober and hardworking, with a strict dress code and a clear leaning toward the clean-cut look—an all-business corporate style, in other words.

Sales trainees earn somewhere between $22,000 and $24,000 a year. The average sales executive rakes in $50,000 and up. Commissions and bonuses are restricted to management, so sales excellence is almost entirely rewarded with a firm hire-and-promote-from-within policy.

A college degree is not a requirement—nor are prior sales experience and specialized technical knowledge. Training takes place deep in tobacco country—Richmond, Virginia. One week of classes is followed by two weeks of on-the-job training in the field under the supervision of experienced reps. Additional training takes place on one day every two months for the first year, with evaluations after six months, and once a year after that.

Reps spend almost all their time on the road, working mostly alone, covering territories that vary from three rural states to a small part of a large city. Expense accounts are a given, and access to top management is provided through the first division manager to the section manager, and on up straight to the top.

Reps never train customers or install or demonstrate products (hardly necessary for Post Toasties or Marlboro Lights), but they do set up displays, rotate stock, and perform such promotional tasks as handing out free cigarettes.

Sales are accomplished strictly through an established marketing and merchandising procedure, lending little room for creative leaps and personal innovation. Trouble-shooting is a critical element in the client-rep relationship, with reinforcements on hand if needed.

Benefits include: full medical and dental insurance, tuition assistance, paid vacation, company car (no travel allowance), profit sharing, and disability insurance. Sales support encompasses administrative/clerical, advertising, market research, monthly meetings, and promotional programs.

"Backing each of our best selling brands are the individual talents of 113,000 committed employees," says Philip Morris management in its 1987 annual report. That's a slogan certified by *Fortune* magazine, which ranked Philip Morris second only to Merck on its 1987 list of Most Admired Corporations in its "ability to attract, develop, and keep talented people." This regard for employees is good news for its salespeople.

THE PILLSBURY COMPANY

VITAL STATISTICS

Entry Level Salary for Sales: **$23,000–$26,000**
Senior Level Salary for Sales: **$45,000–$50,000**

Benefits

medical/dental: **Yes**
life insurance: **Yes**
disability: **Yes, short and long term**
travel allowance: **Yes**
company car: **Yes**
profit sharing plan: **No**
stock purchase plan: **Yes**

child care: **Yes**
retirement plan: **Yes**
savings investment plan: **Yes**
tuition assistance: **Yes**
relocation assistance: **Yes**
memberships: **Smokenders**
Weight Watchers
Wellness program
On-site fitness center

Corporate Culture Index (1 = lowest, 10 = highest)

training: **7**
support: **9**
benefits: **10**

security: **9**
mobility: **9**
intangibles: **9**

Address: Pillsbury Center, Minneapolis, MN 55402
Contact: Human Resources; telephone 612/330-4966

Consistently listed among *Fortune*'s Most Admired Corporations, Pillsbury ranks 61st on the Fortune 500 list. Net sales in 1987 hit a record $6.1 billion, up 5% from 1986. A London-based firm, Grand Metropolitan, acquired Pillsbury in late 1988.

This highly regarded company started out milling flour on the banks of the Mississippi 130 years ago. It has since grown into an international food conglomerate with interests in restaurants, agricultural products, and processed and convenience foods that have been canned, dried, and frozen.

Lately the company's restaurant business, which includes Häagen-Dazs and Steak & Ale, has not proven to be the cash cow it once was. Both Burger King and Godfather's Pizza (once the darling of the industry) have been sold off, while Steak & Ale, Bay Street, Key West Grill, and Quick Wok have all been sharply scaled back as Pillsbury focuses on its core businesses. Pillsbury has always done better on the packaged food side, and though frozen pizza and dessert mixes are not selling quite so well as they used to, its new line of microwave foods has been a hot hit.

The sales force is divided along product lines: dry and frozen groceries, fresh vegetables, feed products, and so on. All over the company, reps start out as "sales merchandisers," calling on retail stores, introducing new products, improving product presentations, and building sales volume. Sales reps set up food displays, but are rarely called on to demonstrate products (maybe a microwave biscuit). The sales force of 500+ (700+, including sales managers) sells almost exclusively to food retailers, and to a few wholesale distributors. Reps stay within product lines: dry groceries (such as Gold Medal flour), frozen groceries (Green Giant frozen peas, and microwave frozen pizza), or prepared doughs (rolls, breads, and breakfast biscuits).

More important than any college degree, management insists, are personal qualities such as self-discipline, motivation, organizational skills, and a willingness to relocate on request. Nonetheless, college degrees are a plus, and business majors are definitely preferred.

The goals of the training program are "increased self-confidence, and sales ability," as trainees learn about different accounts and Pillsbury's vast line-up of products. A trainee spends about four days in class, learning selling skills, territory management, key accounts, and negotiations. This is followed by 12 weeks of on-the-job training in the field, closely supervised by the district sales manager.

For reps with a yen to climb the corporate ladder, Pillsbury has a welcome attitude, for management stresses promotion from within, from account manager to sales manager, on up to marketing staff. The turnover rate is a respectable 13% to 15%, about standard for the industry.

Reps spend nearly all their time on the road, always alone, covering territories that range from one city to two to three states. Expense accounts are part of the package, with average salaries running in the $23,000–$26,000 range for a trainee and $45,000–$50,000 for a senior executive. There are bonuses, but no commissions.

Salaries are standard, but the benefits are tops: group life insurance; full medical, dental, and disability (long- and short-term) insurance; tuition assistance (100%); a company car; relocation expenses; pension/retirement and 401K plan; profit sharing; stock purchase and savings plans; and dependent child care. Pillsbury also throws in membership in Smokenders and Weight Watchers, a wellness program, and the use of a fitness center.

Pillsbury's corporate culture was sharply (some would say contentiously) divided between the Miami-based Burger King and the more traditional, button-down crowd at Pillsbury Minneapolis headquarters. Today the focus is on the bottom line at Pillsbury as the company struggles to maintain its ascendancy in prepared and processed foods—yet keeping a strong foothold in the fast-food restaurant business.

As long as Americans want to eat quickly and easily, Pillsbury's convenience foods, whether on the supermarket shelf or by the interstate exit, will keep the company healthy and strong. Of course, the company also has the Jolly Green Giant on its side.

RJR NABISCO, INC.

VITAL STATISTICS

Entry Level Salary for Sales: **$21,000–$22,000**
Senior Level Salary for Sales: **$100,000**

Benefits

medical/dental: **Yes**	child care: **No**
life insurance: **Yes**	retirement plan: **Yes**
disability: **Yes**	savings investment plan: **N/A**
travel allowance: **Yes**	tuition assistance: **Yes**
company car: **Yes**	relocation assistance: **Yes**
profit sharing plan: **N/A**	memberships: **No**
stock purchase plan: **N/A**	

Corporate Culture Index   (1 = lowest, 10 = highest)

training:	**8**	security:	**8**
support:	**7**	mobility:	**8**
benefits:	**8**	intangibles:	**8**

Address: Reynolds Boulevard, Winston-Salem, NC 27102
Contact: Personnel; telephone 919/773-2000

RJR Nabisco has more than $17 billion in assets, and its 1987 net sales were nearly $16 billion, with net earnings up 14% from 1986, to over $1 billion.

RJR Nabisco recently made history, when it became the subject of the largest corporate bidding session ever, finally selling for $25.07 billion to Kohlberg Kravis Roberts & Company. But that was far from the first major change this company has experienced.

In April 1986, the RJ Reynolds Industries became known as RJR Nabisco, reflecting a more even balance between the company's food and tobacco products. Nabisco's brand names sound like a trip down memory lane or into your mother's kitchen: Lorna Doone and Oreo Cookies, Ritz Crackers, Ginger Snaps, Cheese Nips, and Comet Cones. Then there are Winston, Salem, Vantage, and Doral.

In today's health-conscious age, you might think a company specializing in selling sugary munchies and tobacco would be hurting. Yet RJR Nabisco has never done better. Even if you discount the snack foods and cigarettes, the larders at RJR Nabisco have plenty of other products: A1 Steak Sauce, Vermont Maid Maple Syrup, Planter's Peanuts, Del Monte Fruit, Fleischmann's Margarine—and the list goes on.

That list is not so long as it used to be, however. CEO Ross Johnson—*Fortune* calls him a "tough cookie"—spun off Heublein, Kentucky Fried Chicken, and Canada Dry in a move to concentrate the business on what it knows best.

For sales trainees, RJR prefers a college degree, but is willing to consider candidates from more varied backgrounds. Training for new hires starts off with something called STEP (Sales Training Entry Program), a comprehensive 13-week course combining on-the-job training with classroom work, bolstered with 500 pages of printed material and eight full-length video tapes. But the main thrust of the program is on-the-job training at the work location.

"We strongly believe that the proper training up front will pay dividends in the long run for the company," says Dick Luongo, national manager of sales training and development. "We expect a lot out of our people. So we do what we can to give them the proper tools."

Some tools that trainees are expected to supply themselves are high motivation, eagerness to try new procedures, and flexible goals. To build on these basics, management works closely with trainees for about half of the initial training period, after which the trainees are counseled on an ongoing basis, depending on individual needs. All sales reps receive performance evaluations annually.

An RJR Nabisco sales career includes a four-day sales program open to all reps within the first two years. If a rep gets promoted to an entry-level management position, this special Management Training Program focuses on oral presentation, conducting meetings, stress and time management, and other supervisory management techniques.

Access to top management comes through divisional and regional meetings in the different divisions: Domestic Tobacco; International Tobacco; and Foods, Spirits, and Wines. Travel time varies according to territory, which consists of between 25 and 30 accounts, rural or urban. There are no formal expense accounts, but expenses are reimbursed. Reps rarely work alone, but are frequently managed in teams to make sales primarily in a direct bid to the retailer, to whom all new products are introduced, and who must be instructed in those products' benefits. (The philosophy is that, at the end of the line, it is the grocery retailer who actually sells the product to the end-user.) Staff turnover is a low 10% at RJR Nabisco.

Trainees start out at $21,000–$22,000; senior executives at the VP level hit the $100,000 mark, generously supplemented by bonuses of about 15% of salary (but no commissions). Other benefits include travel allowance;

tuition assistance; company car; medical, dental, life, and disability insurance; and retirement, profit sharing, and stock purchase plans.

Currently whipping rival Procter & Gamble's Duncan Hines brand in the "cookie wars," developing a highly touted "smokeless cigarette" (code-named Spa), and promoting its coin-sized Ritz Bits, RJR Nabisco is clearly ploughing ahead doing what it does best: dreaming up new tobacco and food products and winning the public over with them.

"The company's top managers say the sales force is too good to let them screw up the business," *Fortune* recently reported, extolling the virtues of Nabisco's salespeople, who "make sure that Nabisco gets every inch of shelf space it can." How about fudge-covered Oreos? Sinful, sure, but Oreo sales topped $160 million in the past three years. It is just those types of figures that give your local retailer something to munch on, with enough left over to generate a serious bonus.

SYSCO CORPORATION

VITAL STATISTICS

Entry Level Salary for Sales: *$26,000–$32,000*
Senior Level Salary for Sales: *$100,000+*

Benefits

medical/dental: **Yes**
life insurance: **Yes**
disability: **Yes**
travel allowance: **Yes**
company car: **No**
profit sharing plan: **Yes**
stock purchase plan: **Yes**

child care: **No**
retirement plan: **Yes**
savings investment plan: **Yes**
tuition assistance: **Yes**
relocation assistance: **N/A**
memberships: **Smokenders**

Corporate Culture Index (1 = lowest, 10 = highest)

training: **8**
support: **9**
benefits: **8**

security: **9**
mobility: **8**
intangibles: **8**

Address: 1390 Enclave Parkway, Houston, TX 77077
Contact: Personnel; telephone 713/584-1390

SYSCO Corporation is the largest marketer and distributor of foodservice products in the U.S. In 1987 it had total sales of more than $3 billion, up 15% from 1986. The company ranks 189th in sales in the *Forbes* 500.

SYSCO, an acronym for Systems and Services Company, is a corporate giant whose products are well known, but whose name is not. The products, foodstuffs (wholesale groceries), are distributed nationally to restaurants, hotels, schools, hospitals, and other institutions. The company also supplies frozen food products to supermarkets and retail stores in certain areas. It operates from 83 distribution centers and self-service centers located in 46 states.

Since its inception in 1969 and with the merger of nine independent and geographically dispersed companies, SYSCO has held to a decentralized management philosophy. At present, SYSCO's 54 autonomous operating companies service about 150,000 customers around the country. Each company has the responsibility of determining its own business, deciding what products to stock, establishing its pricing policies, developing its marketing strategies, and so on. With this type of organization, each company is best able to compete effectively in its own different geographical markets and to meet the disparate needs of its own very diverse customers.

Working together under the SYSCO umbrella, however, these companies can take advantage of economies of scale and of efficiencies in distribution to revolutionize the way food reaches the away-from-home dining tables of the nation. With more and more Americans dining out, SYSCO sees healthy growth prospects for the future. At present, the company has a 4% share of the $85-billion national foodservice distribution market, and it sees great opportunities to expand that share and increase sales significantly. Geographic expansion of its distribution centers has already proved a rewarding strategy for SYSCO, and it now has service capabilities in over 80% of the major urban areas in the U.S. It is also actively working to increase its customer base and to broaden the line of products it offers to its customers.

SYSCO's basic marketing and sales approach is to demonstrate to its customers—a restaurant chain, say, or a hospital complex—how the proper use of its products will enhance the customer's own performance. Because variety and nutrition are increasingly important to consumers in their meals away from home, foodservice providers must have access to high-quality, fresh, natural foodstuffs at reasonable prices in order to succeed. Satisfying this need is the business of SYSCO and its affiliated companies.

It is also the business of the nearly 4000-strong sales and marketing force of the corporation. The sales reps and marketing associates (senior salespeople) call on restaurants and institutions to discover their foodservice needs and concerns and to show how SYSCO products and services can meet them. The company supports activities by employing product specialists who bring professional expertise to bear on a customer's problems. For instance, SYSCO used a number of talented and customer-oriented dietitians to assist health-care operators in adapting to new government and economic pressures while still providing the required quality meals. This led to a substantial increase in the corporation's health-care customer base. Although R&D for new products doesn't play much of a role in SYSCO's operations, study and analysis of its customers' industries certainly does.

Sales training for new reps at SYSCO is, like the rest of its management style, decentralized. Held in some central urban area, training takes place at the local (company) level and is spread out over a period of one week a month for three months. The program consists of a mix of company/ industry orientation, product knowledge, and selling skills. The product knowledge area also involves such topics as menu planning, recipes, maintenance of specific stock levels—all related to food (frozen, dry, dairy, meat and poultry, baked goods, and so on) and foodservice concerns.

SYSCO also offers advanced training programs that bring marketing associates into direct contact with suppliers, customers, product and marketing specialists, and other experts from all areas of the food and beverage business. Sales and marketing classes are also routinely conducted at each of the company's distribution centers, and are augmented by week-long training programs held in conjunction with the Conrad H. Hilton College of Hotel and Restaurant Management at the University of Houston. There are also classes for management personnel at all levels, which in part concentrate on improving leadership and people-management skills.

SYSCO looks for stable, family-oriented college graduates for its sales reps. Selling experience is helpful, but not necessary. The pace is hectic, though, with reps working alone and under high pressure every day; so a real desire to sell is a big factor in future success. There is a definite career ladder; the rep advances to marketing associate to district sales manager to national sales manager to vice president of sales, *within* the rep's company. A few from sales may also go on to management positions at the corporate headquarters.

Salaries for sales personnel vary from company to company. One representative company has a salary range of $26,000 to $32,000 (including bonus and incentive) for beginning reps. After three years, the reps go on a straight commission basis where experienced marketing associates have a good chance to earn $100,000+ once they learn the territory and the customers. Other benefits include: medical, dental, and life insurance; disability and retirement plans; profit sharing and stock purchase plans; a 401K plan; tuition assistance; and a company car.

SYSCO has a very ambitious growth schedule planned, and it looks for good dynamic salespeople who can make it happen. For people who like food and selling, the market is there, and the money is there.

WETTERAU INCORPORATED

VITAL STATISTICS

Entry Level Salary for Sales: *$16,000–$24,000*
Senior Level Salary for Sales: *$45,000–$50,000*

Benefits

medical/dental: **Yes**	child care: **No**
life insurance: **Yes**	retirement plan: **Yes**
disability: **Yes, long term**	savings investment plan: **No**
travel allowance: **N/A**	tuition assistance: **Yes, 75%**
company car: **Yes**	relocation assistance: **Yes**
profit sharing plan: **No**	memberships: **Smokenders**
stock purchase plan: **Yes**	**Weight Watchers**

Corporate Culture Index   (1 = lowest, 10 = highest)

training:	**7**	security:	**9**
support:	**8**	mobility:	**9**
benefits:	**8**	intangibles:	**8**

Address: 8920 Pershall Road, St. Louis, MO 63042
Contact: Human Resources; telephone 314/524-5000

Wetterau, the nation's third-largest full-service food distributor, supplies and supports more than 2500 grocery retailers in 27 states throughout the eastern half of the U.S. In 1988 sales exploded to $4 billion from under $1 billion in 1979, a fantastic 300% gain.

Wetterau is one of the nation's largest diversified service companies, operating in two basic sectors: wholesale and retail food distribution, and service and manufacturing activities related to food distribution.

After 118 years, Wetterau's focus remains the development and support of independent grocery retailers. The Food Distribution Group supplies and services grocery store owners mostly in the eastern half of the country. Though this activity still accounts for around 95% of sales and 80% of profits, the company's dynamic expansion has resulted in a highly diversified range of services in the foodservice sector, including a Retail Group that creates and develops new stores (and supports company-owned units); an Industries Group that offers merchandise distribution, insurance protection, commercial construction, and printing to foodservice companies across the country; a Bakery Products Division, now the second-largest producer of frozen dough products nationwide; and Wetterau Builders, which constructs warehouses, shopping centers, stores, restaurants, office complexes, medical centers, factories, and even churches. Wetterau's Communications Group provides the company and external clients with communications consultants for everything from executive skills training to video and A/V production. Finally, the Creative Management Institute (CMI) researches, designs, and conducts professional management programs for food industry clients.

According to Bob Stross, vice president at CMI, Wetterau does not consider its reps to be "salespeople" in the traditional sense, but foodservice "counselors" who spend less than 10% of the time actually selling. Instead, their main activity is to call on grocery store owners and managers and to consult with them on how they can improve profits, product line-ups, and general foodservice management.

Counselors cover large territories, up to 150 miles across, often comprising 25 to 30 major accounts. They are trained to discuss and evaluate profit statements, staff turnover, stale merchandise, and even whether doughnuts or bagels sell better in a certain region—the wide range of problems facing a grocery store operator on a day-to-day basis.

Wetterau is looking for counselors who have prior experience in the grocery business, whether as a stock person, front office clerk, sandwich maker, or even grocery bagger. Sales experience is a plus, and a college degree is a requirement. Training is condensed into a one-week program held in major cities five times a year followed by several four- and three-day sessions during the rep's first six months working his or her assigned territory.

Reps climb the company ladder from small territory to large, from field counselor to district sales manager to marketing manager to vice president for sales. Reps spend almost all their time on the road, either alone or in teams, with easy access to top management by phone to any one of 17 distribution centers. Turnover in this 200+ sales force stays on the low side (around 10%).

A rep's earnings are completely salary-based; there are no commissions, no incentives—just expense accounts. Sales trainees earn between $16,000 and $24,000 (depending on the region), whereas the senior sales executive's salary runs somewhere between $45,000 and $50,000. Benefits include medical and dental insurance, tuition assistance (75%), group life and disability insurance, a retirement/pension plan, a stock purchase plan, a company car, a credit union, and a fitness center. On the down side, the company offers no profit sharing, savings plan, or 401K retirement plan.

Selling for Wetterau is generally low-key, stressing the consulting approach and the development of a partnership between the independent retailer and the "counselor." Though Wetterau's largely invisible but essential services may strike some as too "meat and potatoes," the business keeps growing each year, offering reps a solid job in a solid industry.

INDUSTRIAL AND AGRICULTURAL EQUIPMENT

Henry Adams, John Adams's great-grandson and one of the great writers of the nineteenth century, said that the best symbol he could think of for America was the dynamo. When you think of this country's awesome industrial strength, the first image that comes to mind is some huge piece of machinery, whirring and clanging away.

The dynamo that Henry Adams wrote about and that still shapes our lives has many different forms and does many different things. Not surprisingly, the success of a particular piece of machinery will be closely tied to the fortunes of the industry whose needs it services.

Sales of construction machinery were up in 1987, but still only half of what they were eight years previous. Little future growth is expected in mining or in residential and commercial building, and as the costs of industrial labor increase, more and more construction firms are looking abroad for their equipment. However, experts do predict growth in industrial construction and in public works.

Machine tools constitute a small but essential part of the industry. These power-driven tools shape and form metals by cutting, pressure, impact, and electricity. Imports now account for nearly half of the machine tools in the United States. Many firms are trying to turn this situation to their advantage by creating joint ventures with foreign companies.

Pumps and compressors are used by manufacturers in a number of industrial processes involving liquids and gases. With the recent rises in oil prices, petroleum manufacturers, who are prime consumers of pumps and compressors, have upgraded their facilities and bought new machinery. At the same time, there has been a resurgence of government activity in public works like bridges and water systems, which rely heavily on pumps. These developments have spurred the sales of pumps and compressors to a 2% annual growth rate, amounting to nearly $9 billion in 1987.

Ever since Cain was told that he had to live by the sweat of his brow, people have looked for bigger and better ways of working the land. Agricultural equipment is now an $8-billion-a-year business. Although some downward trends of recent years have begun to ease up, there is no denying that, as farms and farmers have fallen on hard times, so have the companies that supply them with tractors, combines, and haying machines.

The drought that swept the farm belt in 1988 has had a major effect on current sales of farm equipment, which is usually purchased one harvest season in advance. But the drought may turn out to have been a blessing in disguise for major manufacturers like Deere and Harvester, who have fallen behind in production in the past few years and are using the drought as an opportunity to replenish their inventories. Once the drought ends, there will be other crops and new harvests.

As more and more Americans move off the farm, domestic demand for farm equipment will probably decline. At the same time, however, more and more developing countries are moving toward growing their own food, which creates new foreign markets for reliable, heavy-duty American farm equipment and keeps the dynamo in demand.

TRADE ASSOCIATIONS

American Supply and Machinery Manufacturers Association 216/241-7333
Farm and Industrial Equipment Institute 312/321-1470
Farm Equipment Manufacturers Association 314/991-0702
Farm Equipment Wholesalers Association 319/354-5156
National Farm and Power Equipment Dealers Association 314/821-7220
National Industrial Distributors Association 215/564-3484

PERIODICALS

Farm and Power Equipment
Farm Equipment
Industrial Equipment News
New Equipment Digest: Equipment, Materials, Processes, Designs, Literature

BLACK & DECKER, INC.

VITAL STATISTICS

Entry Level Salary for Sales: **$29,400–$44,100**
Senior Level Salary for Sales: **$34,200–$51,300**

Benefits

medical/dental: **Yes**	child care: **N/A**
life insurance: **Yes**	retirement plan: **Yes**
disability: **Yes**	savings investment plan: **Yes**
travel allowance: **Yes**	tuition assistance: **N/A**
company car: **Yes**	relocation assistance: **N/A**
profit sharing plan: **N/A**	memberships: **N/A**
stock purchase plan: **Yes**	

Corporate Culture Index   (1 = lowest, 10 = highest)

training:	**10**	security:	**9**
support:	**10**	mobility:	**9**
benefits:	**10**	intangibles:	**9**

Address: U.S. Power Tools Group, 10 North Park Drive, P.O. Box 798, Hunt Valley, MD 21030-0748
Contact: Human Resources; telephone 301/683-7701 ext. 7811

Black & Decker ranks 195th on the Fortune 500 list. In the period from 1983 to 1986 its sales jumped from $1.1 billion to $1.8 billion, despite heavy foreign competition. In 1986 all but one of its groups showed a sales gain of 4% or more.

Black & Decker is a major manufacturer of power tools for industrial and consumer use. As recently as the early 1980s, the company was experiencing difficulties in sales. What followed wasn't so much a major breakthrough in sales and marketing as a change of focus. "We're going from a culture that made its decisions financially to a company that is very much a marketer," as Mike Convey, vice president of sales, put it. The new emphasis on marketing and detailed sales planning spells good news for the sales staff; it's now seen as the driving force behind the company's improved performance in opening new accounts and in innovation—areas in which B&D had been weak.

One thrust of this change was for the company to get closer to its customers. It started distributor advisory councils, instituted a formal sales training program, and helped the salespeople of its distributors by going on calls with them. That way, the distributors were pushing the Black & Decker line of power tools and farm equipment, along with B&D's own 250 sales reps. In addition, the company jettisoned its emphasis on a financial approach to management and reorganized its sales force into four distinct sales groups designed to handle industrial, consumer, national, and retail accounts, respectively. "Each of these basic components has a specific selling strategy," Convey says, "and that's what's driving our business."

All of B&D's industrial and construction sales and 25% of its consumer sales come through distributor channels, which in turn sell to the end user or retailer. The marketing strategy is to select the very best accounts in each category in each geographical area and then to work with those distributors and their salespeople to "drive" the business with *their* accounts. B&D reps are not so much pressured to add new accounts as they are encouraged to work with existing accounts to ensure that they are successful in profitably selling B&D products to their customers.

Such an approach means that the reps must not only know their products thoroughly, but must also know how to develop creative sell-through programs tailored specifically to individual accounts. Moreover, they must be able to identify emerging new channels of distribution and to help their accounts cope with changes in the marketplace.

To help reps attain these skills, B&D built a state-of-the-art training center at the corporate headquarters in Towson, Maryland, and introduced a comprehensive, ongoing program. After six weeks of supervised training, the new rep spends the next seven to eight months on the job, accompanied by a sales manager at least two days out of every six weeks. After nine months, the rep goes back to the center for three weeks of selling and advanced product knowledge training. After this seminar, the two-day "work-withs" continue, and the rep will return once a year to attend a one-week seminar on important current topics. Additional training supports include a Training Resource Library, a system of manuals that enhance selling skills, and a collection of video cassettes to train reps in the applications and demonstration techniques for power tools.

B&D supports its sales staff in other ways, too. It carefully regulates the amount of information mailings each rep receives, thus keeping the staff informed but not overwhelmed. It arranges for each district and regional office to provide many of the administrative duties required of sales reps (for instance, typing, copying, filing, and completion of various administrative reports). In the field, each member of the sales organization is supplied with a Plus 1 portable computer terminal that can be linked to the main computer by a modem. This makes fast, interactive communications available to each rep, no matter where he or she is. Reps are also provided with a four-door, mid-sized company car with all car expenses paid, plus additional travel accident insurance protection of $50,000 to $100,000.

Clearly, Black & Decker is serious about developing each sales rep to his or her full potential. It looks for new hires who have demonstrated the following characteristics: goal orientation, leadership, solution orientation, interpersonal skills, and organizational ability. In 1988 it instituted a summer internship program targeted to college freshmen and sophomores, with an eye to bringing bright young people into the corporate family.

Salaries run from a low range of $29,400–$44,100, to a high of $34,200–$51,300, with a minimum range of $25,300–$38,000. Salary is based on years of experience and size and complexity of accounts. Merit increases are considered annually, based on achievement of overall job objectives. Bonuses have a high range of $10,000–$12,000, and a low range of $0–$3000, with an average of $3500.

In addition, B&D offers sales personnel the regular companywide package of benefits that includes group medical and life insurance, retirement and savings plans, and optional individual protection plans. These include a variety of personal insurances such as homeowner, automobile, excess liability, and others.

Most important of all, perhaps, Black & Decker is a user-friendly employer. During 1987, for instance, B&D promoted 44 individuals from the sales organization. Because of the accelerated growth in the size of the field force in 1987–1988, opportunities for promotion and career growth should continue to be excellent. Black & Decker likes to promote from within, and it taps sales for marketing positions as well. Thus its field salespeople have two possible avenues of growth—field sales management and marketing management. And for those who are good sales reps and who don't want to move into management, the company provides a climate that allows for both longevity and fulfillment.

CUMMINS ENGINE COMPANY, INC.

VITAL STATISTICS

Entry Level Salary for Sales: **$36,000 with MA**
Senior Level Salary for Sales: **$62,000**

Benefits

---

medical/dental: **Yes**
life insurance: **Yes**
disability: **Yes, long term**
travel allowance: **Yes**
company car: **No**
profit sharing plan: **Yes**
stock purchase plan: **Yes**

child care: **No**
retirement plan: **Yes**
savings investment plan: **Yes**
tuition assistance: **Yes**
relocation assistance: **Yes**
memberships: **No**

Corporate Culture Index   (1 = lowest, 10 = highest)

---

training: **10**
support: **9**
benefits: **9**

security: **9**
mobility: **9**
intangibles: **10**

Address: P.O. Box 3005, Columbus, IN 47202-3005
Contact: Marketing Personnel; telephone 812/377-3201

Cummins Engine Company, Inc., ranks 148th on the Fortune 500 list. In 1987, it had record sales of more than $2.7 billion, up 20% from 1986. It returned to the black in 1987 after a $14 million loss in 1986.

Cummins is a leading worldwide designer and manufacturer of in-line and V-type diesel engines. It also produces and markets a broad range of engine-related components, power systems, and services. Cummins's largest market is the North American heavy-duty truck industry. The company divides its operations into four business groups: Engine Business, Components, Power Systems, and Information and Services.

The Engine Business group supplies diesel engines ranging from 41 to 2400 horsepower. It claims 54% of the heavy-duty truck engine market in North America, with every major truck manufacturer offering Cummins engines as standard or optional equipment on its line. In addition, the company enjoys off-highway sales of its engines among major construction, mining, agricultural, and other industrial equipment manufacturers. The Components group produces crankshafts, turbochargers, filters, and piston rings as well as remanufactured (overhauled and rebuilt) engines and parts. The Power Systems group includes heat transfer equipment, transmissions, electronic control systems, and electric generator sets. The Information and Services group provides software for automotive dealers, computerized operating information for truck fleets, financial services, electronic cash transfer, truck permits, driver training, and road services. The service products include lubricating oil, tools, engine diagnostic equipment, and truck heaters.

After rapid expansion in the 1960s and 1970s, growth in the heavy-duty diesel engine industry has been slow with considerable industry over-capacity and strong foreign competition. To meet these adverse conditions, Cummins adapted a strategy of four elements: (1) it concentrated on rede-signing its engine production capacity for greater efficiency and in order to enter the medium-duty and light-duty diesel engine markets; (2) it up-graded its quality and delivery controls to meet and surpass those of foreign competitors; (3) it cut prices to a world competitive range (this lowered returns but kept or increased market share); and (4) it restructured the company into four operating groups for greater concentration on its core markets.

Cummins's crucial remaining problem is how to bring manufacturing and related costs into line so it can return to solid earnings on its business operations. Cummins is fully persuaded that it's on the right track to achieve these goals. There will still need to be plenty of hard selling and careful managing ahead, however.

Although Cummins operates four business groups, the discussion here will concentrate on the engine business, which provides more than two-thirds of Cummins's total revenue. In the Engine Business, there are several Marketing/Sales organizations, including Automotive, Construction, Mining, Agriculture, Defense, Marine, and Generator Sets. The sales effort described below applies to the Automotive market, which is Cummins's largest market. There are two different sales forces selling Cummins Automotive engines. One sells to original equipment manufacturers (OEMs), for example, Ford, Chrysler, Peterbilt, Navistar, Kenworth, Volvo-GM, Freightliner, and Western Star. The other is a Field Sales force that acts as "regional managers" and calls on Cummins distributors. (Cummins distributors have their own sales staffs selling directly to the end customers.) The sales representatives introduce and explain the features and benefits of new engines to the customers, and are supported by Cummins engineers. To sell effectively, reps have to be knowledgeable about maintenance costs, engine operating costs, truck specifications, service intervals, and the like. Representatives are trained in the use of portable lap-top computers and electronic mail for communication with marketing services or engineering groups at the Columbus, Indiana, headquarters.

The Original Equipment Manufacturer sales force works primarily out of the Columbus Corporate Headquarters, and they can expect to be on the road about 25% of the time. Reps typically work in teams of four: an account executive, who supervises the team, and a representative from each of Marketing, Manufacturing, and Engineering. Representatives frequently fly to a city, rent a car to make their rounds to their OEM locations, and then fly home.

The Field Sales force works out of six division and regional offices, and regional managers are assigned to one of these offices. Their territories will cover anywhere from one to three states and they can expect to spend up to 50% of their time on the road. The field force works on the *pull* principle, that is, persuading truck fleet owners to specify Cummins engines in their next order of new trucks.

Cummins typically looks for new sales representatives who have a degree in business or engineering. Prior sales experience is helpful but not necessary; mechanical aptitude, however, is required. New sales representatives must have some affinity with heavy-duty diesel engines to succeed in this industry. Cummins relies on work experience more than on formal training programs to prepare new employees for sales assignments. The new employee's early assignments can be in a variety of areas—marketing, application engineering, or customer service—that provide excellent exposure to Cummins customers, products, and to the automotive business in general. This training usually lasts one to three years. Once the new employee achieves the right level of experience, he or she is then assigned to either the OEM or Field Sales groups. Management positions within OEM sales or Field Sales are usually filled by promotions from within these groups.

Salaries for trainees with a master's degree average about $36,000; senior sales reps can make about $62,000. A bonus of 3% to 6% can be awarded, based on companywide performance, and a profit sharing program is included in the compensation package. Profit sharing participation level is dependent on the rep's job responsibility level. The pay-out is based on companywide performance. Other benefits include: medical, dental, and life insurance; disability and retirement plans; stock purchase plans; tuition assistance; and paid relocation expenses.

Cummins is a tough company in a tough industry facing strong international competition. In its favor, it has a strategy, a respected family of products, and a professional sales force it supports all the way down the line.

DEERE AND COMPANY

VITAL STATISTICS

Entry Level Salary for Sales: **$38,000–$40,000**
Senior Level Salary for Sales: **$57,000**

Benefits

medical/dental: **Yes**
life insurance: **Yes**
disability: **Yes**
travel allowance: **Yes**
company car: **Yes**
profit sharing plan: **Yes**
stock purchase plan: **Yes**

child care: **No**
retirement plan: **Yes**
savings investment plan: **Yes**
tuition assistance: **Yes**
relocation assistance: **Yes**
memberships: **No**

Corporate Culture Index (1 = lowest, 10 = highest)

training: **7**
support: **8**
benefits: **10**

security: **8**
mobility: **8**
intangibles: **10**

Address: John Deere Road, Moline, IL 61265-8098
Contact: Recruiting Management; telephone 309/765-8000 ext. 4126

Deere and Company ranks 108th on the Fortune 500 list. In 1987 it enjoyed sales of more than $4 billion, up 18% from 1986; it also posted a net loss of $99 million, compared with a net loss in 1986 of $229 million.

Founded in 1837, Deere & Company celebrated its 150th anniversary in 1987. The 1980s, however, have not been kind to the company, and it is a real tribute to Deere's management and workers that it was able to mark its sesquicentennial year with a celebration and with plans for the future.

The prolonged farm slump of the 1980s had brought Deere and other manufacturers of farm equipment to the point of going under; in fact, some did. Deere didn't. Now Deere is looking to build up its fortunes again. It is well positioned to do this because it has dominated the farm machinery market for a long time and still has about 45% of the U.S. market sewn up. If the lean years of the recession are followed with fat years of farm prosperity, Deere would appear to be in an excellent position to cash in on the farmers' pent-up demands for new equipment. In addition, Deere is now preparing to unveil the largest new product line-up in its history. At the same time, the company has made itself respond to market changes more rapidly. It can now bring a new product from the conception stage to production in two years instead of the six-year lead time it used to take.

Admittedly, the great farm boom of the 1970s is very likely over, but Deere believes it can do well even at a slower pace of business than in the bonanza years. For one thing, Deere itself is leaner, although it was the only farm equipment company *not* to close any U.S. plants during the recession. It did cut its work force, though, and it brought in cost-saving equipment so that now it can break even when it's producing at only 35% of its capacity; this compares with a break-even point at 75% of capacity only ten years ago. In addition, there has been some diversification. Deere is now supplying some components to other manufacturers and is expanding its line of nonfarm equipment.

At present Deere manufactures, distributes, and finances the sale and lease of mobile power farm and industrial equipment. The farm sector deals with a full range of agricultural machines—for example, tractors, and tillage, planting, and harvesting equipment—and some consumer equipment, such as small tractors for lawn and garden use, riding lawnmowers, golf course equipment, and the like. The industrial component produces a broad range of heavy earth-moving and forestry equipment. Even with diversification, though, Deere looks to its farm machinery line to supply about 60% of its revenues. Whereas some feel this makes Deere vulnerable in case of another downturn in farm income, Deere CEO Robert A. Hanson is confident that the company can remain profitable in the long term. Of the farm equipment, he says: "It's still a good business and we dominate it."

To maintain that domination in the face of lower overall sales and increased competition, Deere needs a dynamic and skilled marketing force. Selling for Deere is similar to selling for other automotive manufacturers in the sense that Deere sales reps do not sell to the end user, the farmer, but to dealerships, which in turn use their sales reps to make sales to individual farmers. It's a two-stage sell, in other words.

The sales process works this way. Deere sets up what it calls *product announcements* to which it invites the dealers in the territory. There, the Deere rep demonstrates the new product (tractor, truck) to the dealers and to their reps, if possible. The Deere salespeople have videos, catalogues, and piles of promotional printed materials to sell from. Also, in the farm equipment field, the name of Deere is a proud one, one that commands loyalty and respect from both dealers and end users.

Training as a Deere rep is intense but relatively short. The formal part may take only a week or so. It takes place in the field, at dealerships, and at hotels, and it concentrates primarily on applied selling techniques (basic selling skills, psychology of selling, and coaching). Refresher courses are offered frequently, and there is an advanced session called MOVE (Making Others More Effective), which is designed to help Deere reps in their relations with dealers and in motivating dealer reps to sell Deere products.

Deere requires reps to have a college degree. Sales experience is desirable but not necessary; this holds true for technical knowledge, too. The Deere rep covers a territory with an approximate 100-mile radius and is on the road most of the time, visiting dealerships. Most sales jobs at Deere will be found in the Midwest where there is a major concentration of large-scale farming, but dealerships can be found around the country wherever farming is part of the local economy.

The average salary for a Deere trainee sales rep is an outstanding $38,000, with a bonus when the company performance is good. A senior territory manager will earn about $57,000 plus bonus. These salaries are at the top of the industry. Other benefits include: full medical and dental insurance, group life insurance, disability and retirement plans, a profit sharing plan, tuition assistance, paid moving expenses, and a company car. Also available are a stock purchasing plan and matching funds for the savings plan.

At 150 years of age, Deere has a warm and family-like atmosphere. Employees are on a first-name basis, and there are many long-term employees, who, like the company, are survivors—and proud of it!

DRESSER INDUSTRIES, INC.

VITAL STATISTICS

Entry Level Salary for Sales: **$30,000–$45,000**
Senior Level Salary for Sales: **$33,000–$49,000**

Benefits

medical/dental: **Yes**	child care: **No**
life insurance: **Yes**	retirement plan: **401K**
disability: **Yes**	savings investment plan: **N/A**
travel allowance: **Yes**	tuition assistance: **Yes**
company car: **Yes**	relocation assistance: **Yes**
profit sharing plan: **No**	memberships: **No**
stock purchase plan: **Yes**	

Corporate Culture Index   (1 = lowest, 10 = highest)

training:	**8**	security:	**8**
support:	**8**	mobility:	**3**
benefits:	**9**	intangibles:	**8**

Address: 1600 Pacific Avenue, Dallas, TX 75201
Contact: Corporate Headquarters; telephone 214/740-6000

Dresser Industries, Inc., ranks 138th on the Fortune 500 list. In 1987 it posted sales of more than $3 billion, down 15% from 1986. Profits though, at $49 million, were up an incredible 409% from $10 million in 1986.

Dresser Industries, Inc., has suffered, as has the entire petroleum industry, during the mid 1980s from falling demand, overcapacity, and low prices. The company is a major manufacturer and distributor of industrial equipment, primarily to large oil and gas companies. Dresser's operations involve 25 divisions grouped in four basic business segments: petroleum operations, energy processing and conversion, mining and construction equipment, and general industry.

Dresser's petroleum operations segment is one of the world's leading suppliers of specialized products and services for oil and gas exploration, drilling, production, and marketing. The decline of oil prices in the 1980s led to significant reductions in capital spending by energy producers, resulting in lowered sales for this operating segment. Dresser restructured this part of the company, however, reducing costs and company size, and improving earnings.

The energy processing and conversion segment of Dresser is involved in the designing, manufacturing, and marketing of highly engineered systems and products for oil and gas production, gas transmission, and the processing or conversion of oil, gas, and coal into value-added energy forms. Since Dresser expects increasing world demand for petrochemical end products, the company is working on new product specifications and on the modernization of plant facilities.

Dresser's mining and construction equipment segment is a global supplier of equipment for mining, earth-moving, and road maintenance operations. This segment, too, has suffered from recent slow growth in the mining and construction markets. Again, Dresser downsized, reduced its break-even level, and improved and broadened its product lines and quality of service.

The general industry segment supplies U.S. and foreign industries with a broad range of specialty products. The industries served by this segment, however, have also experienced soft markets; consequently they provide significantly less business than they did in the past. Therefore, Dresser's strategy is to concentrate its resources in those product and service areas where it has a distinct competitive edge in technology, expertise, management skills, and market knowledge.

Since so much of what Dresser does is energy related, the company will have to use all its expertise to maintain and improve its share of the stable, mature, and slow-growing energy market. It will concentrate on making its own operations as efficient as possible and on offering new and innovative products and services that will help make its customers' businesses more efficient as well.

To accomplish this, Dresser needs sales reps who are thoroughly familiar with the company's complicated products and services, who understand the needs and concerns of their customers' operations, and who can come up with cost-effective, Dresser solutions to high-tech problems. Training such reps is an intensive operation undertaken at the division level. This means that there may be as many as 25 different kinds of training programs, depending on the division and the market involved. Generally, a training period lasts from six months to a year, with heavy emphasis on developing product knowledge and selling skills. Most of the training takes place on the job in conjunction with an experienced rep.

No matter what division or business segment of Dresser a rep works for, he or she is expected to solve problems for customers. For instance, reps may have to recommend a piece of heavy equipment that will answer a customer's needs economically and efficiently. Thus, Dresser reps need technical knowledge. A background in energy is necessary, and a degree in petroleum, electrical, or mechanical engineering is required. Very few new hires are recent graduates; most new reps have a few years of work experience under their belts before they start at Dresser. Sales experience is not necessary, but it is a big plus.

Dresser reps spend most of their time on the road, and their territories are usually quite large. They may expect to spend up to 50% of their time on overnights. They work alone and are expected to set their own schedules. They sell equipment and expertise to major industries—big construction companies, oil refineries, pipeline and mine operators, original equipment manufacturers, and the like. The reps are technical experts in their fields, but they can count on good technical backup from their division, if necessary. Some reps are equipped with personal computers in their cars to track orders, and all receive good advertising and promotion materials, and clerical and administrative assistance.

Beginning reps can earn from $30,000 to $45,000, depending on experience and education. Senior sales reps' salaries run much the same ($33,000 to $49,000) but incentive payments make a difference. At the lower end, incentives (generally based on group goals) may equal 20% to 30% of the base salary; at the upper levels, the incentives may amount to much more—50% of total salary and up. Each of Dresser's divisions has its own compensation plan. Other benefits include: full medical and dental insurance, group life insurance, disability and retirement plans, a 401K savings plan, a stock purchase plan, a company car, paid moving expenses, and full tuition assistance.

The atmosphere at Dresser is corporate, professional, and technically oriented. Sales reps generally stay in the field where they can exercise their technical and problem-solving skills, an excellent position for committed engineers. While often formal in manner, Dresser does reward its skilled sales staff, offering them a more open and relaxed atmosphere on the job site.

NORTON COMPANY

VITAL STATISTICS

Entry Level Salary for Sales: **$25,000**
Senior Level Salary for Sales: **$50,000++**

Benefits

medical/dental: **Yes**
life insurance: **Yes**
disability: **Yes**
travel allowance: **Yes**
company car: **Yes**
profit sharing plan: **No**
stock purchase plan: **Yes**

child care: **No**
retirement plan: **Yes**
savings investment plan: **Yes**
tuition assistance: **Yes**
relocation assistance: **Yes**
memberships: **Pays part of health
maintenance
Smokenders
Weight Watchers
YMCA**

Corporate Culture Index   (1 = lowest, 10 = highest)

training: **10**
support: **9**
benefits: **9**

security: **9**
mobility: **9**
intangibles: **10**

Address: Norton Company World Headquarters, 120 Front Street, Worcester, MA 01608-1446
Contact: Personnel; telephone 508/795-5732

The world's leading manufacturer of industrial abrasives, Norton ranks first in the U.S. building materials industry and 272nd on the Fortune 500 list of top industrial corporations. Profits for 1987 were $66 million from sales of $1.26 billion.

For over a century Norton's business has been abrasives: grinding wheels, and sandpaper—rough stuff. In 1858 master potter Franklin Norton started the business in a Worcester, Massachusetts, plant, which rapidly grew from pottery to petroleum. Nowadays, bonded abrasives, coated abrasives, superabrasives, construction products, advanced ceramics, performance plastics, and various chemical products and processes form the bulk of Norton's line-up.

Norton reps manage their own territories almost as if they were small independent contractors, behaving much like business consultants, problem-solvers, and trouble-shooters to a wide range of industrial customers, from "Joe's welding shop" to Chrysler Corporation or Sikorsky Aircraft.

"Most people entering sales for the first time are concerned about having sales experience," says Donald Ricci, District Sales Manager for the northern New England area. "But Norton has the best technical and sales training of any manufacturer in the business." According to Ricci, who started out with a BS degree from Worcester State College, "Most of our sales people move up from their first assignments within four to five years." Ricci himself went from sales rep to product manager, and account manager to assistant district sales manager, in rapid succession before assuming his current job.

Norton recruits heavily from Midwestern and Southern colleges (Sunbelt grads tend to tolerate relocation better), looking for candidates with an ability and willingness to relocate (this is a high priority) and a certain degree of comfort in a blue-collar environment.

Except for the requisite college degree, neither technical knowledge nor prior sales experience is required. Training combines classroom and book work with on-the-job training and visits to product distributors, as well as Territory Management and Professional Selling Skills (PSS), lasting a total of 30 weeks (20 in class, ten in on-the-job training) conducted at the Worcester headquarters.

Promotion is from within, and runs up the ladder from sales rep to product engineer to product manager, on up to various marketing and management positions, for which sales reps are looked upon favorably. Overnight stays are rarely the rule, since reps tend to live within a 50-mile radius of their territories' borders. Norton reps work alone, on expense account, and according to strict ethical guidelines (a very strong Norton selling point, and a critical element in Norton corporate policy).

Access to top management is just a phone call away: to a product engineer, who often then pays a visit to the client. At 8%, rep turnover is fairly low and largely dependent on how well a rep handles the heavy technical aspect, the strict ethical code, and the unusual degree of independence reps have to follow their entrepreneurial bent.

Salary plus commissions and other incentives total about $25,000 for a trainee, running up to $50,000 or more for a senior sales executive with a bonus but no commission. Benefits include: medical and dental insurance, disability insurance, tuition assistance (100% up to $2500/yr) a company car, a stock purchase plan, paid relocation expenses, and membership in such organizations as Weight Watchers, Smokenders, and the local YMCA.

Norton literature is literally packed with real-life short stories of enthusiastic young graduates armed with little more than a strong BA or BS and an honest urge to get ahead, who were able to move into management and leadership ranks. Clearly, Norton offers a wide world of products, challenges, techniques, and services well suited to such a career.

INSURANCE

How many times have you listened to someone begin a joke with, "Didya hear the one about the insurance salesman . . . ?"

Insurance agents are as firmly entrenched in our folklore as cowboys and farmers' daughters. Because, when the joking is said and done, insurance is something that nearly everybody needs. People want to provide for their loved ones and take care that life's inevitable misfortunes don't leave them broke. So they've been taking out insurance ever since the sea captains who mapped out the New World came up with the idea centuries ago. And along the way, insurance companies have become some of the most powerful financial institutions in the country. In 1987, for example, the assets of U.S. life insurance companies came to more than $937 billion, up 13.5% from the previous year.

There are two kinds of life insurance companies: stock companies, owned by shareholders, and mutual companies, owned by the policyholders. Only about 5% fall into the second category. Half of the nation's life insurance policies are "ordinary" policies of $1000 or more with premiums paid on some sort of time-fixed basis—annual, quarterly, or at other intervals. The other half consists of group insurance (usually taken out by employers for employees) and industrial life insurance issued in small amounts.

With inflation abated and more disposable income available, more and more people are buying new life insurance policies. The face value of all policies nationwide is more than $6 trillion! Two-thirds of the U.S.

population has some sort of life insurance coverage. Nearly 46 million people also have private pension plans provided by insurance companies.

There are 3500 companies in the property and casualty insurance business, earning roughly $20 billion last year. These companies write the policies that protect businesses against losses that result from their liability for things like pollution, defective products, and property damage. After some losses in the mid 1980s, property and casualty insurers seem to be bouncing back.

The biggest problem facing the industry as a whole is the AIDS crisis. Industry analysts estimate that by the mid 1990s, AIDS-related deaths will account for more than 10% of the claims filed against life insurance companies. This has caused some insurance stock to drop and many companies to think hard about the future. As one CEO put it, "We won't be around to keep our promises . . . if we can't accurately assess our risks from AIDS." In response to this problem, insurance companies are lobbying for mandatory AIDS testing of prospective policyholders.

Life insurance companies derive their income from the premiums paid by policyholders and from the returns on their investments, income that came to nearly $300 billion in 1986, up 10% from the previous year. Most insurance companies are in good financial health, and most states have guaranty funds that protect policyholders in the event that their insurer goes belly up.

By all accounts, however, the insurance industry is poised for steady growth in the 1990s. It's an industry with a solid reputation for salesmanship and a good launching pad for a people-oriented career.

TRADE ASSOCIATIONS

American Council of Life Insurers 202/862-4000
Insurance Services Office 212/487-5000
National Insurance Association 312/842-5125
Professional Insurance Agents 703/836-9340

PERIODICALS

Insurance Advocate
Insurance Journal
Insurance Week

AETNA LIFE & CASUALTY

VITAL STATISTICS

Entry Level Salary for Sales: **$25,000–$30,000**
Senior Level Salary for Sales: **$100,000**

Benefits (Not for independent agents)

Corporate Culture Index   (1 = lowest, 10 = highest)

training:	**10**	security:	**3**
support:	**9**	mobility:	**3**
benefits:	**1**	intangibles:	**9**

Address: 151 Farmington Avenue, Hartford, CT 06156
Contact: Human Resources; telephone 203/273-0123

Aetna Life & Casualty is a leading worldwide provider of insurance and financial services. In 1987 it posted revenue of over $22 billion, up 8% from 1986. Profits, at $921 million, were down 11% from 1986.

Aetna Life & Casualty has six main operating units: five divisions (Employee Benefits, Personal Financial Security, Commercial Insurance, Financial, and International Insurance) and the American Re-Insurance Company. In 1987 the company enjoyed record operating earnings of $867 million, up 21% from 1986. The big factor in this improvement was the performance of Aetna's three casualty-property operations—the Commercial Insurance Division, the Auto-Homeowners segment of the Personal Financial Security Division, and the American Re-Insurance Company. The combined operating earnings of these three businesses in 1987 were $592 million, 70% above 1986's figure and 68% of Aetna's total 1987 operating earnings.

The Employee Benefits Division markets a full range of group insurance (life, health) and group pension plans and services. Customers include corporations, government agencies, associations, and collectively negotiated welfare trusts. Earnings in this unit dropped in 1987 and 1986 primarily because of large, unexpected increases in group health insurance claim costs. Also, the division sustained some losses from its development of alternative health-care operations. Aetna is seeking to develop, finance, manage, and market new types of health benefit plans, particularly ones including alternative health delivery systems (for example, health maintenance organizations), as a way of containing ever-rising health costs.

The Personal Financial Security Division markets personal insurance protection to individuals, small businesses, and other employer-sponsored groups. Types of coverages include automobile and homeowners' insurance, retirement and annuity funds, and life and health insurance. The auto and homeowners' insurance segment contributed the largest operating earnings of the group.

The Commercial Insurance Division underwrites most types of casualty-property insurance and bonds for large and small businesses. The American Re-Insurance Company underwrites reinsurance on commercial property and liability risks, in both the domestic and international markets. The Commercial Division had an especially good year in 1987 and American Re-Insurance has enjoyed a favorable market since 1984. The International Insurance Division manages operations in countries in Asia, Latin America, and Europe. The Financial Division manages the company's investment portfolios supporting its insurance, pension, and financial services operations.

Aetna agents (reps) are generally, but not necessarily, college graduates. The company looks for candidates who are open-minded problem-solvers for their customers and have a real drive for self-improvement. Agents have to know their inventory of policies (called "products" in the trade) so that they can recommend the most appropriate ones for each particular customer. An agent may be dealing with an individual, in the client's office or home, making sales in the evening or at some other time convenient for the client. Such a call may involve personal life insurance, health insurance, auto or home insurance, or any combination. The sale has to be right for the client *at the time*. As times and needs change, the agent must know what changes to recommend in the client's insurance coverage to cope with the new situation.

Agents also sell group insurance to businesses where they must deal with the concerns of managers to keep costs down while offering the best possible mix of coverages. Agents must be good communicators because they have to explain the provisions of the various policies they write and also help business managers understand how different options affect their costs and the benefits they can offer.

Training for Aetna agents is quite intensive initially, and it continues through the agent's career with periodic seminars, workshops, and the like. The emphasis both in initial and in follow-up training is on product knowledge and on selling skills. Many of these courses are offered at the Aetna Institute for Corporate Education in Hartford, Connecticut. In addition, the Personal Financial Security Division, in 1987, instituted a new nationwide support system that extends to its agents many training and planning capabilities that in the past had only been available to large corporations. What's more, agents from across the country were involved in the planning of the program and in presenting it for approval to the home office. Not only does Aetna support its agents, it also listens to their input on what that support should contain.

Although Aetna agents begin with a salary in the $25,000 to $30,000 range, after a certain time they move on to a straight commission basis. There are no company benefits for agents, who work alone and manage their relatively small territories as if they were in business for themselves. There is no cap on what they can earn through commissions, and reps who stay with the job can be earning $100,000 in ten years. The turnover rate for agents, though, is very high, over 50% in the first year, so the job is not for everyone. Aetna offers a pre-appointment orientation (internship) that lasts for two months, with the aim of introducing prospective agents to the job via videos, lectures, role-playing exercises, and the like. There is no pay during this session; it is simply a way both sides can check each other out with no commitments by either party.

The climate at Aetna is informal and friendly. The company offers good support, good training, and good income potential, but with no guaranteed salary and no corporate benefits, agents have to be good just to make a go of it. For those who thrive on this sort of thing, the rewards of considerable personal freedom and high potential income more than compensate for the challenges.

THE EQUITABLE

VITAL STATISTICS

Entry Level Salary for Sales: **$30,000+**
Senior Level Salary for Sales: **$50,000–$100,000+ (straight commission after fourth year)**

Benefits (Offered even after fourth year)

medical/dental: **Yes**	child care: **No**
life insurance: **Yes**	retirement plan: **Yes**
disability: **Yes**	savings investment plan: **Yes**
travel allowance: **No**	tuition assistance: **Yes**
company car: **No**	relocation assistance: **No**
profit sharing plan: **Yes**	memberships: **No**
stock purchase plan: **Yes**	

Corporate Culture Index   (1 = lowest, 10 = highest)

training:	**10**	security:	**2**
support:	**9**	mobility:	**4**
benefits:	**7**	intangibles:	**9**

Address: 787 Seventh Avenue, New York, NY 10019
Contact: Human Resources; telephone 212/554-1234

The Equitable Life Assurance Society (and affiliates) is the third largest life insurance company in America. In 1987, new individual premium income soared to a record $3.1 billion, new individual life insurance sales amounted to $43 billion, and the total amount of life insurance currently in force exceeded $213 billion.

In 1987, Equitable managed to flourish during a period of widespread financial turbulence, a remarkable performance widely credited to outstanding salesmanship on the part of Equitable's 11,000-strong agency field force. Faced with the first major downturn in stock and bond markets since the advent of investment-sensitive life insurance products, Equitable's policyholders refused to panic, in marked contrast to some pretty panicky selling by investors in other insurance companies.

The business of insurance is assurance (in England, they're called "life assurance societies") and during a period of financial turmoil, the underlying strength of "the enterprise" is revealed. "The Equitable Enterprise" includes the Wall Street brokerage firm of Donaldson, Lufkin & Jenrette, the investment manager Alliance Capital Management Corporation, and Equicor, a health-care subsidiary.

Despite Equitable's diversification into new areas, traditional life insurance is still the most profitable sector in the whole group. The Individual Financial Management Group, which makes up the bulk of the company's life and health insurance business, has consistently profited from steady growth in life insurance sales by field agents.

Everyone, the saying goes, needs insurance—it's just a question of how much and which type. This company is following a policy of promoting "basic insurance products," forgoing some of the frills currently flooding the burgeoning financial services marketplace.

As is the case with most insurance companies, training at Equitable is ongoing and never-ending: a permanent fact of life. It is particularly intensive during the first four years, when a new agent survives on "salary support," until commissions (one hopes) begin to roll in.

The average salary for a sales trainee is $30,000, while a senior sales executive may earn $50,000 or $100,000 or more. Since compensation for senior sales execs is straight commission, the sky is truly the limit.

The Equitable likes self-motivated, self-educated, and presentable candidates. Sales experience is also helpful, and a college degree is required. The average age for new recruits is the late twenties to early thirties. Although some agents are recruited right out of college, most have tried something else before. The notoriously high industrywide turnover rate of 90% (within the first four years), due largely to the high level of independence and self-motivation required to become an effective agent, is being met on The Equitable front by an increased stress on "needs selling"— trying to understand what a particular client or professional group needs by way of coverage. Preliminary training focuses on certification to sell securities by the National Association of Securities Dealers, and on becoming licensed by the individual state to sell insurance.

Training takes place at 100 agency offices around the country, combining classroom work in selling skills and product knowledge with self-study programs, computer-assisted and video instruction, and on-the-job training closely supervised by a trainer and district manager.

Territories here are highly localized, demanding little or no overnight travel. Reps work alone, without an expense account, with access to top management provided through the district sales manager.

A rep's job is to explain the provisions of an insurance policy—to outline the features and benefits. To do this effectively, agents are routinely supplied with the latest advertising and promotional materials, often at regular sales meetings. In accordance with regular industry practice, agents are rarely promoted to senior management—not because they don't deserve to be, but because they wouldn't want to go.

One area in which Equitable diverges from industry custom is in the benefits department, where benefits continue after the four-year apprenticeship period has ended. The package includes full medical and dental insurance, tuition assistance, group life and disability insurance, a retirement/pension and savings plan, and a profit sharing plan.

The corporate atmosphere is "aggressive and dynamic": "very tense" was one agent's terse comment. But if selling insurance appeals to you, both for the lucrative commissions and unparalleled independence, The Equitable is one of a handful of firms where the company and the product form a challenging combination.

"Like many good agents," says Marshall Wolper, an Equitable agent in Miami and New York, "I enjoy exploring the unknown. Nobody hands an agent success, or gives him a weekly paycheck. We have to build a practice, much like a doctor or dentist. However, that's where the thrill comes in, especially for creative self-starters."

If exploring the unknown is for you, Equitable can supply plenty of uncharted territory.

JOHN HANCOCK MUTUAL LIFE INSURANCE COMPANY

VITAL STATISTICS

Entry Level Salary for Sales: **$26,000**
Senior Level Salary for Sales: **$33,000**

Benefits (For approximately 5000 agents out of a total of 7500)

medical/dental: **Yes**	child care: **No**
life insurance: **Yes**	retirement plan: **Yes**
disability: **Yes, long and short term accident**	savings investment plan: **N/A**
	tuition assistance: **Yes**
travel allowance: **N/A**	relocation assistance: **No**
company car: **No**	memberships: **On-site fitness**
profit sharing plan: **Yes**	**center for**
stock purchase plan: **No**	**headquarters staff only**

Corporate Culture Index   (1 = lowest, 10 = highest)

training:	**9**	security:	**7**
support:	**9**	mobility:	**6**
benefits:	**9**	intangibles:	**9**

Address: John Hancock Place, 200 Clarendon, Boston, MA 02117
Contact: Human Resources; telephone 618/572-4500

John Hancock Financial Services is a leading, worldwide provider of products and services relating to the financial and physical well-being of individuals and organizations. In 1987 its total assets stood at $28.2 billion, up 1.4% from 1986.

John Hancock is an old-line mutual (not a stock) insurance company that offers a broad range of insurance and financial products and services to consumers and businesses in three main marketing sectors: the retail sector, the corporate sector, and the investment and pension sector.

The retail sector is made up of the Consumer Insurance Products Group and the Consumer Financial Services Group. Consumer insurance includes individual life insurance, disability income coverage, annuities, a long-term care policy for the elderly, and property and casualty insurance.

Consumer financial services include banking services, mutual funds, and mortgages. In marketing these products and services, John Hancock is customer-driven. As the company points out, "No one needs a life insurance policy, an annuity, or a mutual fund. But people do need family income, emergency funds, or income for retirement." Meeting these needs realistically is John Hancock's business.

Employee Benefits Services, the corporate sector, offers a complete range of group life and health programs that can be customized to fit the needs of large and small employers and their employees. The company recognizes that the greatest threat to employee benefits is runaway costs, and its stated goal in this sector is to provide employers with the cost containment that they need in the face of rising health-care costs while providing employees with the quality health care that they need. The Investment and Pension sector provides a wide array of institutional finance, investment management, and pension products and services designed to help businesses and organizations meet their financial needs for capital management, mortgages, expansion, and pension obligations.

In 1987 the company underwent a major restructuring of its internal organization. At that time, the three marketing sectors were clearly defined, and responsibility for those areas was given to the three sector presidents. In addition, personnel and management costs were reduced, and "ServiceLine," a program initiated in 1986 that put Hancock management in direct contact with customers who call the home office, was vigorously pursued. The principal aim in the restructuring was to make Hancock's products and services and all its personnel from top management down responsive to its customers' needs. "Real life, real answers" is the theme of Hancock's advertising—and of its operations, too.

Hancock is committed to "relationship selling." As someone from Hancock's Hall of Fame put it, "It is not the agent who knows the most about insurance who sells to the most people. It is the agent who knows the most about people who sells the most insurance." Whether the sale takes place in someone's living room at 9 P.M. or in a corporate boardroom at 11 A.M., the process takes a lot of face-to-face selling and personal commitment. Policies have to be explained, plans modified, and situations analyzed to present the right choices to the client. In addition, agents' incomes depend largely—and in the case of independent agents, solely—on commissions, which in turn depend largely on renewals; agents have to sell their clients and then continue to keep them sold. Agents must be aware, too, of changes in their clients' situations that require rethinking of their insurance or financial needs. A Hancock agent, particularly in the consumer sector, becomes personally involved with his or her customers in a way that a rep selling cars or corn flakes, for instance, does not.

Insurance agents must have persistence, hustle, and the ability to withstand rejection at a peculiarly personal level. As a hedge against this last problem, Hancock stresses forcefulness, communication, and smoothness (the ability to close a sale) when selecting new agents.

Hancock generally looks for agents who have a college degree, but this is not absolutely essential. Sales experience, however, is required. Training for new agents lasts about four months and it takes place both at the Boston headquarters and in the field. The content is heavy on product knowledge (different policies, how they can be customized to fit a specific situation, and so on) and also on the selling skills required for different clients (individuals, small businesses, or corporations). Training is ongoing to acquaint reps with new policies or new coverages. Also, agents who move up the corporate ladder undergo several management training programs.

Hancock deploys a sales force of about 5000 agents, plus another 2000 independents. The independents are essentially in business for themselves and do not receive a salary or benefits from the company. Agents who are company employees receive a salary plus commission, totaling about $26,000 for trainees and about $33,000 for senior salespeople. The salaried agents do enjoy the protection of a regular income and company benefits, but they also may hit income ceilings that do not apply to the independents on straight commission. Superstars can earn into six figures, but most agents will make considerably less than that. For salaried agents, the company benefits include: medical, dental, and life insurance; disability and retirement/pension plans; a 401K plan; and tuition assistance for job-related courses. The company offers support in the field with good media advertising and promotion, clerical/administrative help, and new products for changing times.

John Hancock is an old and conservative company with a dress code and corporate atmosphere. But with stiff competition on all sides, the pace has quickened, and new—and successful—ideas are welcome and hard work rewarded.

NEW YORK LIFE INSURANCE COMPANY

VITAL STATISTICS

Entry Level Salary for Sales: **$34,000–$36,000**
Senior Level Salary for Sales: **$100,000+**

Benefits (For first three years only)

medical/dental: **Yes**	child care: **No**
life insurance: **Yes**	retirement plan: **No**
disability: **Yes**	savings investment plan: **No**
travel allowance: **N/A**	tuition assistance: **Yes, after first year**
company car: **No**	
profit sharing plan: **No**	relocation assistance: **No**
stock purchase plan: **No**	memberships: **No**

Corporate Culture Index (1 = lowest, 10 = highest)

training:	**10**	security:	**5**
support:	**9**	mobility:	**2**
benefits:	**1**	intangibles:	**9**

Address: 51 Madison Avenue, New York, NY 10010
Contact: Agency Department; telephone 212/576-7000 ext. 6841

In 1986 New York Life was the world's eleventh largest insurance company. Sales totaled $5.4 billion in 1987. Total insurance coverage provided came to $250 billion in 1987, on assets of $40 billion.

The poet Jonathan Swift once said that "vision is the art of seeing things invisible." This is the challenge of New York Life's 11,000 sales agents—to turn an intangible image of future financial security into a lucrative present-day reality.

The "product" is invisible: life, health, and disability insurance, and mutual funds—no casualty coverage. To meet what the company believes is the major crisis facing the insurance industry today, New York Life is underwriting an extensive and expensive AIDS information and prevention campaign for the New York City area, where the disease has hit hardest.

Because of October's stock market crisis, 1987 was not a good year for insurance brokers. But New York Life has rebounded with remarkable resiliency, coming off the stock panic with a more valuable portfolio owing to a sharp jump in bond values. In addition, the company launched its first global mutual fund, purchased a major interest in a third-party insurance administrator, acquired a controlling interest in the largest privately held health-care company in the country, and opened a new administrative subsidiary. Not a bad showing for troubled times.

The latest increase in sales agents to more than 11,000 is part of a comprehensive strategy to boost the sales force to 12,000 by 1990. New York Life is recruiting sales agents with graduate degrees in finance, but a college degree is sufficient if the candidate displays the ability to close a sale, social skills, an articulate sales presence, and skill with numbers. Prior sales experience and/or technical knowledge are helpful, but not essential.

Training New York Life agents is an intensive three-year program, combining on-the-job training with classroom instruction in sales skills and specialized product knowledge. Trainees learn something about each different account, but may specialize during the long training period. The program is conducted at any of the 200 branch offices around the country, and has an employee/trainer ratio as low as 1:1. The branch manager or trainer makes weekly evaluations during the three-year trial period, with monthly evaluations after that.

At New York Life, training goes on "forever." Reps report regularly to their assigned trainers and branch managers even after the three-year program is over. The branch managers' job is to keep agents in the field informed and motivated about new products and policies, and to provide them with access to top management, which meets regularly with an Agents Advisory Council to discuss product development and marketing.

After a trainee's grace period comes to an end, the subsidized salary of $34,000 to $36,000 is simply cut off, and the new agent is on his or her own. There are no more benefits, salary, perks—compensation becomes straight commission.

But becoming an independent agent and New York Life rep can hardly be described as a prescription for penury. Senior agent incomes can run from $100,000 up to *$1 million*. In this line of work, the sky is the limit, and the only restrictions are how effectively an agent can sell to individual buyers, to companies interested in purchasing group policies, to physicians, senior executives, retail store owners—anyone the agent can establish a good business relationship with. In this line of work, sales can take place practically anywhere: on the golf course, or in the living room or the board room.

This is a high-risk, high-turnover job (a 25%–30% drop-out rate within the first year is not uncommon), but the rewards can be staggering. The "corporate culture" is defined by the individual agent—the kind of client he or she attracts, the territory, and the product. However, the company does like to describe both its clients and agents as basically "upper-middle-class."

New York Life is tops in its industry in training and sales support, but not job security, benefits, corporate mobility, or other typical support systems. Senior sales reps pride themselves on being corporate entities unto themselves who just happen to belong to a very powerful "family" ready and willing to lend a hand when needed. Reps rarely move on to top management—at a million a year, they hardly have to. During training, benefits are quite comprehensive: full medical, dental, tuition assistance (after one year only), group life insurance, and disability insurance.

Life at New York Life can be sweet, if financial independence, personal motivation, and individual risks and rewards are what you are searching for. If not, independent contracting can be risky, a risk judged by successful Lifers as more than commensurate with the rewards.

NORTHWESTERN MUTUAL LIFE INSURANCE COMPANY

VITAL STATISTICS

Entry Level Salary for Sales: *Usually straight commission, in the $20,000– $45,000 range*

Senior Level Salary for Sales: *Usually straight commission, in the $90,000– $1,000,000 range*

Benefits (No benefits)

Corporate Culture Index (1 = lowest, 10 = highest)

---

training:	**10**	security:	**1**
support:	**9**	mobility:	**4**
benefits:	**1**	intangibles:	**9**

Address: 720 East Wisconsin Avenue, Milwaukee, WI 53202
Contact: Human Resources; telephone 414/271-1444

Northwestern Mutual Life is the nation's tenth largest insurance company with $22 billion in assets, $157.1 billion of insurance in force, and $3.6 billion in premium and annuity income in 1987, up 21% from 1986.

This 130-year-old, Milwaukee-based mutual insurance company ranks 73rd in assets of all business enterprises in the U.S. Among the ten largest life insurance companies, Northwestern is the only one specializing in individual coverage. In 1988, for the sixth time in as many years, Northwestern was ranked by *Fortune* magazine as "the most admired" of the nation's top ten insurance companies.

Known in Milwaukee as the place where all employees get a free lunch, "The Quiet Company," as Northwestern proudly calls itself, is known to its more than 6000 independent agents around the country by another name: "The Supportive Company."

"This company has a deep respect for our agency force," says Dennis Tamscin, vice president of sales and agency operations. "If you want to harness the energy of an army of independent agents, you have to give them constant sales support."

This support extends to supplying the latest in insurance products, like flexible coverage and adjustable premiums, extra-ordinary life, extra-ordinary term, whole life, and variable life—all backed by a state-of-the-art computer network and ongoing, intensive sales training.

"Education is a journey, not a destination," proclaims one company motto, a slogan Northwestern agents take seriously. Every July, thousands of agents converge on the Milwaukee headquarters to attend the annual four-day sales conference. "We learn to concentrate on doing a professional job so that people will continue to buy our products over the long term," comments Chicago agent Dennis Giertz, member of a study group of 25 agents who sell some $10 million worth of insurance per year, per person—a performance in no way minimizing the fact that fully one-fourth of their Northwestern colleagues qualify as members of the Million Dollar Round Table.

It takes a truly independent, highly motivated person to thrive on selling insurance, particularly individual coverage, Northwestern's specialty. There are no salary, bonus, incentives, or other perks—just commissions, straight commissions.

The motivation needed to last on this course begins at the beginning: in training. Northwestern's program combines classroom courses on life underwriting, client building, advanced personal planning, business planning, and advanced underwriting, with five years of on-the-job training apprenticed to an experienced agent.

When the apprenticeship comes to an end, training has only just begun. Even senior agents attend seminars and clinics ranging from estate planning to personal dynamics, from role-playing to interactive technology. This training is what binds the "army" of independents together and forms the basis of support from the parent company.

A college degree is not a requirement, but fewer than 6% of Northwestern agents start out without the benefit of at least some college background—preferably in accounting, economics, finance, business, liberal arts, marketing, or management.

Northwestern aggressively recruits "confident types who seek what they want out of life"—in other words, the emotionally sturdy sort who are not intimidated by frequent rejection, the type who make not just good insurance salespeople, but good salespeople in general.

Reps hardly ever move up to corporate headquarters, which is again standard industry practice, since the financial rewards for successful field work far outstrip all but top-level staff salaries. Reps spend a great deal of time on the road covering territories too small to require many nights out.

"Northwestern is a solid company with a warm, family feel to it," testifies one satisfied NW agent, who undoubtedly has acquired more than a few satisfied customers. NW ranked first in the industry in a recent A. M. Best survey of life policies sold over the last twenty years. There's no doubt that NW is a good bet for a career as an insurance rep, especially when there's so much competition out there.

THE PRUDENTIAL

VITAL STATISTICS

Entry Level Salary for Sales: *$25,000–$27,000*
Senior Level Salary for Sales: *$120,000+ (straight commission after third year)*

Benefits (Offered even after third year)

medical/dental: **Yes**	child care: **No**
life insurance: **Yes**	retirement plan: **Yes**
disability: **Yes**	savings investment plan: **No**
travel allowance: **No**	tuition assistance: **Yes**
company car: **No**	relocation assistance: **No**
profit sharing plan: **Yes**	memberships: **No**
stock purchase plan: **No**	

Corporate Culture Index   (1 = lowest, 10 = highest)

training:	**10**	security:	**2**
support:	**9**	mobility:	**4**
benefits:	**8**	intangibles:	**10**

Address: Prudential Plaza, Newark, NJ 07101
Contact: Human Resources; telephone 201/802-8984

Prudential is the world's fifth largest corporation, and the largest American corporation on the Fortune list of the 50 largest insurance companies. Prudential's total consolidated assets and assets under management reached $187.6 billion in 1987, nearly two-and-a-half times the record $79.5 billion set just five years earlier.

Prudential's world-famous Rock of Gibraltar is as rock-solid as ever, even after the potentially devastating stock market crash of October 1987. Despite these severe market pressures, Prudential has continued to reach new and impressive heights. New business sales and premiums rose a respectable 5% to $12.8 billion, while net investment income reached $8.9 billion in 1987, virtually guaranteeing that "getting a piece of the Rock" will be a solid investment decision for decades to come.

Prudential is a mutual life insurance company (owned by its policy-holders) offering a broad line of insurance products: life, health, and disability insurance, annuities, Keogh plans, IRAs, mutual funds, mortgages, credit cards, group life, and just about everything under the sun when it comes to financial services.

"Serving Diverse Needs" is one of the company's slogans, and it is backed up by high-quality products and services, as well as the steady, no-nonsense success of its 24,000 field agents.

The Prudential sales network consists of two distinct tiers: 4000 agents working out of "ordinary" agencies serving the upscale market, and 20,000 agents operating out of "district" offices serving middle-income accounts. In all, some 120 insurance agencies nationwide sell Prudential products.

A rep's job, pure and simple, is to explain product provisions clearly, simply, and persuasively, whether he or she is trying to sell an IRA, a Keogh plan, or a no-load mutual fund. Sales are mainly to individual consumers, in board rooms, on golf courses, anywhere that an agent and a potential customer might meet. Candidates for sales positions must have a college degree. Three groups of people are encouraged to apply: new graduates, agents from competitors, and those who have had several years of experience selling something or other. The company actively encourages "career-change artists" interested in trying something new, challenging, and independent in spirit.

Reps rely on "support commissions" for the first three years, after which they are pretty much on their own, financially speaking. The average salary for a sales trainee runs from $25,000 to $27,000. A senior sales executive, operating on a straight commission basis, can earn an impressive average of $120,000 and up. In this business, million-dollar incomes are hardly unheard of, while healthy six-figure sums are certainly not uncommon.

As is the case with nearly all insurance organizations, training is an ongoing activity. To avoid the distressingly high drop-out rate plaguing most insurance companies, Prudential has instituted a policy of requesting reps to complete a "job sample" within the first six to eight weeks of training, to determine whether the candidate is truly cut out for this line of work. This "job sample" is, in essence, a temporary contract that gives new hires a chance to prove to themselves and to the company that this is the appropriate position for them. The training begins with classroom instruction and proceeds to field training with an individual trainer. Although no salary is paid during this training period, commissions commensurate with performance are awarded. Of the 50% of the candidates who make it past this first cut, Prudential retains nearly 85%. This low turnover rate is very unusual for the insurance industry.

No single agent can hope to be knowledgeable about all aspects of the insurance business, so the real training begins with each agent becoming a "general practitioner." At this point agents become involved in the process of selling insurance, learning how to set up appointments and how to prospect for new clients. In addition, every new rep needs to be licensed to sell health and life insurance, right off the bat, by the state. Reps are also required to pass the National Association of Insurance Dealers test for selling securities, which makes up a large part of today's insurance business. As reps specialize, after three years of intensive training, some get master's degrees in insurance from the American College in Pennsylvania, while others become certified financial planners.

Rep territories are very small, requiring few overnight stays. Most reps work alone, without expense accounts (remember, these are independent agents), reporting to a head agent, a trainer, or a general agent.

America's largest insurance company also provides its agents with one other advantage: benefits. Contrary to standard industry practice, it offers full medical and dental insurance, tuition assistance, group life and disability insurance, a retirement/pension plan and a 401K plan to all nominally independent agents, who are still the most critical component in "The Prudential family."

This is a business where it pays to be personable. First-name-basis relationships are the norm. The dress code is simply what is "appropriate" for a particular place, a particular time, or a particular professional class.

If the entrepreneurial spirit has you in its grasp, Prudential has "a piece of the Rock" suitable for just about everyone.

THE TRAVELERS
CORPORATION

VITAL STATISTICS

Entry Level Salary for Sales: **_Usually straight commission_**
Senior Level Salary for Sales: **_Usually straight commission, but may reach_**
_$100,000+_

Benefits (No benefits)

Corporate Culture Index (1 = lowest, 10 = highest)

training:	**9**	security:	**1**
support:	**9**	mobility:	**6**
benefits:	**1**	intangibles:	**8**

Address: One Tower Square, Hartford, CT 06183
Contact: Personnel; telephone 203/277-0111 ext. 2994

The Travelers is the nation's seventh largest insurance company, with assets exceeding $50 billion and $170 billion worth of life insurance in force. In 1987 earnings climbed 47%, to over $400 million, and revenues were up 9%, to $17.5 billion.

The Travelers is a broadly based, multiline insurance firm offering a wide range of products from today's far-flung financial services marketplace. You'll find everything you might need on The Travelers menu: property, casualty, life, accident, and health insurance; investment banking, pension and mutual funds, commercial mortgages, IRAs, Keogh plans—the works.

Still, The Travelers is and will always be an insurance company at heart, a leader in an industry that has lately suffered a series of shocks to its system: the 1987 stock market crash, the AIDS crisis, high inflation in the health-care industry, and declining energy and soft real estate markets.

To its credit, The Travelers has not just survived these debacles, it has prospered, having been unusually successful in adapting the latest financial services technology to delivering more varied products at lower cost, processing claims quickly, and offering a wide range of services beyond the traditional domains of an old-line insurance firm, such as the

Keystone Group of mutual funds, the commercial banking services of the Massachusetts Company, and the investment banking services of Wall Street's Dillon Reed.

In keeping with long-established industry practice, The Travelers sells its products through independent agents who receive no company benefits other than straight commissions. In recent years, this rule has been broken to some degree, as a small minority of agents have signed on to receive a subsidized "draw" before buying into an agency.

Reps spend two-thirds of their time setting up calls, and the rest on the road actually selling. Territories are never very large—a town or a small city, or part of a large one at most. Turnover is average for the industry: 50%–85%. That might sound high, but the former figure applies mainly to multiline policies, while the real drop-outs hit the wayside trying to sell life insurance alone.

A college degree is always a help for new hires, but not a necessity. Management also considers prior sales or business experience secondary for success in this field. More important is a self-confident attitude and a high tolerance for rejection.

Sales training lasts from three to nine months (long enough for a candidate to obtain a state license) and includes classroom work at the Hartford headquarters in product knowledge and selling skills, followed by plenty of closely supervised on-the-job training in the field.

Even after formal training concludes, training goes on forever. A multiyear apprenticeship requires close contact with head agents and senior sales reps, making calls, contacting prospective clients, polishing skills, closing deals. And this is only the beginning of a process potentially resulting in promotion to more senior territory. In all but rare cases, the career ladder ends either at branch manager or head agent, where compensation easily outclasses even the highest HQ staff salary scales.

Selling insurance is no piece of cake, but most experts agree that success or failure depends largely on a rep's personality. The Travelers' products are competitive, and if you feel you might thrive selling them face-to-face, the risks could be worth it, in return for the enormous financial rewards (symbolized by that all-powerful Million Dollar Round Table). Hazards are high, and the hours irregular (sales frequently take place in the evening), but the strong possibility of hitting the jackpot still beckons to the best and the brightest salespeople.

PAPER AND ALLIED PRODUCTS

Does money grow on trees? Analysts predict that profits in the $85 billion paper products industry will have grown by as much as 25% in 1988, to sales of nearly $5 billion. Lumber consumption keeps on growing, and Congress has used protectionist laws to stave off the Canadian competition. The wood and paper industry has seen boom-and-bust cycles before, though, and these good times won't necessarily last forever.

The industry employs some 625,000 people, with the primary products—pulp, paper, and paperboard—concentrated in the South. The pulp mills are by far the largest component of the industry, and paper accounts for a huge 85% of their output. Demand for paper keeps growing with the expansion of American business. In mid 1987, pulp inventories totaled nearly 250 tons, or enough to supply the entire United States for two weeks.

New technologies are a major factor in the pulp industry. The traditional chemical cooking process that has been the backbone of pulping is giving way to electrical grinding techniques that should increase worldwide pulp capacity by nearly 4 million tons by 1991. At the same time, new markets for American pulp products are emerging in developing countries like Japan, Mexico, and South Korea, which don't have the raw materials to suit the needs of their increasingly sophisticated economies. Analysts also project solid growth in paperboard products, as well as in corrugated paper and paper boxes.

The paper industry serves a stunning array of needs—newspapers and magazines, laser printers, toilet paper, shopping bags, direct mail, surgical gowns, diapers, photographs, books, and construction—all requiring vast amounts of paper of different qualities and specifications. As a result, sales reps can expect to deal with a wide variety of customers: suppliers of office products, construction firms, food wholesalers, publishing houses, medical suppliers, and manufacturers of baby products. These are just some of the customers whose businesses paper reps will get to know and understand.

The paper industry has come a very long way since Paul Bunyan and Babe, his Blue Ox. But it is all the result of our unending use of one of nature's most extraordinary creations—wood.

TRADE ASSOCIATIONS

American Forest Institute 202/797-4500
National Forest Products Association 202/797-5800
National Paper Trade Association 516/829-3070
Sales Association of the Paper Industry 212/340-0648

PERIODICALS

Forest Products Journal
Paper Trade Journal
Pulp and Paper
Pulp and Paper Week

ALCO STANDARD CORPORATION

VITAL STATISTICS

Entry Level Salary for Sales: **$24,000**
Senior Level Salary for Sales: **$50,000–$55,000**

Benefits

medical/dental: **Yes**
life insurance: **Yes**
disability: **Yes**
travel allowance: **No**
company car: **No**
profit sharing plan: **No**
stock purchase plan: **Yes**

child care: **No**
retirement plan: **Yes**
savings investment plan: **Yes**
tuition assistance: **Yes**
relocation assistance: **Yes, if as a result of promotion**
memberships: **No**

Corporate Culture Index   (1 = lowest, 10 = highest)

training: **7**
support: **7**
benefits: **8**

security: **8**
mobility: **6**
intangibles: **7**

Address: P.O. Box 834, Valley Forge, PA 19482-0834
Contact: Human Resources; telephone 215/296-8000 ext. 301

In 1987 Alco Standard Corporation had sales of $3.6 billion, up 15% from 1986. Alco's profits for this period were $69.3 million, an increase of 16% over 1986.

Alco Standard Corporation, a publicly held distribution and manufacturing company, undertook a major review of its operations in 1987. With one eye on the future and the other on past experiences of the company in various distribution and manufacturing ventures, Alco's management decided to concentrate on its three core businesses that offered good promise of stability and future growth: paper distribution, office products distribution, and the manufacturing of foodservice equipment and specialty food products.

A fourth group, the Triumph Group, comprises the most profitable of Alco's aerospace and metal companies, and future developments will decide whether or not this group becomes another major part of the corporation's business core. Alco also has additional businesses in specialty manufacturing and in service companies in the aerospace and steel converting industries. Alco plans to divest itself of its other operations if it becomes apparent that they do not fit its growth strategies.

For its main businesses, Alco has adopted a unique form of management, one it calls the "Corporate Partnership Concept." This is essentially a form of controlled decentralization, whereby each of the Alco operating companies is supported by the considerable resources of the corporation while maintaining a significant degree of independence. This type of organization has proved its worth over the years for the corporation, and it will remain the cornerstone of its operating philosophy for the future.

The largest of Alco's core businesses is its paper group, Paper Corporation of America, the largest distributor and converter of paper and paper-related products in the country. It (1) supplies quality paper and paper-related products for printing, publishing, and office use; (2) produces and distributes such products as envelopes, tablets, filing supplies, book cover materials, and foodservice disposables; (3) distributes packaging equipment and supplies, and maintenance and sanitary products for office and industry; and (4) operates the trademark "Paper Plus" stores that serve offices and small printers. Alco Office Products sells and leases photocopiers, typewriters, and facsimile and other automated office equipment, and provides copier supplies and maintenance. Alco Foodservice manufactures food handling and processing equipment, beverage dispensing equipment, and packaging equipment for food and dairy products.

Because of the decentralized nature of the corporation, the many products it makes, and the diverse markets it serves, one can speak of the sales rep position only in general terms. There is a slot for nearly every kind of selling at Alco, but the major part of its business comes from its paper group, so that is what will be emphasized here. Alco generally looks for new reps who have some experience in sales. A college degree is very helpful, but it is not essential for most openings. Training stresses on-the-job learning, with the rep accompanying the sales manager to call on accounts in the territory before taking over that territory. For the janitorial part of the paper group, the formal training is brief and concentrates on selling skills. The quality paper part of the operations requires more product knowledge training, and so there is more emphasis on the differing needs of the customers and how Alco products can answer those needs. In any case, reps are expected to pick up much of what they need to know on the job, selling wholesale to publishers and printers, to large retailers of office supplies, to institutions, and the like. The rep is customer-driven, looking for ways to introduce Alco products to the customer as a way of improving the customer's operations.

Alco reps generally work alone, managing their territories and accounts as they think best. They need to make their quotas, but they are on their own as to how to do so. In those divisions where the reps are on straight commission selling, the position is rather like being in business for oneself. There is no company car or travel expense, but the territories are often small and no overnights are required. The company generally supports its reps with administrative/clerical help where possible and product information materials as needed and as dictated by the product line. Again, support will vary depending on the division and class of customers serviced. Alco provides a career ladder for its reps and a consulting psychologist to help them set career goals for themselves. Many reps, however, find staying in the field offers them the most satisfaction.

Salaries are dependent equally on the product and on whether the rep is on straight commission or not. For new hires, there is always salary support for at least the first nine months or until the reps' sales generate sufficient commissions. The average income for new hires is about $24,000, and senior salespeople average an income of about $50,000 to $55,000. Commissions are generally not limited, though, so earnings can go as high as the rep can take them. Other benefits include: medical, dental, and life insurance; disability and retirement plans; a profit sharing plan; a 401K plan; and tuition assistance (up to a maximum of $1000). Incidentally, the company has a drug testing and employee assistance program, which emphasizes its commitment to the well-being of its employees.

Alco is an enormous corporation with diverse selling needs and strategies. One of its stated future goals is to improve productivity by increased employee training programs, emphasizing in all cases customer satisfaction and quality service—in all core businesses. The businesses themselves have strong growth potential for the future—always an encouraging sign.

BOISE CASCADE CORPORATION

VITAL STATISTICS

Entry Level Salary for Sales: *$25,000–$30,000*
Senior Level Salary for Sales: *$60,000–$80,000*

Benefits

medical/dental: **Yes**	child care: **No**
life insurance: **Yes**	retirement plan: **Yes**
disability: **Yes**	savings investment plan: **401K**
travel allowance: **Yes**	tuition assistance: **Yes**
car allowance: **Yes**	relocation assistance: **Yes**
profit sharing plan: **Yes**	memberships: **Yes, health clubs,**
stock purchase plan: **Yes**	**country clubs**

Corporate Culture Index   (1 = lowest, 10 = highest)

training:	**8**	security:	**9**
support:	**8**	mobility:	**9**
benefits:	**9**	intangibles:	**9**

Address: One Jefferson Square, Boise, ID 83728
Contact: Human Resources; telephone 208/384-6161

Boise Cascade Corporation ranks 113th on the Fortune 500 list. In 1987 it had sales of $3.8 billion, only 2% above 1986. Profits, however, at over $180 million, jumped an impressive 80% above 1986.

Boise Cascade Corporation is a major forest products manufacturer, distributor, and marketer, with operations principally in the United States and Canada. Its operations are basically divided into three business groups: paper and paper products, office products, and building products. The company also owns and manages large tracts of timberland to support these operations.

The Paper Group provides various kinds of paper stock for all business communication needs: newsprint, groundwood stock for catalogues and advertising supplements, high-quality paper for book publishers and businesses, and coated stock for magazines and ad pieces. It has also developed a family of "advanced technology papers" to be used in today's demanding electronic printing systems such as laser and ink-jet printers. The group produces specialty paperboard products, such as its "Genuine Pressboard" products used for report and computer printout covers, and maintains a corrugated container business that manufactures heavyweight packaging, specially coated containers, and point-of-purchase displays. The paper and paper products group is the corporation's chief moneymaker, bringing in more than half the revenue in 1987.

The Office Products Group distributes office products nationally to businesses in every industry. This group is noted for its rapid service, including delivery within 24 hours. It maintains a network of computerized systems that helps it provide responsive—and cost-effective—service to its customers. Building products are handled by the Timber and Wood Products Group and the Building Materials Distribution Division. Boise manufactures building commodity items, such as studs, particleboard, and the like. In addition, the distribution division uses state-of-the-art computer systems to track product price, availability, and freight information for more than 500 lumber mills in the U.S. and Canada. This information is directly accessible to Boise sales reps so they can give immediate, accurate responses to their customers.

Boise Cascade is well on its way to realizing its three-way goal of (1) increasing manufacturing efficiency and productivity across the board, (2) developing and maintaining a "distinctive competence" by adding value to its goods and services and thus gaining a competitive edge, and (3) focusing its growth in the high-potential segments of its business. As its net earnings increase of 80% in 1987 demonstrated, Boise is containing costs and upping efficiency. With its development of new products and its use of sophisticated delivery systems, the company is working to give each of its products and services a distinctive edge. As part of its plan to focus on high-potential areas of business, Boise sold off its Consumer Packaging division because it saw that plastic bottles were replacing composite cans as the preferred package for motor oil. The company plans to pursue these strategies as vigorously in the future.

Boise is a large, complex corporation. Other than the company's general strategies, there are few specific procedures or requirements that apply to its divisions. In training, Boise offers programs for sales managers and tech support people, and at least two training sessions for sales reps. Training in the Paper Group, which fields the largest sales force, is short and intense. It lasts about a week and involves classroom work on selling skills and product information and on-the-job training in sales presentations.

The primary job of the Boise sales rep is to help solve customer problems, to help the customer become more profitable. For instance, newspapers and magazines always need different kinds of papers with different kinds of properties. The rep's job is to understand the customer's needs *for a particular project* (type of paper required, amount, delivery date, price, and so on) and develop a Boise Cascade solution that works. Boise paper reps sell to publishers, business executives, shipping people, graphic artists, and production people, to name a few. The size of a rep's territory varies, too, but most of a rep's time is spent on the road with clients. Reps generally work alone, but at any time they can call on experts at the plant or at headquarters for help with complex customer problems.

Boise wants bright young people it can promote from within. The managers of some divisions require a college degree. In any case, some selling experience is very helpful. Technical knowledge is not a requirement; Boise will teach the rep what he or she needs to know. Boise does run some summer internships, and this is a good way to get to know the company and its products while still in school.

Forest products reps work on straight salary at Boise. Trainees average from $25,000 to $30,000, depending on education and prior experience. Salaries of senior sales reps range from $60,000 to $80,000. Reps get other support, too: good advertising and promotion materials for Boise products and services, clerical/administrative help where possible, and the constant development of new products and more efficient ways of delivering services. Other benefits include: medical and dental insurance plans, group life insurance, disability and retirement plans, a travel allowance, a 401K savings plan, a stock purchase plan, tuition assistance, paid moving expenses, and a car allowance.

Boise Cascade is very serious about giving its products and service a competitive edge with "distinctive competence." It is equally serious about working with its reps to make this happen.

GEORGIA-PACIFIC CORPORATION

VITAL STATISTICS

Entry Level Salary for Sales: **$20,000**
Senior Level Salary for Sales: **$40,000–$60,000**

Benefits

medical/dental: **Yes**	child care: **No**
life insurance: **Yes**	retirement plan: **Yes**
disability: **Yes**	savings investment plan: **Yes**
travel allowance: **Yes**	tuition assistance: **Yes**
company car: **Yes**	relocation assistance: **Yes**
profit sharing plan: **Yes**	memberships: **No**
stock purchase plan: **Yes**	

Corporate Culture Index   (1 = lowest, 10 = highest)

training:	**9**	security:	**9**
support:	**9**	mobility:	**9**
benefits:	**9**	intangibles:	**10**

Address: 133 Peachtree Street, N.E., Atlanta, GA 30303
Contact: Personnel for Distribution; telephone 404/521-5129

Georgia-Pacific ranks 44th on the Fortune 500 list. In 1987 it enjoyed net sales of $8.6 billion, up 17% from 1986. It manufactures and distributes building products, industrial wood products, pulp, paper, packaging, and related chemicals.

Founded in 1927, Georgia-Pacific is the leader in all areas and stages of manufacture and distribution of forest products to the building construction industry: lumber (the company owns 5.5 million acres of timberland), wood panels, plywood, gypsum wallboard, roofing, and industrial wood products.

Georgia-Pacific began as a lumber wholesaler, and, to this day, building products still account for two-thirds ($5.7 billion in 1987) of the company's sales. G-P's profits from building products have been steadily on the rise through the 1980s. Strangely enough, the national decline in housing construction has had almost no effect on G-P, where management had the foresight to secure a strong position as a ready and reliable supplier to home—and industrial—improvement markets, which posted $100 billion in sales in 1988.

Sales reps for G-P don't have to come in with any technical knowledge of the building industry or of sales, though a college degree is essential and a major in forestry, communications, marketing, or psychology a real plus. G-P also values people with good telephone skills. Most of all, a potential sales rep must be friendly and self-motivated—a go-getter.

Georgia-Pacific's 153-branch Distribution Division serves every metropolitan area in the United States. Sales trainee programs convene at conference centers in a number of major cities. To gain entry into the training program, prospective sales reps must pass a pre-employment test. If you pass the test, which emphasizes personal skills, G-P believes that you are almost certain to finish the training course with good marks. The training program lasts for six months, during which sales trainees learn about the company and study sales strategy and G-P's product lines. G-P also has customized training programs that emphasize phone sales and self-pacing, and it runs regular refresher courses for its sales reps. Videos and computers augment the program with training on how to "sell with style."

Some graduates of the program become G-P specialists who provide sales reps with easy access to top management for sharing information and ideas. This system is one of the key ingredients of G-P's success. As T. Marshall Hahn, Jr., the company chairman, recently put it, "We look for intelligence from every major market so we can better meet the needs of customers and find opportunities for value-added, higher-margin products."

G-P fields 2500 sales reps, each of whom covers an assigned area. Each sales rep reports to one of G-P's 153 branch managers, who also set the sales goals for sales reps. Reps sell to wholesalers as well as retailers, particularly lumber retailers. One of their responsibilities is teaching and training customers about G-P products. They benefit from the continuous support of G-P's research and advertising departments, as well as from G-P's especially good administrative and clerical teams. Reps have an expense account and are given a company car.

G-P is a salary-oriented company, with salaries beginning at $20,000 for trainees, and senior sales executives earning anywhere from $40,000 to $60,000 a year. There is a 25% commission on sales and a very full package of benefits, including medical and dental insurance, life insurance, pension and disability plans, tuition assistance, profit sharing, and stock purchase plans. G-P also picks up the moving expenses for its sales reps.

Beginning as a sales rep at G-P provides especially good opportunities for advancement. Starting out at G-P is the only way to make it to the top ranks of the company, since all management slots are filled from within. The current president of G-P started out as a sales rep, as have many of those in the company's top management slots. This is because starting as a sales rep for G-P is especially good training for higher positions, for several reasons. Sales reps at G-P benefit from exceptional training throughout their careers. Refresher courses keep each sales rep abreast of all new developments in all of G-P's divisions and product lines. The company maintains an informal, first-name, family-like atmosphere (though reps are expected to dress conservatively) and eagerly rewards initiative and skill. Some G-P reps eventually go off on their own to rewarding opportunities. One former G-Per, for example, is now the CEO of his own $800 million chemical corporation.

Thanks to prudent management and a number of solid product lines, all of G-P's enterprises look forward to steady expansion over the next decade. It is an especially promising place to begin a challenging career.

INTERNATIONAL PAPER COMPANY

VITAL STATISTICS

Entry Level Salary for Sales: **$35,000–$50,000**
Senior Level Salary for Sales: **$46,000–$72,000**

Benefits

medical/dental: **Yes**
life insurance: **Yes**
disability: **Yes**
travel allowance: **N/A**
company car: **Yes**
profit sharing plan: **N/A**
stock purchase plan: **N/A**

child care: **N/A**
retirement plan: **Yes**
savings investment plan: **Yes, including Employee Stock Ownership Plan (ESOP)**

tuition assistance: **N/A**
relocation assistance: **N/A**
memberships: **N/A**

Corporate Culture Index   (1 = lowest, 10 = highest)

training: **10**
support: **10**
benefits: **10**

security: **10**
mobility: **8**
intangibles: **9**

Address: Department P.M., International Place I, 6400 Poplar Avenue, Memphis, TN 38119
Contact: Manager, Staffing and Development; telephone 901/763-6000

International Paper Company ranks 52nd on the Fortune 500 list. In 1987 it had worldwide sales exceeding $7.7 billion, up 41% from 1986. It is the world's largest paper company.

Founded in 1898, International Paper Company is a leading manufacturer of pulp, paper, and packaging, and ranks among the top lumber and plywood producers. IP owns more than seven million acres of U.S. timberland, making it the country's largest landowner as well. It also has 24 paper mills around the world, 93 packaging plants, numerous lumber mills, plywood facilities, and other plants. Other operations include oil and gas drilling, and the manufacture of chemicals, formed fabrics, and laminated products. IP employs 45,500 people worldwide, including more than 600 sales/marketing professionals.

IP's basic business strategies apply both to its core forest products business (coated and uncoated paper, bleached packaging board, liquid containers, and so on) and to its diversified businesses (chemicals, minerals, and so on). The company stresses quality and the development of new products to make its customers more competitive. To implement these strategies, IP has committed itself to the philosophy that its employees are responsible for its past accomplishments and provide the foundation for its future growth.

This philosophy together with the company's size and diversity of operations creates a corporate climate that strongly encourages individual growth and career development among all employees. For those in sales, International Paper offers several diverse career paths. Sales professionals are individuals who make sales their career. Typically, they prefer not to move into sales management, but they can move from entry-level positions up through four or five levels of professional sales positions. Marketing professionals begin in sales, but broaden out to staff marketing positions. Such individuals may move on to more senior marketing or general management positions, or they may return to sales. Sales managers are those whose goal is to move into management. They may progress up the ladder in one sales division or transfer from one division to another. The most successful move on to senior marketing and general management positions. Additionally, IP provides for cross-functional moves, involving transfers from one function to another (for instance, sales to purchasing). Such transfers occur on a limited and very selective basis.

Progress up the ladder is facilitated by IP's policy of filling most positions from within. IP does this through its internal selection process called "job slating," a formal procedure that makes every effort to match qualified employees with open positions.

Naturally, IP very carefully selects among applicants for sales positions and then provides those chosen with a comprehensive—and continuing—set of training programs. IP looks for new hires who have demonstrated sales/marketing interest (a proven track record for experienced reps), leadership skills, strong academics (BA or BS degree, or a technical degree with a strong sales interest, and grades in the top 25% from a select school), excellent written and oral communication skills, and solid business experience for an entry-level rep or customer orientation for an experienced rep.

Sales training for new hires begins with the Sales Training Education Program (STEP), consisting of two modules scheduled several months apart.

Module I comprises a two-week company orientation program given at the Memphis headquarters. It includes training in sales and marketing skills, papermaking, quality control, and safety, and units on career development and IP's human resources policies. Tours of selected woodlands, primary mills, packaging operation facilities, a wood products plant, and a distribution center are also incorporated into this module.

The new rep is then assigned to an operating division for specific training for six to eight months in the division's product line and customer needs. Module II of STEP begins during this period and consists of a one-week program directed at developing the rep's personal selling skills. It also includes tours of selected packaging facilities and meetings with customers and company salespeople. During the next four to six months, the rep continues to work with other aspects of the division's selling organization and becomes better acquainted with customers' product problems and product development. The plan is to have the candidate up and running, fully trained to fill the responsibilities of an IP sales representative, in 18 months. In different divisions, training may last anywhere from 3 to 12 months.

Advanced training can take the form of one-day workshops, three-day programs, or more formal affairs such as the sales/marketing management programs given at Columbia University. Other ways in which International Paper helps its sales staff include administrative staff support (typing, filing, and so on) and a company car. IP companywide benefits offer several sources of protection, including: an employee stock ownership plan, medical/dental plans, life insurance plans, disability plans, and a retirement plan.

Compensation at IP varies from division to division; some product divisions use bonuses and commissions, others pay their reps a straight salary. Salaries run from a low range of $35,000–$50,000 to a high of $46,000–$72,000, with a minimum of $29,000. Commissions and bonuses, when given, have a high range of 16%–22%, a low range of 1%–7%, and an average range of 8%–15%.

International Paper reps have no responsibilities other than the sales of their division's products. Depending on the product line, these sales will be made to retailers, wholesale distributors, or individual consumers or end users. Thus, IP sales reps must be well versed in various kinds of selling and selling techniques and acquire product knowledge across a wide spectrum of products with diverse uses and technologies. International Paper is a blue-chip company with top-notch products that offers blue-chip opportunities for highly qualified, ambitious salespeople. Although the demands are high, so are the rewards, financially and professionally.

MEAD CORPORATION

VITAL STATISTICS

Entry Level Salary for Sales: **$25,000 (estimate)**
Senior Level Salary for Sales: **$50,000–$75,000 (estimate)**

Benefits

medical/dental: **Yes**		child care: **Flex plan**	
life insurance: **Yes**		retirement plan: **Yes**	
disability: **yes**		savings investment plan: **Yes**	
travel allowance: **Yes**		tuition assistance: **Yes, 75%**	
company car: **No**		relocation assistance: **Yes**	
profit sharing plan: **No**		memberships: **Smokenders**	
stock purchase plan: **Yes**		**Partial dues to YMCA**	

Corporate Culture Index   (1 = lowest, 10 = highest)

training:	**10**	security:	**8**
support:	**9**	mobility:	**9**
benefits:	**9**	intangibles:	**10**

Address: Courthouse Plaza, N.E., Dayton, OH 45463
Contact: Director of Sales Support, Mead Data Central; telephone 513/865-6882

Mead Corporation manufactures paper and corrugated containers, school and office supplies, and rubber products. Ranked 102nd on the Fortune 500 list of America's largest corporations, it is 7th in the forest products category, with more than $4 billion in sales for 1987. In that year, Mead's profits jumped a stunning 500%, to $218 million.

Mead Corporation started out 150 years ago as a food and beverage packager. These days, most of its profits are still built on paper products, pulp and wood products, distribution, and paper converting and include the proceeds from over 1.4 million acres of prime U.S. timberland. But this company, founded on the primacy of paper, is getting to be better known for its contribution to the paperless segments of industry. The Mead Data Central division's hugely popular electronic data services, including the LEXIS legal reference database, the NEXIS journalistic database, and the MEDIS medical reference service, have virtually revolutionized the information industry. This division represents 7% of the corporation, but is growing at a faster rate than any other segment. When paper is but a memory, Mead Data Central should still be growing at breakneck pace.

Mead is a classic "customer-driven" company, with a diversified, highly motivated, and professional sales force, reflecting the basic characteristics of its client base: top-flight, top-notch, and elite.

Mead Data Central's 350+ reps install and demonstrate products— "all the time." The goal is to develop long-term relationships with major clients who will subscribe to Mead's data services on an ongoing basis. Though law firms and physicians make up the bulk of the present subscriber base, the potential for broadening the market is as limitless as the number of people who need information: just about everyone.

MDC recruits college graduates (computer science and business majors are preferred) as well as more experienced reps from other industries. The company also hires PhDs, MDs, and JDs, who can work well in this critical market.

Mead wants all new recruits to "think how other people think," to grasp the nuances of a client's need, to determine how to solve a client's problems—perhaps when even the client can't fully understand what he or she is missing.

It's hard to imagine more sophisticated target markets than lawyers, doctors, schools, hospitals, and medical and legal libraries. But not all customers are sophisticated at managing information, manipulating databases, or all the other skills and techniques of the "Information Age."

It's all part of "needs selling," whereby reps learn to "sell the question," rather than the answer. Training is heavy on product knowledge, imparted in an initial eight-week training program for recent graduates, or a four-week compressed course for reps with real-life selling experience.

As one way of ensuring that the "right" reps are assigned to the "right" market, Mead follows a practice of "targeted selection," carefully matching the newly trained rep to his or her territorial assignment.

Reps are typically assigned to a specific market: law schools or medical schools, news organizations, or major corporations. To deal effectively with this sophisticated customer base, reps are trained to be "politely assertive," not "overtly aggressive." When dealing with publishing companies, accounting and law firms, and large government organizations, hard sell is rarely the way to close a sale.

Reps spend very few nights on the road, covering territories usually consisting of half a state at the most. Though team selling does happen, it's more common for reps to work alone, on an expense account, and reporting directly to their branch manager. Mead's rep turnover rate of 10% strongly suggests that the mysterious "targeted selection" personnel process actually works in the long run.

Trainees earn an estimated $25,000, while senior sales executives receive an estimated $50,000–$75,000, plus commission and certain nonfinancial incentives such as becoming a member of the "circle of excellence" when exceeding certain goals, which awards exotic travel as a reward.

Benefits include: medical and dental insurance, tuition assistance (75%), a car allowance, group life and disability insurance, a retirement/pension plan, a credit union, a linked 401K and savings plan, and a "flexi" plan for dependent and child care.

Mead Data Central is the company of the future. "A world of knowledge at your fingertips," Mead Data Central's slogan, might sound like good copy, but it's also true. Since it pioneered the development of full-text, computer-assisted information retrieval in the early 1970s, Mead has taken a somewhat intangible service and made it into a virtually indispensable product.

WEYERHAEUSER COMPANY

VITAL STATISTICS

Entry Level Salary for Sales: **$21,000 plus up to $6000 incentive**
Senior Level Salary for Sales: **$45,000 plus up to $10,000 incentive**

Benefits

medical/dental: **Yes**
life insurance: **Yes**
disability: **Yes**
travel allowance: **Yes**
company car: **Yes**
profit sharing plan: **Yes**
stock purchase plan: **Yes**

child care: **No**
retirement plan: **N/A**
savings investment plan: **N/A**
tuition assistance: **Yes, 80%**
relocation assistance: **Yes**
memberships: **Company health center**

Corporate Culture Index   (1 = lowest, 10 = highest)

training: **9**
support: **9**
benefits: **10**

security: **9**
mobility: **9**
intangibles: **10**

Address: Tacoma, WA 98477
Contact: College Relations and Recruiting Office, Box C; telephone 206/924-2345

Weyerhauser Company ranks 58th on the Fortune 500 list. In 1987 it enjoyed record sales of $7 billion, up 24% from 1986. At the same time it posted profits of more than $400 million, 61% above 1986.

Weyerhaeuser Company is one of the country's largest and most diversified forest products companies. It has four distinct business operating units: Weyerhaeuser Forest Products, Weyerhaeuser Paper Company, Weyerhaeuser Real Estate Company, and Diversified and Specialty Businesses. The forest products segment is the main source of revenue worldwide. It markets seeds, seedlings, and raw materials, and it manufactures a full line of softwood products from lumber to engineered composites and laminated products. It also operates the country's second largest wholesale building materials distribution system.

The pulp, paper, and packaging segment had a record year in 1987, with the bulk of the sales coming from the pulp, containerboard, and newsprint lines. Demand for these and other paper products looks very promising for future growth. The real estate and financial services segment had some problems in 1987, as did the U.S. housing market as a whole, largely due to the stock market crash and high mortgage rates. The diversified and specialty building segments include a chemical business, a line of personal-care products, gardening supplies, and specialty products such as commercial architectural doors, gypsum wallboard, and others. In addition, Weyerhaeuser is a major landowner with over 6 million acres of productive commercial forest for which it employs more foresters than anyone else except the U.S. Park Service.

The Weyerhaeuser training program for new sales reps is carefully laid out and executed. The program is geared to handle three different types of trainees: those with no prior training or sales experience, those with some sales experience, and sales managers who are more advanced. For those with no prior experience, the program runs for eight months, in seven-week cycles: one week of classroom work in the office followed by six weeks of on-the-job training in the field. The training is progressive, and it is tailored to the individual needs of the sales rep and the company. Trainees with experience or sales managers doing advanced work will take only those courses they need; others will be exposed to the whole cycle.

For its sales trainees in the forest products segment, Weyerhaeuser is looking for aggressive, bright people with leadership potential. About 80% of the reps are recent college graduates, most with business or liberal arts majors. Sales experience is a plus, but only if it is relevant to the kind of selling done at Weyerhaeuser. Technical knowledge of forestry, construction, or paper is not necessary; the company is prepared to teach what is needed on the job.

Weyerhaeuser's 600 to 700 reps in the forest products segment do not call on the end user of the products as a whole. Theirs is more of a "consultative selling" type of operation. They try to help their customers— retailers and wholesale distributors (for example, lumber yards, manufacturers, mill-direct chains)—become more profitable. They can offer their customers Weyerhaeuser's high-quality construction products, needed for residential and commercial construction. In addition, through the company's building materials distribution system (there are 55 distribution centers around the country), the reps can satisfy customer needs for a whole range of construction materials.

Reps can spend a lot of time on the road, but overnight trips are infrequent. Much depends on the size of the territory. Some Weyerhaeuser reps also work at headquarters in telemarketing. Typically, reps work on their own, but there can be some teamwork if an account needs special attention. In any case, reps concentrate on building a long-term relationship with the customer rather than on making a quick killing.

The company offers significant in-the-field support to its reps, including a company car equipped with a personal computer. It assists reps with their administrative/clerical chores where possible, and it does heavy research to develop new products all the time—making sure that the reps get promotion materials and new product information as soon as possible. Technical support is available whenever a rep feels it is necessary to make a sale, and there is ready access to top management for all reps.

Weyerhaeuser reps work on a salary-plus-incentive basis. The average salary for a trainee is about $21,000, plus an incentive of about 30% of base salary for a total of about $27,000. Salaries for senior sales reps run to about $45,000, plus an incentive of up to $10,000, for a total of $55,000. The incentive, however, is based on each unit's achieving the profitability goals set for it by management. If not, the incentive is scaled back from 30% to 20% or even to 10%. The idea is to have each unit—a paper mill, for instance—pull together as a team to achieve its planned goals.

Other benefits provided by Weyerhaeuser include: full medical and dental insurance, group life insurance, a long- and short-term disability plan, a travel allowance, an optional profit sharing plan, a matching stock purchase plan, tuition assistance of up to 80%, and a company health club, reflecting the company's concern with fitness.

Weyerhaeuser is a very large company with the sensibility of a smaller, close-knit enterprise. The people are friendly, but professional; everyone is on a first-name basis and, for example, there is no assigned parking. More to the point, employee turnover is low. The company has a long-term, growth attitude, with its forests, with its customers, and with its employees.

PHARMACEUTICALS AND HEALTH CARE

The 1980s have been good for the pharmaceutical business. In the past five years, worldwide sales of American-made pharmaceuticals have nearly doubled and now total more than $40 billion annually. The eight pharmaceutical companies we will be looking at account for more than $15 billion, or 40%, of that total. By cutting the costs of raw materials and manufacturing, pharmaceutical companies nationwide have been able to reduce their debt burdens, spend more on research and development, and be more competitive in foreign markets.

Working in the pharmaceutical industry brings many rewards. *U.S. Industrial Outlook* recently reported that employees of the pharmaceutical industry enjoy greater job satisfaction than employees in any other major industry. This is because these companies offer good working conditions, good benefits, and the chance to work with high-quality people at all levels, although they may not necessarily offer the best chances for advancement or job security.

The overwhelming share of activity in this industry takes place in pharmaceutical prescriptions, namely, over-the-counter and prescription drugs. This means that sales reps, more often than not, deal directly with physicians who prescribe and recommend drugs for their patients. Biological products (such as diagnostic drugs and vaccines) and agricultural biochemicals account for the rest of the industry.

As explained in the following pages (see especially page 270), the pharmaceutical business has unusual selling procedures that position the rep in a quite specialized field of sales.

Pharmaceuticals are a high-risk business. Generic products have flooded the market. There is lengthy lead time between the introduction of a new product and its appearance on the market, sometimes as much as a decade. And once a product has appeared, a company has a limited number of years to recover its costs and make a profit before its patent runs out.

In this climate, active research and the development of new products are the key to success in the pharmaceutical industry. Companies such as Merck, which has been able to develop new products in its own laboratories and get them speedily approved by the Food and Drug Administration, have been able to maintain solid growth. This is not so easy as it sounds when you realize that only one out of every ten thousand chemicals synthesized in a laboratory eventually makes it into the open market. A good pharmaceutical product will find new applications and sometimes lead to the development of whole new families of products. For example, some of the drugs that were originally developed to treat high blood pressure are now used to treat diabetes and even memory loss.

Another reason for the success of the pharmaceutical industry has been that, as the costs of a hospital stay get steeper and the federal government cuts back on health insurance programs, more and more physicians are turning to pharmaceuticals as a less costly method of treating their patients. If these trends continue, and it certainly looks as if they will, the pharmaceutical industry will be a fine place to begin a career for the 1990s.

TRADE ASSOCIATIONS

American Pharmaceutical Association 202/628-4210
National Association of Pharmaceutical Manufacturers 212/838-3720
Pharmaceutical Manufacturers Association 202/835-3400

PERIODICALS

American Druggist
Drug and Cosmetic Industry
Drug Store News

BAXTER TRAVENOL LABORATORIES, INC.

VITAL STATISTICS

Entry Level Salary for Sales: **$25,000–$35,000**
Senior Level Salary for Sales: **Unlimited, often straight commission**

Benefits

medical/dental: **Yes**	child care: **No**
life insurance: **Yes**	retirement plan: **Yes**
disability: **Yes**	savings investment plan: **Yes**
travel allowance: **Yes**	tuition assistance: **Yes**
company car: **Yes**	relocation assistance: **Yes**
profit sharing plan: **Yes**	memberships: **No**
stock purchase plan: **Yes**	

Corporate Culture Index   (1 = lowest, 10 = highest)

training:	**7**	security:	**8**
support:	**10**	mobility:	**9**
benefits:	**9**	intangibles:	**9**

Address: One Baxter Parkway, Deerfield, IL 60015
Contact: Professional Staffing; telephone 312/948-2000

Baxter Travenol Laboratories, Inc., ranks 66th on the Fortune 500 list. In 1987 it had sales of over $6 billion, up 10% from 1986. Its profits were $331 million, a 25% decrease from 1986, but the company had extraordinary income from the sale of discontinued units in 1986.

Baxter Travenol Laboratories, Inc., is an international supplier of health-care products, systems, and services. The company in its present state was formed in a 1985 merger between Baxter Travenol and American Hospital Supply. Baxter now comprises three business operations: Hospital Products and Services, Medical Systems and Specialties, and Alternate Site Products and Services. The company offers 120,000 products to health-care providers in over 100 countries.

The Hospital Products and Services group is Baxter's largest income producer, accounting for 53.8% of total sales in 1987. The unit offers the broadest line of hospital products and services in the industry, with products ranging from tongue depressors to complex intravenous solutions. All told, Baxter can satisfy more than 65% of any hospital's supply needs. It also helps hospitals reduce inventory, consolidate shipments, automate purchasing, and streamline billing, all of which serve to reduce waste and cut hospital costs. Baxter's goal is not only to provide hospitals with the high-quality, low-cost products they need but also to help them cope with the very real economic pressures they face.

The Medical Systems and Specialties group concentrates on providing products used in specialty areas within a hospital, notably those that fulfill clinical and diagnostic needs. For example, it develops and markets blood and diagnostic therapies, medical specialty devices, and cardiac-care equipment. It also provides, through its hospital information systems business, computer programs that link a hospital's medical and business departments with doctors' offices for more efficient communications.

The Alternate Site Products and Services group concentrates on fulfilling the needs of patients who are being treated at home. For example, the unit supplies home-care needs for those suffering from cancer, hemophilia, diabetes, and other diseases. It offers the industry's largest array of products and services for patients at home through a network of more than 150 centers that provide the best available technologies for intravenous nutrition, cancer therapy, antibiotic therapy, and dialysis therapy.

Baxter sees a very strong future growth for the company, based on the expanding health market. To service this market, Baxter is following four central strategic directions: (1) It is positioning itself to work as a partner with hospitals, showing that it understands their needs and can meet them better than anyone else. (2) It is concentrating on selected medical specialties where advanced technology (a Baxter strong point) is often the key to successful competitiveness. (3) It is redoubling its efforts in the nonhospitals marketplace, where it expects a surge of interest on the part of employers, insurance companies, and government in their efforts to cut health-care costs. (4) It is looking to world trade for increased business.

This discussion will center on a division in the Hospital Products and Services group. Baxter's current approach to selling to hospitals is an extension of its "Corporate Program," which provides large purchasing groups (major hospitals, medical centers, multihospital systems) with a single point of contact for acquiring their medical supplies—Baxter products and those Baxter purchases for resale. Its reps must therefore be familiar with hospitals' overall supply needs and how Baxter can meet them, rather than concentrating on selling individual products.

The company looks for reps who have a college degree *and* successful sales experience, at least three years' worth. Technical knowledge is not required, however; Baxter will furnish trainees with what they need. It does this with a month-long, intensive, initial training program given at headquarters in Deerfield, Illinois. The program consists of two two-week sessions, one devoted to product knowledge and the other to advanced clinical training (case studies, presentations, and the like).

The reps sell directly to hospitals, frequently calling on the same hospital several times a week (the territories are relatively small). They come to know their customers very well and to work in concert with them; that's the kind of selling this Baxter group does. Reps are expected to demonstrate new products to doctors and hospital personnel and to handle some in-service training after a sale.

Salaries for trainees vary with division and product line, but generally they range from about $25,000 to $35,000. After an initial selling period, most reps (but not all) go on a straight commission basis or on a small-salary-plus-big-incentive basis. Remember, Baxter emphasizes sales experience and orientation in its reps, so a largely commission-based sales force makes good sense for the company. Other benefits include: medical, dental, and life insurance; disability and retirement plans; profit sharing and stock purchase plans; tuition assistance; paid relocation costs; and a company car. In addition, advancement prospects are good; the career ladder runs from sales rep to sales instructor to regional sales manager to marketing director.

Baxter has a warm, friendly atmosphere, perhaps the result of its generally family-oriented reps. The turnover rate is on the low side, and the sales force represents a stable and very highly motivated group. The compensation is good, the products and services are excellent, and the company's prospects in an expanding market are very promising. Professional salespeople should do very well for themselves here.

BERGEN BRUNSWIG

VITAL STATISTICS

Entry Level Salary for Sales: **$25,000**
Senior Level Salary for Sales: **$50,000**

Benefits

medical/dental: **Yes**	child care: **N/A**
life insurance: **Yes**	retirement plan: **N/A**
disability: **N/A**	savings investment plan: **Yes**
travel allowance: **N/A**	tuition assistance: **Yes**
company car: **No**	relocation assistance: **N/A**
profit sharing plan: **N/A**	memberships: **N/A**
stock purchase plan: **N/A**	

Corporate Culture Index (1 = lowest, 10 = highest)

training:	**9**	security:	**7**
support:	**9**	mobility:	**8**
benefits:	**8**	intangibles:	**9**

Address: 4000 Metropolitan Drive, Orange, CA 92668
Contact: Director of Sales or Group Vice President of Sales; telephone 714/385-4000

Bergen Brunswig is made up of three subsidiaries, a drug wholesale unit, a medical supply unit, and an electronic products unit. In 1986 the drug unit, the corporation's leader, posted sales of $2.4 billion, up 26% from the previous year.

Bergen Brunswig gains 80% of its annual revenues from its drug wholesaling unit, Bergen Brunswig Drug Company, which has enjoyed 13 consecutive years of sales increases. The company racked up this enviable record, first by introducing innovative technologies to the industry, and then by providing such an array of services that it locked in its customers.

For instance, in the early 1970s, BB introduced several important innovations into drug retailing. It fostered the concept of single-supplier drug wholesaling and it led the way in using the computer as a marketing and sales tool as well as an operations aid. BB created programs that allowed pharmacists to use their computers to solve their financial and asset management problems as well as for electronic entry, inventory and shelf control, and other day-to-day operations. At that time, *Chain Store Age*, the premier trade journal of the industry, said: "Bergen Brunswig is without equal in drug wholesaling in its use of the computer to develop a range of innovative services and programs."

As all wholesale drug companies followed suit and computerized their operations, too, BB soon found it would have to do something more to maintain its drug unit's sales. That something more involved concentrating not only on creating new merchandising plans for pharmacists, but on implementing them as well. "Other wholesalers send pharmacists photos of planograms, but we execute plans. We make them work. We have a second field force of merchandisers who go into pharmacies, implement the plans, and keep them updated," explains Leo Granucci, Bergen Brunswig Drug Company's group vice president.

Service is stressed at all new sales trainee meetings and with senior executives as well. Because salespeople must be able to implement any programs BB offers, they receive intense initial training and continued support. The initial program lasts from 15 to 40 working days, depending on the new trainee's skill level. There is no expense involved for the trainee, and the training takes place in the division and territory to which the new rep has been assigned. Each new trainee is "sponsored" through the training period by experienced sales or management personnel.

The program itself consists of a training manual/workbook and video and audio tapes for specific areas of study. Each topic and skill covered in the program is reinforced with direct field experience in order to keep the training realistic. This helps new reps transfer their skills and knowledge to the marketplace, and it also tests the validity of the program against actual selling conditions. The overall program is designed to be implemented through individualized training plans, which are able to accelerate participants through areas they know well while allowing them to spend more time on areas in which they need intensive work.

After that, all sales and management personnel attend a minimum of six training sessions a year and all are individually assessed for additional training needs. In addition, all sales personnel are encouraged to continue their formal education—and are helped financially by the company if they do.

In selecting new sales reps, Bergen Brunswig looks for: excellent communications skills, good business sense coupled with a sincere desire to help customers, and a good knowledge of the retail drug environment. Formal graduate education is not required.

Benefits include an annual bonus, complete medical package, group life insurance, group investment insurance programs to cover many special-need areas, an education assistance program, and a recognition program that includes free trips and vacations with spouses. For all field reps, administrative assistance is provided as needed, and a large staff of regional support people is also available.

Bergen Brunswig fields a sales force of around 330, who sell into three basic markets: independent retail drug outlets, food/drug chains, and hospital and other managed health-care facilities. Because BB salespeople have total account responsibility within their territories, reporting only to their division sales managers, the reps have challenging positions.

The company supports its sales staff in other ways. It offers customers co-op advertising and promotional programs, and, in addition, builds goodwill in pharmacies with free services. These include one-stop coupon redemption and a magazine allowance program—even though BB does not distribute publications. The goodwill pays off: BB has increased its market share from 6% to 14% in ten years.

Salaries at Bergen Brunswig range from a high of around $50,000 to a low of around $25,000, with a minimum of $22,000. There are no commissions, but bonuses are available for all levels of field salespeople. Bonuses are based on measurable goals; a portion of the bonus is paid quarterly, with the balance paid at the end of the company's fiscal year.

Highly motivated salespeople can look forward to excellent opportunities for advancement at BB. The company president and 80% of its vice presidents have come from the sales ranks—direct proof of the company's commitment to advancement from within. In addition, all top managers, including the president, are expected to make 100 sales calls a year. Thus BB sales reps are assured that the top echelon are in the trenches with them and aware of the real conditions they cope with every day.

BRISTOL-MYERS COMPANY

VITAL STATISTICS

Entry Level Salary for Sales: *$30,000+*
Senior Level Salary for Sales: *$50,000–$60,000*

Benefits

medical/dental: **Yes**
life insurance: **Yes**
disability: **Yes**
travel allowance: **Yes**
company car: **Yes**
profit sharing plan: **No**
stock purchase plan: **N/A**

child care: **No**
retirement plan: **Yes**
savings investment plan: **N/A**
tuition assistance: **Yes**
relocation assistance: **Yes**
memberships: **No**

Corporate Culture Index   (1 = lowest, 10 = highest)

training: **10**
support: **9**
benefits: **8**

security: **9**
mobility: **9**
intangibles: **10**

Address: 345 Park Avenue, New York, NY 10154
Contact: Human Resources; telephone 212/546-4000

Bristol-Myers Company ranks 76th on the Fortune 500 list. In 1987 it posted sales of more than $5 billion, up 12% from 1987. Profits, at $710 million, were up 20% from 1986.

Heading into its second century as of 1988, Bristol-Myers pursues the three business objectives that made its first 100 years a success: performance, product leadership, and excellence in research. In 1987 B-M racked up its fifteenth consecutive year of improved profit margins, and it increased its R&D funding to $342 million. It is confident of continued worldwide growth in its four core businesses: the Consumer Products Group, the Health Care Group, the U.S. Pharmaceutical and Nutritional Group, and the Science and Technology Group.

The Consumer Products Group makes and markets proprietary medicines and toiletries; skin-care, hair-care, and hair-coloring products; and a variety of household cleaning and specialty products in the U.S. and Canada. Included among these products are such widely known brand names as: Nuprin, Bufferin, Excedrin, and Datril (pain relievers); Comtrex (cold reliever); Ban (anti-perspirant); Clairol (hair-coloring products); and Windex and Drano (home-care products).

The Health Care Group develops, manufactures, and markets medical devices and other nonpharmaceutical (nonprescription) health-care products. Among these are hip replacement products; surgical instruments; and specialty medical products in such areas as urology, burn care, vascular problems, and ear, nose, and throat disorders.

The U.S. Pharmaceutical and Nutritional Group manufactures and markets a wide range of nutritional products and pharmaceuticals. The latter include anti-cancer drugs, antibiotics, cardiovascular products, dermatological products, and drugs for the central nervous system. B-M's Institutional Marketing Division sells these products to the large-volume users like hospital buying groups, nursing homes, and HMOs (Health Maintenance Organizations). The pharmaceutical and medical products segment of B-M's business is the company's largest, accounting for 41% of B-M's sales and 42% of its profits. The Science and Technology Group directs and coordinates all of B-M's pharmaceutical research efforts. Moreover, it is responsible for all the licensing activities involved in the company's pharmaceutical, processing, and technology products.

B-M now seems particularly well situated to meet the challenges of the end of this century and the beginning of the next. Although it sells in highly competitive markets and locks horns with some of the strongest and best managed companies in the world, B-M is not without resources of its own. It has excellent plants and equipment. Its laboratories and R&D staff are first rate. Its patents and trademarks are among the most valuable in the business. Its financial situation places it in the top rank of the world's industrial companies, and its sales forces are well trained and aggressive.

The Pharmaceutical Group, the unit featured here, runs a carefully articulated training program that involves home study, classes at the group's headquarters in Evansville, Indiana, and frequent on-the-job sessions with district and regional managers. The typical course lasts from nine months to a year and comprises six phases. Phase 1 runs from five to eight weeks and consists of meetings with a district trainer and home study. Trainees are tested on material and repeat and retest until they attain 80% or better on all tests. Phase 2 involves classroom work in Evansville with two instructors and ten to 12 trainees. Phase 3 consists of ten weeks to four months in the field with the district manager calling on accounts. In Phase 4 the trainee goes back to headquarters for a week of reinforcement and concentration on marketing presentations. Phase 5 comprises four to six months of field work, with supervision, and Phase 6 is a week of recaps back at headquarters.

During the training, the new hires learn about the company's career paths for reps (who can move to marketing or training or sales management). Most promotions to B-M's top management levels come from sales. For the most part, B-M reps work alone. Territories vary in size, but no reps have more than two overnights a week. Reps sell primarily to doctors (this group concentrates on ethical—meaning prescription—drugs and related medical products), and so they sell indirectly, as is typical in the rest of the pharmaceutical industry.

B-M looks for new sales reps who are college graduates with some pharmacy or science background. Prior selling experience, preferably in the pharmaceutical field, is very desirable. (*Note:* Other B-M divisions recruit from colleges and take liberal arts graduates as well as those with degrees in business or marketing. B-M has prepared a video presentation that shows what selling is like at the company, so college seniors can get a look at the real world of selling, a world their college courses may not have covered in any detail.) Make no mistake, B-M is very serious about hiring, training, and deploying a class A sales force. It also supports its salespeople with top-quality ad and promotion materials, clerical/administrative help where possible, and major commitments to R&D in all product areas.

Salaries for trainees average about $30,000; senior salespeople average about $50,000 to $60,000. Bonus and incentive plans are also part of the compensation package. B-M, and particularly the pharmaceutical segment, offers compensation to its salespeople that is competitive with any company in the business. Other benefits include: medical, dental, and life insurance; disability and retirement plans; 401A and 401K plans; a travel allowance; tuition assistance; paid relocation expenses; and a company car.

B-M has a corporate but warm atmosphere. It is proud of its history and dedicated to staying at the top of its demanding and competitive industry. Its reps are known for their professionalism and commitment, and they are backed up by a company that knows where it has been and where it wants to go—and that possesses the resources and the determination to get there.

ELI LILLY AND COMPANY

VITAL STATISTICS

Entry Level Salary for Sales: **$31,000**
Senior Level Salary for Sales: **$70,000**

Benefits

medical/dental: **Yes**
life insurance; **Yes**
disability: **Yes, short and long term**
travel allowance: **Yes**
company car: **Yes**
profit sharing plan: **Yes**
stock purchase plan: **Yes**

child care: **No**
retirement plan: **Yes**
savings investment plan: **Yes**
tuition assistance: **Yes**
relocation assistance: **Yes**
memberships: **Employee Activities Group sponsors 39 activities**

Corporate Culture Index   (1 = lowest, 10 = highest)

training: **10**
support: **8**
benefits: **10**

security: **9**
mobility: **10**
intangibles: **8**

Address: Lilly Corporate Center, Indianapolis, IN 46285
Contact: Corporate Recruitment; telephone 800/428-4592

Eli Lilly and Company ranks 111th on the Fortune 500 list. In 1987 it posted sales of more than $3.6 billion, up 10% from 1986. At the same time, it had profits of $644 million, an increase of 15% from 1986.

Eli Lilly and Company is a research-based corporation that develops, manufactures, and markets pharmaceuticals, medical instruments, diagnostic products, and agricultural products. It markets its products in more than 130 countries around the world. The company concentrates its resources on product areas that are research-based and have a life sciences orientation. Consequently, the company has divested itself of ventures that fall outside this commitment, such as the Elizabeth Arden cosmetics unit.

Lilly divides its business operations into two major segments: human health and agriculture. The human health segment is by far the larger of the two, accounting for nearly $2.9 billion in 1987, about 79.4% of the company's total revenues. Included in this segment are oral and injectable antibiotics, medical instruments, diagnostic products that incorporate monoclonal antibodies, and a substantial array of other human health products, such as analgesics, anti-arthritics, anti-diabetic agents, anti-depressants, anti-ulcer products, cardiovascular products, and others. This segment also includes medical instruments and devices, medical monitoring systems, and diagnostic testing materials used in hospitals.

The agricultural segment comprises plant science products and animal health products. These include herbicides, cattle feed additives, and other products for livestock and poultry. The agricultural segment accounted for sales of $748 million in 1987, approximately 21% of the company's total revenue.

The key to long-term success in pharmaceuticals is constant research resulting in a steady stream of new products. The corporation's resources are being directed to product areas that have a research-based, high-technology, life sciences orientation. In this respect, Lilly is in the forefront of research in important therapeutic areas such as diseases of the central nervous system, pulmonary and cardiovascular diseases, diabetes, cancer, infectious diseases and even recombinant DNA technology. In the medical instruments area, it is continuing its emphasis on what it calls "total quality control" systems. In its agricultural operations, the company is further tailoring its products and customer service capabilities to the needs of agricultural producers. In 1987 the company experienced its twenty-seventh consecutive year of increased net income. It sees more of the same in the future.

Lilly looks for sales reps who have a college degree (BA or BS) and preferably a pharmacy degree. The company does not hire from competitors, relying on graduates from good schools who have good grades and good communication skills, and have demonstrated leadership qualities. Prior sales experience is not necessary.

The initial training program for new hires lasts three to four weeks and is conducted at the Sales Training and Development Center at the home office in Indianapolis. Training programs, however, continue throughout the entire career of a sales rep. Six months after the initial program, another training session takes place, and a third program is held approximately one year after that. Then subsequent formal programs occur on a routine/scheduled basis approximately every four years. In addition, training programs are conducted outside the Indianapolis headquarters on a regional basis, with sales reps attending approximately every two years.

The initial training program combines a mix of formal classroom sessions (which focus on developing expertise in both product/medical knowledge and selling/communication skills) and on-the-job training conducted by the district manager. Later programs comprise primarily classroom and seminar sessions. In addition, training also includes special on-site clinical orientation programs in teaching institutions throughout the U.S. to further enhance product and medical knowledge. The trainee/instructor ratio for the formal sessions varies but averages around 14:1. Evaluations and monitoring of continued sales-skill development occur on the job with the rep's district manager.

New hires are taught about all different kinds of accounts because Lilly sales reps call on a variety of workers in the health-care industry— physicians, physicians' assistants, nurses, pharmacists, and so on. Calls are made to doctors' offices, hospitals, pharmacies, and wholesalers. As with most of the pharmaceutical industry, Lilly representatives do not sell directly to the end user. Lilly products (including over-the-counter, nonprescription items as well as the prescription drugs) are sold only to selected wholesalers, who in turn sell them to hospital and retail pharmacies. The sales reps generally convey information about the products through individual or group presentation techniques. Because they deal exclusively with health professionals, reps need to know their products thoroughly and be able to explain precisely what they can—and cannot—do. Sales reps' activities are supported by first-class advertising and promotion materials and by leading-edge research.

Sales reps generally work alone, but they are all part of a district sales team. The size of their territories varies, with representatives in suburban areas experiencing few overnights and those in rural areas having some overnight travel. There are approximately 1500+ Lilly reps divided into four divisions: Lilly, Dista, Lilly Hospital, and Lilly Select Products. Advancement opportunities are excellent. Lilly views its representatives as a primary source of talent throughout all levels of sales and marketing management. As a result, Lilly is a promote-from-within company; for example, all the current vice presidents in the sales and marketing divisions began their careers as sales reps.

Salaries for new reps average around $31,000; senior sales reps can earn a total of around $70,000. There is also a merit-based, corporate-performance incentive payment that is awarded when certain goals are met. Other benefits include: medical, dental, and life insurance; disability and retirement plans; an excellent company-matching savings plan; profit sharing and stock purchase plans; tuition assistance; paid relocation expenses; and a company car.

Lilly is a 112-year-old pharmaceutical company that is highly regarded for both its products and its integrity. Sales reps in this industry have a lot of responsibility—they are, after all, selling life-supporting products—and Lilly demands top performance and commitment from its employees. In turn, the company offers a solid growth opportunity in a vital field for all who qualify.

MERCK & COMPANY, INC.

VITAL STATISTICS

Entry Level Salary for Sales: **$33,000**
Senior Level Salary for Sales: **$60,000**

Benefits

medical/dental: **Yes**	child care: **Yes, in HQ only**
life insurance: **Yes**	retirement plan: **Yes**
disability: **Yes**	savings investment plan: **N/A**
travel allowance: **Yes**	tuition assistance: **Yes**
company car: **Yes**	relocation assistance: **Yes**
profit sharing plan: **No**	memberships: **No**
stock purchase plan: **Yes**	

Corporate Culture Index   (1 = lowest, 10 = highest)

training:	**10**	security:	**9**
support:	**9**	mobility:	**9**
benefits:	**9**	intangibles:	**10**

Address: PO Box 2000, Rahway, NJ 07065-0909
Contact: Corporate Headquarters; telephone 201/574-4000

Merck & Company ranks 80th on the Fortune 500 list. In 1987 it had sales of more than $5 billion, an increase of 23% from 1986. Profits for this period were more than $900 million, up 34% from 1986.

Merck & Company is a leading, worldwide pharmaceutical company with no fewer than 13 major drug products that generate $100 million or more apiece in annual revenues. When *Business Month* named Merck one of the five best-managed companies of 1987, it was only acknowledging the fact that this research-driven organization was producing more breakthroughs than any other drug maker—and was likely to continue doing so. This kind of performance has doubled Merck's profits in the four-year period from 1984 to 1987.

Merck develops, produces, and markets products and services for the maintenance or restoration of health. Its business is divided into two industry segments: Human and Animal Health Products and Specialty Health Products. The Human and Animal Health Products group includes therapeutic and preventive items, most often sold by prescription, for the treatment of human disease. In this area, Merck provides a line of anti-hypertensive and cardiovascular products that are leaders in the field. Animal medicinals include products that are used to control and alleviate disease in poultry and livestock. The Specialty Chemical Products group manufactures chemicals that have a wide variety of applications in various industries such as water treatment, papermaking, oil field drilling, and food processing.

At present, Merck is working to make itself the world leader in pharmaceuticals. The company's immediate goal is to double its now leading 8.5% share of the U.S. market and to pull ahead of the deadlocked pack that is tied at 3% to 4% of the global market. As part of its strategy to accomplish this, Merck is now aggressively looking at acquisition possibilities. More to the point, in this highly competitive industry, Merck maintains an intensive and very successful research program, recruiting top talent from the world's universities. Says John Lyons, Merck's executive vice president, "Marketing is crucial here, but research is the engine of growth."

This drive for excellence in product is matched with a high degree of professional marketing savvy. The "absolute key" to marketing prescription drugs is the relationship of trust that a highly trained salesperson builds with the customer, according to Jerry Keller, the vice president of sales for Merck Sharp & Dohme, the company's pharmaceutical division. This means a top-notch sales force, and in 1987 Merck was cited by *Sales & Marketing Management* magazine as having the best sales force in the pharmaceutical industry.

Merck maintains an excellent mix in its sales force, recruiting some 40% of its reps from recent college graduates and the remaining 60% from a variety of sources such as pharmacists, doctors, nurses, teachers, and the competition. Merck looks for people with some science or health-care background; sales experience is helpful, but not required. Training, in any case, is intense because the field is so competitive and because the end user's life and well-being are at stake as well as sales. For instance, legal requirements now demand that drug sales reps tell a doctor not only what a drug product *can* do but also what it *can't* do.

Merck salespeople receive thorough training in three distinct areas: (1) a primer on basic medicine including anatomy, physiology, and diseases; (2) a six-month to one-year course on presenting Merck products in their territory; and (3) a wrap-up on medical knowledge concentrating on maladies treated with Merck products. In addition, once every two years, Merck reps are sent to medical school for a week to update their knowledge of current procedures. Reps also receive individual training on products from an assigned physician/mentor in a special course that concentrates on the real-world aspects of delivering medical care. Moreover, a district meeting is convened monthly to focus on specific topics of immediate interest. The program itself consists of a combination of self-study materials, classroom work, plant tours, and on-the-job training both in the field and in the home office.

Like other pharmaceutical companies, Merck relies on indirect selling to get its products to the end users. Merck reps call primarily on doctors (either in their offices or at hospitals), trying to persuade them to prescribe Merck products. Territories are generally rather small with little or no overnight travel; about one-half of the reps will have three or four overnights a month, however. Reps file call plans and call reports with their managers, and there is close supervision by, and access to, management.

Salaries for trainees average about $33,000, with salaries for senior salespeople averaging about $60,000. Bonuses are available, too, but they are linked up with performance and with product line. Merck's aim is to pay at the upper 10% of the industry. Good reps can *double* their beginning salary in 10 to 15 years. They also receive excellent support from high-quality ad and promotion materials, from administrative/clerical assistance, and, especially, from the company's commitment to R&D. There are good advancement opportunities, too: from sales associate to sales rep to senior sales rep. Then reps are eligible (if they so desire) to go on to sales trainer to marketing and to general management (almost all of Merck's positions are filled by internal promotions). Other benefits include: medical, dental, and life insurance; disability and retirement plans; a stock purchase plan; tuition assistance; child care for headquarters employees; a company car; and paid relocation expenses.

The atmosphere at Merck is aggressive and dynamic, and the business is very competitive. Reps must be the kind of people who like study and medicine and feel they are part of the healing professions. With top products, top sales training, and continuous support and recognition, Merck offers a fine career opportunity.

PFIZER, INC.

VITAL STATISTICS

Entry Level Salary for Sales: *Highly competitive*
Senior Level Salary for Sales: *Highly competitive*

Benefits

medical/dental: **Yes**	child care: **N/A**
life insurance: **Yes**	retirement plan: **Yes**
disability: **N/A**	savings investment plan: **Yes**
travel allowance: **N/A**	tuition assistance: **Yes**
company car: **Yes**	relocation assistance: **N/A**
profit sharing plan: **N/A**	memberships: **N/A**
stock purchase plan: **Yes**	

Corporate Culture Index   (1 = lowest, 10 = highest)

training:	**8**	security:	**8**
support:	**8**	mobility:	**9**
benefits:	**9**	intangibles:	**9**

Address: 235 East 42nd Street, New York, NY 10017
Contact: Manager, Employment; telephone 212/573-2323, or the nearest Regional Personnel Manager at offices located in Hoffman Estates, IL; Irvine, CA; Clifton, NJ; Doraville, GA; or Dallas, TX

Pfizer, Inc., ranks 83rd on the Fortune 500 list. In 1987 it enjoyed sales of almost $5 billion, up 10% over 1986. At present, the company possesses one of the most impressive rosters of new products in development.

Pfizer, Inc., is a research-based company conducting business in more than 140 countries. It discovers, develops, manufactures, and sells technology-intensive products in five areas: health care, agriculture, specialty chemicals, materials science, and consumer. The major source of the company's revenues is pharmaceuticals in the health-care segment.

As at all pharmaceutical companies, selling at Pfizer means calling on doctors and explaining the new products to them. Sales reps in this business almost never have contact with the end user of the products and only rarely with retailers. They deal almost exclusively with highly trained professionals, doctors, dentists, and veterinarians. They are also likely to meet with hospital staff physicians, hospital pharmacists, and, less frequently, with independent retail druggists as well.

Because this selling procedure is basically indirect, pharmaceutical companies have developed a special method for keeping track of what sales reps make in order to determine commissions and incentives. (This is also true of Merck & Company and the other drug firms mentioned in this book.) The companies use zip codes to assign sales to the rep. For instance, any sales of a Pfizer product to a pharmacy in a particular postal zone are credited to the rep in whose territory the zip code of the pharmacy falls.

This means, for example, that a rep may persuade a doctor in his or her territory to use Pfizer's Cardura, a brand-new medication for the treatment of hypertension. The doctor then prescribes it for a patient, who, in turn, may fill the prescription at a pharmacy near home that is not in the rep's territory. The sale of the drug in that pharmacy will be assigned to the rep whose territory includes the zip code of the pharmacy, not to the rep who originally made the call on the doctor. This may seem unfair to the original rep, but that rep receives credit for all the pharmacy sales zip-coded to his or her territory. The thinking is that it all evens out in the end.

The reason for this roundabout method of selling and calculating sales lies in the unique nature of the prescription drug business. Although it is the pharmacy that actually buys the medication from the producer, pharmaceutical companies understand that it is the doctor who determines which drugs the pharmacist will dispense and the customer (patient) will use. The physician is the one who drives the sale, and this means that the reps must know each product thoroughly in order to sell it to someone with much more medical knowledge. Consequently, Pfizer takes great pains with the training of new hires.

The company's formal training program lasts a year, taking place at the New York headquarters and in the field. It begins with a basic orientation followed by several weeks of classes in New York. Trainees are exposed to basic human anatomy, physiology, and pharmacology. They must learn about Pfizer's pharmaceutical products and those of other companies as well, and they need to master the techniques of making presentations to the professionals they will be calling on. This is perhaps the most grueling part of the program. Trainees role-play and critique video tapes of their performance again and again.

Pfizer also encourages its reps to continue their education. It pays the tuition costs and costs of books for job-related courses and degrees taken by reps. It offers certificate programs of its own, and there is always ongoing training in new products and market developments with field managers. Other sales support takes the form of rapid answers by the company's research people to any technical questions or problems that a rep may encounter. Also, field managers and the home office are careful to get new product information and industry and medical developments into the reps' hands as soon as possible.

Still, Pfizer reps must be able and willing to work largely on their own. They work out of their own homes, arrange their own call schedules, and do most of their own clerical/administrative chores, even though local offices do offer as much assistance as possible. The job requires independent, self-starter, entrepreneurial types, who see problems as opportunities and competition as a challenge. A college education is essential with a major in the life sciences or business a definite plus, but trainees may be accepted with a variety of college majors if they show a creative and competitive attitude. Those with any prior training or experience in health fields, such as nurses who have become dissatisfied with hospital work, are especially welcomed.

Starting salaries at Pfizer are very competitive with other pharmaceutical houses (the industry average is $24,000 to $30,000) and bonus plans reward the diligent. In addition to bonuses, the company offers other incentives such as sales contests and performance awards. Promotion opportunities from sales up the corporate ladder are excellent; the president, for instance, began as a sales rep.

Benefits are good. They include: a full medical/dental insurance plan, group life insurance, a disability plan, post-retirement benefits such as certain health-care and life insurance coverage, a volunteer savings and investment plan, a stock option plan, and a company car. Best of all, perhaps, is Pfizer's commitment to new products; in this business, R&D is the rep's best friend.

SMITHKLINE BECKMAN CORPORATION

VITAL STATISTICS

Entry Level Salary for Sales: **$27,500**
Senior Level Salary for Sales: **$60,000**

Benefits

medical/dental: **Yes**
life insurance: **Yes**
disability: **Yes**
travel allowance: **Yes**
company car: **Yes**
profit sharing plan: **N/A**
stock purchase plan: **Yes**

child care: **N/A**
retirement plan: **Yes**
savings investment plan: **Yes**
tuition assistance: **Yes**
relocation assistance: **Yes**
memberships: **N/A**

Corporate Culture Index (1 = lowest, 10 = highest)

training: **10**
support: **8**
benefits: **10**

security: **9**
mobility: **9**
intangibles: **9**

Address: One Franklin Plaza, P.O. Box 7929, Philadelphia, PA 19101
Contact: Vice President, Corporate Personnel; telephone 215/751-4000

SmithKline Beckman ranks 100th on the Fortune 500 list. During the 1980s, the company saw its sales more than double. In 1987 alone it enjoyed total sales of over $4 billion, an increase of 16% over 1986.

SmithKline Beckman is a major manufacturer of pharmaceutical and health-care products of three basic types. The Therapeutics line includes pharmaceuticals promoted to the medical profession and nonprescription health-care products that are advertised to consumers. Also covered are animal health-care products such as vaccines, pharmaceuticals, and feed additives.

Contact lenses and products for their care, pharmaceuticals for eye disorders, diagnostic equipment for detecting vision disorders, and products for eye surgery make up the Eye and Skin Care line that is generally promoted to eye-care professionals. Finally, the Diagnostic/Analytical line includes medical instruments and supplies (for use in health-care, biomedical research, and scientific applications) and clinical laboratory services (provided to hospitals and physicians through a network of laboratories in the U.S. and Canada).

SmithKline has had its share of problems. Spectacularly successful with its ulcer medication Tagamet, introduced in 1976 and until recently the world's best-selling drug, the company neglected to continue to do basic research and development. It was, to quote Prudential-Bache Securities analyst Neil B. Sweig, "the only big pharmaceutical house to go through the 1980s without introducing a major drug." But all that is history now for SmithKline's top management. It has acknowledged that growth must come from new products, and it sees these products already emerging in the areas of molecular genetics, diagnostic techniques, immunology, and other disciplines. The company is particularly happy with the growth of the lab testing industry, which, because of physicians' and hospitals' fears of malpractice suits, has become big business indeed and seems likely to continue that way.

Still, the company expects the most growth in its pharmaceutical line. Training for SmithKline's pharmaceutical sales reps takes 17 weeks, involving a mix of home study, core study in Philadelphia, and field work. The trainee spends the first week at home learning the terminology and basic concepts from textbooks. This is followed by two weeks of core study at headquarters, including classes at the Medical College of Philadelphia. After that come four weeks of work in the field, supervised by the District Sales Manager (DSM).

The trainee then returns home for a week to digest what he or she has learned. The next two to three weeks are taken up by more core training at headquarters, and then four to six weeks are spent in the field with the DSM and a trainer-recruiter. The formal training then ends with a week studying professional selling skills at headquarters.

As you can see, trainees are expected to accomplish a good deal of the work on their own. This is in keeping with the style of SmithKline reps, who generally maintain their own home offices and work their territories from there. The territories themselves are smaller than most, and reps average only three nights a month on the road. They must file a weekly work plan with their DSM (each DSM supervises about ten reps), including a doctor call plan (the doctors they expect to see in the course of the week). Each sales rep is assigned an annual sales goal, broken down by district. It is the rep's job to meet the goals established and to work out call plans and appropriate presentations to achieve that end.

SmithKline reps do not call on end users; sales are made to doctors and nurses. As a result, the rep's demonstration must be geared to explaining the uses, procedures, and effectiveness of the company's products to these extremely knowledgeable customers. Reps can count on such support as first-rate advertising, promotion, and new product information materials from the home office; administrative/clerical help when needed; and assistance from the company's various research staffs when necessary.

For instance, SmithKline's management found that competing ulcer medications that needed to be taken only twice a day—as opposed to SmithKline's Tagamet that had to be taken four times a day—were eating up SmithKline's share of the market. So, SmithKline did research and clinical testing and established that Tagamet is as safe and effective when taken just once a day. That wiped out the competition's advantage and left SmithKline's reps with a level playing field. The company's chief executive, Henry Wendt, made the situation clear to his marketing staff and salespeople when he declared: "We won't lose any more market share."

To ensure this, SmithKline looks for sales rep candidates with a science background and from one to three years of experience in nursing or pharmacy. Sales experience is not necessary, but the ability to communicate well and make effective presentations is. Also important is the ability to work on one's own, although team selling is used when the situation requires it.

Salaries at SmithKline average from $27,500 or more for sales trainees to about $60,000 for senior sales executives. DSMs have discretion to reward above-average trainees for exceptional performance. After six months, superstar prospects may be fast-tracked; otherwise, salaries are reviewed annually. Bonuses and incentives are available, too, based on productivity.

Benefits include medical/dental, life, and disability insurance; tuition assistance; retirement plans; a company car for reps; and a companywide stock purchasing/matching savings plan. SmithKline offers plenty of opportunity to advance to top management if the salesperson wishes to do so and demonstrates the necessary ability.

SmithKline has about 1100 sales reps working in nine regions across the country. The reps are highly professional, enthusiastic people, and they find these characteristics mirrored in top management and in the company's basic research and development staffs. Although spread out and working on their own for the most part, the reps feel that they belong more to a close-knit, single-minded group than to a major corporate conglomerate.

WARNER-LAMBERT COMPANY

VITAL STATISTICS

Entry Level Salary for Sales: **$26,200–$29,000 (depending on degree and experience)**

Senior Level Salary for Sales: **$53,800**

Benefits

medical/dental: **Yes**
life insurance: **Yes**
disability: **Yes**
travel allowance: **Yes**
company car: **Yes**
profit sharing plan: **No**
stock purchase plan: **Yes**

child care: **No**
retirement plan: **Yes**
savings investment plan: **N/A**
tuition assistance: **Yes**
relocation assistance: **Yes**
memberships: **Health clubs**

Corporate Culture Index   (1 = lowest, 10 = highest)

training: **8**
support: **8**
benefits: **10**

security: **9**
mobility: **8**
intangibles: **9**

Address: 201 Tabor Road, Morris Plains, NJ 07950
Contact: Corporate Headquarters; telephone 201/540-2000

Warner-Lambert Company ranks 121st on the Fortune 500 list. In 1987 it posted sales of more than $3 billion, up 12% from 1986. Profits were $296 million, up 13% from 1986 (if a net nonrecurring gain for that year is excluded).

Warner-Lambert Company develops, manufactures, and markets quality health-care and consumer products on a worldwide basis. Its broad range of businesses encompasses such items as ethical and nonprescription pharmaceuticals, chewing gums, breath mints, shaving and pet care products, and empty, hard gelatin capsules. It employs 30,500 people in 80 manufacturing plants and nine major research facilities and operates in more than 130 countries. It concentrates on three core businesses—ethical products, nonprescription products, and gums and mints. It also produces a variety of other consumer items.

The company's ethical—that is, prescription—products comprise a line of pharmaceuticals marketed primarily under the Parke-Davis name. Chief among these is the increasing use of the lipid-regulator Lopid. Warner-Lambert, taking into account the forecasts of explosive growth for compounds that inhibit heart disease, has set a strategic objective of becoming a leading force in cardiovascular medicine. In 1987 it began marketing an anti-hypertensive, anti-anginal compound and expects to continue emphasizing research in this area in the future. For example, in 1987 the company budgeted $232 million for such research, a 15% increase from 1986. It budgeted $255 million for 1988, showing clearly that its talk of finding innovative solutions was a lot more than just talk.

The nonprescription products segment of Warner-Lambert's business also did very well in 1987, increasing its total sales by 11%. Among the many over-the-counter products that Warner-Lambert markets are its mouthwashes Listerine and Listermint, its denture cleanser Efferdent, its antihistamine Benedryl, its Halls cough tablets, and its other products: nutritional supplements, antacids, and skin-care and other related items.

In the gums and mints segment of its business, Warner-Lambert enjoyed a successful year in 1987 despite increased competition. Its Trident sugarless gum had its most successful year, and the remaining line of gums also did well. Breath mints like Certs and Certs Mini-Mints likewise shared in the success, and the company is now poised to expand its confectionery business beyond its traditional focus on gums and mints. Warner-Lambert's other products operations include razor blades (Schick), aquarium products (Tetra), and empty, hard gelatin capsules (Capsugel).

Warner-Lambert is confident of its future prospects, and it sees its continued success as resting largely on the company's ability to develop innovative solutions to customers' needs. It emphasizes innovation in research and marketing for both its pharmaceutical and consumer products, and it supports these efforts with major advertising and promotion campaigns.

Selling at Warner-Lambert falls into two separate categories, ethical pharmaceuticals and the rest of the company's products. In its prescription drug operations, the segment covered here, Warner-Lambert is like other pharmaceutical companies. In the nonprescription and confectionery operations, Warner-Lambert is closer to other consumer-item producers who deal with wholesalers and retailers. Reps in this area must know about marketing, setting up displays, attaining the most desirable locations, and maximizing the leverage to be gained from the company's formidable media advertising operations. Selling ethical pharmaceuticals is, of course, a different ball game.

For its Parke-Davis sales reps, Warner-Lambert looks for college graduates, preferably with a degree in pharmacy or some related health science. Prior sales experience is helpful, but not necessary. Training for new reps is intense but not overly long; it takes about eight weeks and is given at the company headquarters in Morris Plains, New Jersey. The initial course includes a mix of classroom work, role playing—including video taping and critique of sales presentations, and home study (product knowledge, human anatomy, diseases, medical terms, and the like). The informal on-the-job training part of the course takes place in the sales territory where the rep will work, under the supervision of the district sales manager.

The training is ongoing as well, especially in the case of new products. There is also a self-administered three-week program of instruction as well as guidance on how to run a home office and a workshop on professional selling skills. The point of the continued training is to bring reps along the five levels of the company's career ladder, each one with increasing responsibility and, presumably, compensation. Promotion opportunities are good at Warner-Lambert; the present CEO began as a sales rep. The territories are generally small and reps typically work alone, calling on doctors and nurses in private offices and hospitals, trying to persuade physicians to prescribe their products for their patients—indirect selling, as it's called.

Trainee salaries range from $26,200 (college graduate) to $28,200 (graduate with pharmacy degree) to $29,000 (graduate with pharmacy degree and several years' experience). Salaries are boosted by a commission of 9%, and senior salespeople can go as high as $59,000, averaging about $44,000. Other benefits include: medical, dental, and life insurance; disability and retirement plans; a travel allowance; a stock purchasing plan; a 401K plan; tuition assistance (100%); paid relocation expenses; and a company car. Reps are supported with high-quality ad and promotion materials, administrative/clerical help when possible, and dedicated R&D of new and innovative products.

Warner-Lambert offers a relaxed but professional atmosphere; there is a formal dress code, but people are on a first-name basis in the office. Market responsiveness and innovation, on the other hand, whether one is selling cardiovascular medicine or bubble gum, are absolute musts, and are, fortunately, taken very seriously here.

PHOTOGRAPHIC AND SCIENTIFIC EQUIPMENT

One picture is worth ten thousand words, the Chinese proverb says. Lots of pictures add up to many dollars, $19 billion to be exact. That was the value of shipments in the photographic industry in 1987. The industry has two sectors—the equipment sector, which produces cameras and projectors, and the sensitized materials sector, which makes photographic film, plates, paper, and the necessary chemicals. Companies have been restructuring in recent years, streamlining and cost-cutting, and by now, most are involved in both sectors of the industry.

In 1987 U.S. imports of photographic equipment were down 2% to $4 billion, the first drop in five years. The weak dollar and the high quality of American products are enabling U.S. export manufacturers to hold their own against stiff competition from Japan.

The standard 35 mm camera continues to account for the single largest share of sales for still photography equipment, but new product lines are heralding the future. Disposable cameras were introduced in 1987, both here and in Japan. This camera is a product with a built-in market niche, namely parks, tourist sites, and hotels, the sorts of places where people would want to snap photos after forgetting to bring a camera along.

Another new product, the ESC, or Electronic Still Camera, bypasses the developing process and immediately processes and transmits an image by computer. Micrographics for storing information is developing as an economical alternative to the bulky metal shelves and filing cabinets with which we are all familiar. This new technology is especially popular with banks, utilities, and communications firms. And new flashes with built-in microprocessors automatically calculate and adjust for the right amount of light in a picture. In today's strong economy, consumers have more disposable income for leisure activities, spurring them to buy cameras, whether they need new ones or, as is more often the case, seek to upgrade the equipment they already have.

American companies' edge results from technological superiority. That superiority would be impossible without significant research and development. And scientific instruments turn that R&D from figures on a blackboard into reality. The market for scientific instruments is directly keyed into trends in R&D. In 1987 R&D began to rise and sales of scientific instruments rose along with it, to a total of $28 billion, an annual growth rate of 4%. Industry analysts predict annual growth rates of 5% for the next five years.

Scientific instruments fall into three basic categories: aircraft instruments—navigational, nautical, and aeronautical equipment, like gyroscopes and altimeters; laboratory apparatus, like balances, centrifuges, and sterilizers; and the largest category, laboratory and optical instruments. Also known as "analytical instruments," these devices enable researchers to measure precisely the nature of, and changes in, matter. Most of the customers for these instruments are in the petroleum, chemical, or pharmaceutical business. And all three categories of instruments are steadily purchased by the federal government. Electronic monitoring devices are another developing area of the scientific instrument field, and are finding their way into a variety of uses, from telecommunications to nuclear power plants.

Scientific instruments is one sector of the economy in which foreign competition will have a long way to go before it can catch up to us. In the meantime, it's more discoveries ahead!

TRADE ASSOCIATIONS

Instrument Society of America 919/549-8411
National Association of Photographic Manufacturers 914/698-7603
Photographic Manufacturers and Distributors Association 212/688-3520
Scientific Apparatus Makers Association 202/223-1360

PERIODICALS

Electronic Business
I.A.N. (Instrumentation and Control News)
INTECH
Review of Scientific Instruments

EASTMAN KODAK COMPANY

VITAL STATISTICS

Entry Level Salary for Sales: **$25,000**
Senior Level Salary for Sales: **$60,000–$70,000**

Benefits

medical/dental: **Yes**	child care: **No**
life insurance: **Yes**	retirement plan: **Yes**
disability: **Yes, short and long term**	savings investment plan: **Yes**
travel allowance: **N/A**	tuition assistance: **Yes**
company car: **Yes**	relocation assistance: **Yes**
profit sharing plan: **Yes**	memberships: **Smokenders**
stock purchase plan: **Yes**	**Weight Watchers**
	Aerobics class

Corporate Culture Index (1 = lowest, 10 = highest)

training:	**10**	security:	**9**
support:	**10**	mobility:	**10**
benefits:	**10**	intangibles:	**10**

Address: 343 State Street, Rochester, NY 14650
Contact: Operations Manager, Marketing Education Center; telephone 716/724-4000

Eastman Kodak ranked 28th on the 1987 Fortune 500 list with worldwide sales in excess of $13 billion, up 15% from 1986. Earnings in 1987 rose an impressive 192% to $2.1 billion!

George Eastman's first Kodak box camera, introduced in 1888, was as revolutionary as the invention that followed a year later: transparent Kodak roll film. And the twentieth century which began 11 years after that would never have been the same without Kodak.

Today, "Father Yellow," as Kodak is known internally, has blossomed into an international giant still profiting from the specialized "imaging" processes that Eastman developed. From Kodak copiers to film emulsions to lithium batteries, most company operations retain at least a distant connection to the photography business (its thriving chemicals business has its roots in photo-finishing, for example). The most glaring and recent exception was Kodak's $5 billion gamble to acquire the Sterling Drug Company, the largest non-oil takeover of 1987.

Kodak has been a leader in employee relations ever since George Eastman's day, when Eastman startled the world by making annual dividend wage payments to all employees. This legacy has led to a firm promotion-and-hire-from-within corporate policy and a generous benefits package that still promotes fierce loyalty and pride.

Liberal arts and/or technical degrees are preferred in nearly all applicants, on top of such interpersonal skills as an ability to function independently and within a team. The hiring process starts out with an objective "job competency assessment" of the prospective employee, but then moves on to judge more subjective criteria such as a candidate's leadership abilities. This is where such achievements as holding class office, outstanding performance in a summer job, or responsibilities in a student organization are scrutinized and taken into account.

Every new sales trainee retains "candidate" status until his or her promotion to territorial sales rep. The training program requires from two to eight months of instruction at Kodak's Marketing Education Center in Rochester, New York. The curriculum stresses a good deal of specialized product knowledge and lab work in addition to general sales and negotiating techniques. Two field trips with experienced sales personnel are a must before territories are assigned.

After graduation, the path up the corporate ladder runs from sales rep to district manager to national sales manager, on up to positions in marketing, assignments overseas, even to a stint on a vice president's personal staff. Successful reps are often asked back to school to be instructors, both an honor and a proven route to advancement. Still, this opportunity is frequently declined by successful reps who prefer to stay out in the field.

Trainees begin at $25,000. Experienced reps pull in an average of $60,000. Superstar members of the 110 Club (the top 10% of the sales force) qualify for generous bonuses in addition to commissions (up to 25% of base salary) and exotic "incentive travel" trips.

Reps are on the road most of the time, although overnight stays are infrequent, and they are expected to move up from rural territories to more complex metropolitan assignments. Expense accounts are provided, as well as access to top management via district sales managers and tech-support reps.

The sales staff is trained to install and demonstrate products, and to teach the end users of those products how to operate such office paraphernalia as photocopiers and image-processors. Reps sell mainly to retailers, wholesale distributors, and some individual customers, depending on the product line.

The 2500+ sales staff is supported effectively with advertising and sales promotion, typing, filing, research, and computer support. "Father Yellow," known the world over for its "Quality" image, explicitly prides itself on being a hotbed of aggressive, confident salesmanship, with a conservative, buttoned-down corporate atmosphere.

George Eastman would approve of Kodak's current benefits policies: the company spends 50 cents on benefits for every salary dollar. These include: medical and dental insurance, tuition assistance (restricted to various percentages on a list of "appropriate" courses), a company car, group life and long-term and short-term disability insurance, retirement/pension plans, profit sharing, a stock purchase plan, a 401K savings plan, fitness programs, and relocation expenses.

As Kodak moves with increasing assurance into foreign markets, helped by the softening dollar, and meets its Asian competitors head-on on its home turf, the effective marketing of a long line of products remains an impressive challenge, demanding a high degree of knowledge and experience. Kodak comes in number two (just below Johnson & Johnson) on *Fortune* magazine's list of Most Admired Corporations for "Community and Environmental Responsibility." Kodak's household brand-name, high-quality merchandise, and tip-top sales image all add up to a tough team to beat.

POLAROID CORPORATION

VITAL STATISTICS

Entry Level Salary for Sales: **$28,000–$32,000**
Senior Level Salary for Sales: **$46,000–$51,000**

Benefits

medical/dental: **Yes**	child care: **Spending accounts**
life insurance: **Yes**	retirement plan: **Yes**
disability: **Yes**	savings investment plan: **Yes**
travel allowance: **Yes**	tuition assistance: **Yes**
company car: **Yes**	relocation assistance: **Yes**
profit sharing plan: **Yes**	memberships: **Wellness program**
stock purchase plan: **No**	

Corporate Culture Index   (1 = lowest, 10 = highest)

training:	**8**	security:	**9**
support:	**9**	mobility:	**9**
benefits:	**10**	intangibles:	**10**

Address: 549 Technology Square, Cambridge, MA 02139
Contact: Personnel; telephone 617/577-3302

Polaroid designs, manufactures, and markets products mainly in the instant image processing field. In 1987 sales topped $1.7 billion. Polaroid ranks 211th on the Fortune 500 list and is also listed among *Fortune*'s Most Admired Corporations.

In 1928 Harvard undergraduate Edwin H. Land invented a way to polarize light that is still the basis for "polaroid" sunglasses. Twenty years later, Land brought out the world's first instant picture camera. In the four decades since 1948, the company has consistently ranked first in instant photography and second (behind Kodak) in camera and film sales.

In recent years, Polaroid has been forced to respond to the maturing of its instant camera and film market. Its new Spectra series of cameras has lately revitalized this ailing sector while the successful litigation of a suit against Kodak for trying to copy Polaroid's instant-film technology has cleared the way for a near monopoly in this still potentially profitable market.

Polaroid, however, is wisely refusing to sit back. Its hottest new technological development is electronic imaging, a computer-aided process now mainly used for ultrasonic fetal tests, but one that has immense untapped commercial potential.

Polaroid was an early leader in sophisticated employee relations, launching subsidized child care back in 1971. The company has both maintained a competitive edge and kept its people happy by consistently offering both salaries and benefits at the leading edge in their class.

A first-year sales trainee earns between $28,000 and $32,000; an average senior sales executive can make from $46,000 to $51,000. Bonuses weigh in at between 15% and 20% of base salary, *sans* commission. Benefits include: medical and dental insurance, tuition assistance, a company car or car allowance, group life and disability insurance, a retirement/pension plan, profit sharing, a 401K savings plan, paid relocation expenses, and a wellness program.

Hiring criteria are strict. All new recruits must come armed with a college degree and a minimum of two years of "successful selling experience" for a Fortune 500 company. Training consists of six weeks of classroom instruction at corporate headquarters in Cambridge, Massachusetts, and ongoing on-the-job training with a trainer and a district sales manager in the field. The goal of the training program is to increase productivity and heighten the sales rep's confidence to sell in a competitive world.

Trainees learn different accounts and acquire standard sales skills and product knowledge (for six kinds of cameras, film, and video film).

The sales hierarchy begins at the MSR (Marketing Support/Service Rep), which leads to becoming a sales rep, then a district manager, national account manager, and so on, up to senior marketing and merchandising posts. Sales personnel are assigned to either the Consumer or the Industrial Division. Reps live in their territories, which makes for few overnights.

Reps are frequently called upon to demonstrate cameras, copiers, and other high-tech equipment. For example, selling high-end Polaroid image-processing equipment such as Freezeframe (a successful recent Polaroid product permitting video images to be instantly transferred to stills) requires an immense amount of specialized product knowledge, for which special training is needed.

Reps sell to a variety of markets: Mom & Pop stores, grocers, drugstores—anywhere and everywhere that John Q. Public is likely to pop in for some new instant film and maybe a new camera if the price is right. The sales uniform may be corporate and the atmosphere may be strictly "New England," but a Polaroid sales rep's job is fast-paced, at the cutting edge of dramatically evolving high-end technology. This is a fiercely product-driven company, and so long as the public keeps demanding Polaroid products—everything from instant cameras to film to complex, computerized instant-imaging—Polaroid will provide a superb line to sell. The current crop of senior executives has been widely credited with waking up yet another sleeping giant, streamlining cumbersome operations, and placing new emphasis on marketing and consumer research. With an all-electronic camera and a new high-density floppy disk under development, Polaroid will always mean something more than lightweight plastic shades.

3M (MINNESOTA MINING AND MANUFACTURING)

VITAL STATISTICS

Entry Level Salary for Sales: *$25,000*
Senior Level Salary for Sales: *$50,000*

Benefits

medical/dental: **Yes**
life insurance: **Yes**
disability: **Yes**
travel allowance: **Yes**
company car: **Yes**
profit sharing plan: **Yes**
stock purchase plan: **Yes**

child care: **No**
retirement plan: **Yes**
savings investment plan: **Yes**
tuition assistance: **Yes**
relocation assistance: **Yes**
memberships: **3M Club**

Corporate Culture Index   (1 = lowest, 10 = highest)

training: **9**
support: **9**
benefits: **10**

security: **9**
mobility: **9**
intangibles: **10**

Address: 3M Center, St. Paul, MN 55144-1000
Contact: Sales and Employee Resources; telephone 612/733-1110

3M ranks 37th on the Fortune 500 list. In 1987 it posted worldwide sales of more than $9.4 billion, an increase of 10% from 1986. 1987 profits were $918 million, up 18% from 1986.

3M is a major diversified manufacturing company operating in the U.S. and in 48 other countries as well. The company's businesses are organized into four sectors, based on the technologies and markets involved: Industrial and Electronic, Information and Imaging Technologies, Life Sciences, and Commercial and Consumer.

The Industrial and Electronic sector manufactures a variety of products ranging from pressure-sensitive tapes, abrasives, and specialty chemicals to electronic connectors. It serves a number of industrial markets (aerospace, packaging, food service, paper, and many others) worldwide. It relies on innovative technology, efficient manufacturing, and strong customer service for its consistent growth.

The Information and Imaging Technologies sector concentrates on three major areas: commercial graphics and audiovisuals, magnetic media, and imaging systems. The group develops technologies used in the processing of information and images. Its products include lithographic plates and films, X-ray films and screens, overhead projection systems, digital processing systems, and others. Hybrid systems match proprietary 3M materials with the latest in electronic technologies in such areas as medical diagnostics, computer systems, and publishing and printing.

The Life Sciences sector produces a range of materials such as pressure-sensitive adhesives, nonwoven materials, glasses, biomaterials, and many others. They are used by physicians, nurses, hospitals, emergency treatment centers, dentists, pharmacists, and veterinarians. The Commercial and Consumer sector products are used in homes and businesses all over the world, and include such brand-name items as "Post-It" notes and Scotch Magic transparent tape.

The driving force behind 3M's growth is its emphasis on product development. Fully 25% of its sales in 1987 was generated by products that came on the market in only the last five years. New technologies like microreplication (used in materials science for making diverse materials with new and valuable properties), and improvements on known technologies like nonwoven materials, help keep 3M in the forefront of all its market areas. In addition, 3M management keeps a tight rein on production costs. In 1987, 3M's cost of goods sold as a percentage of total sales declined to its lowest level since 1981. 3M is confident that its R&D and its structure, emphasizing individual responsibility and initiative, will add up to continued success.

With so many operating businesses, product lines, and markets, 3M is a company that encompasses many different kinds of selling. 3M reps generally do not sell to retailers but rather to wholesale distributors, such as large printers and their major suppliers in the publishing and printing end of 3M's business. In this instance, they are selling such products as lithographic plates, color proofing systems, graphic film materials, and the like. Territory size varies; it may be small, like a single urban area, or as large as several states. Overnight travel is rare, however. All told, 3M has about 3000 reps on the road selling its products. The company looks for sales reps who have a college degree, preferably in the sciences, engineering, marketing, business, or management. In some divisions, as in the one featured here—publishing and printing—a degree is not absolutely necessary if the candidate has good prior selling experience, and has knowledge of 3M products or of industries served by 3M.

Sales trainees receive formal classroom training at the St. Paul headquarters and on-the-job training in the field. The initial program lasts six months, with short courses in advanced selling later on. The program covers a mix of product knowledge, professional selling skills, analysis of markets, and territory management. Video taping is also used for role playing in order to learn how to deal with different kinds of sales calls and situations.

The advancement opportunities are very good for all 3M sales reps. One career ladder allows a rep to stay in sales and advance from rep to senior account rep to district sales manager. Reps may also elect to try for a career in general management, moving into positions in training, branch management, national account management, corporate marketing, and so on. Reps, of course, have the option to remain in the field selling, and many do.

Salaries for trainees are competitive with the industry the rep is selling in. For printing and publishing, this means a beginning salary of about $25,000, plus or minus a bit, depending on experience and education. Senior sales personnel can double that to around $50,000. Bonuses are also available, but they depend on individual performance and the division and product lines involved. Other benefits are good, including: medical, dental, and life insurance; disability and retirement plans; profit sharing and stock purchase plans; a 401K plan; tuition assistance; paid relocation expenses; and a company car.

The company also offers its reps good field support with excellent ad and promotion materials, administrative/clerical help when possible, and top-flight R&D to create new products and improve existing ones. Although reps often work alone, there is some team selling on major accounts and in other situations, with marketing providing close support for the reps in the field. Technical help is readily available when needed; reps can jump the chain of command whenever they feel the need to obtain specific information or help.

3M maintains a close-knit atmosphere, even though it operates in aggressive and competitive markets. Employees are on a first-name basis, but all, like the company, are goal-driven. 3M is a successful company, and it knows how to encourage and reward success.

PUBLISHING AND PRINTING

"Words, words, words." Hamlet's speech has never rung more true than today. Americans read more—more books, newspapers, magazines, newsletters—than ever before. Between sales and advertising revenues, the 53,000 printing and publishing firms across the country do nearly $130 billion in business annually and make up the sixth largest employment sector in American manufacturing. Theirs is a great success story, in a country in love with the printed word.

There is more to publishing than newspapers, books, and magazines. Commercial printers' shipments totaled $40 billion in 1987, in everything from annual reports and newsletters to menus and business cards. Business forms and greeting cards are whole industries in themselves. They have enjoyed an upswing in the past few years and in 1987 did business amounting to, respectively, $7 billion and $3 billion. And then there are the printers who produce phone books, maps, almanacs, clothing patterns, calendars, directories, and catalogues. This is one industry with more niches than you can count!

After sluggish times in the mid 1980s, newspapers are coming back. In 1987, total receipts came to $31 billion, 80% of which was from advertising and the rest from circulation. Circulation has been falling over the past few years, so today's newspapers must compete even harder with other media (network TV, radio, and cable TV) for advertising dollars. In recent years they have developed new products—like special targeted editions and promotional supplements—that take advantage of the unique advertising opportunities that they have to offer. Local suburban papers have been especially successful at attracting new advertisers.

Periodicals are growing, but more slowly than other media. In 1987, the periodicals business saw $17 billion in receipts. Half of that came from advertising revenues. The wave of the future in periodicals seems to be special-interest magazines that deal with health, fashion, sports, child-rearing, and computers; and regional consumer magazines that focus on women, the business community, and lifestyles. The more precisely targeted a magazine is, the more likely it is to attract advertisers. The interests of the baby-boomers, who are prime consumers of magazines, will determine the magazine trends of the future.

People bought $11 billion worth of books in 1987, up nearly 5% from the previous year. More than half of that was spent on the two mainstays of the industry, elementary school textbooks and hardcover trade books. (Trade books are the books we buy in bookstores, including adult and juvenile fiction and nonfiction.) Technical, scientific, and professional books account for nearly 20% of sales. Religious books, book clubs, reference works, and university presses account for the rest.

The book publishing business is going through some changes. Publishers may now require authors to submit their manuscripts in formats that are readable by machine, thus cutting down on production costs and shortening the process. The industry has seen lots of mergers, which have enabled companies to streamline and consolidate their production. This is especially significant because most publishers have no production facilities and, in the past, have had to contract out the actual printing.

With a growing, older population, the spread of higher education, and the nationwide rise in disposable income, the publishing business is looking toward a best-selling future.

TRADE ASSOCIATIONS

American Newspaper Publishers Association 703/620-9500
Association of American Publishers 212/689-8920
Magazine Publishers Association 212/752-0055

PERIODICALS

American Book Publishing Record
Editor and Publisher
Publishers Weekly

DOW JONES & COMPANY

VITAL STATISTICS

Entry Level Salary for Sales **$25,000+**
Senior Level Salary for Sales **$60,000+**

Benefits

medical/dental: **Yes**	child care: **Yes**
life insurance: **Yes**	retirement plan: **No**
disability: **Yes**	savings investment plan: **N/A**
travel allowance: **N/A**	tuition assistance: **Yes**
company car: **N/A**	relocation assistance: **Yes**
profit sharing: **Yes**	memberships: **Up to $200 toward**
stock purchase plan: **Yes, after**	**health club dues**
three years	

Corporate Culture Index (1 = lowest, 10 = highest)

training: **10**	security: **9**
support: **10**	mobility: **7**
benefits: **10**	intangibles: **10**

Address: World Financial Center, 200 Liberty Street, New York, NY 10281
Contact: Employee Relations; telephone 212/416-2484

Dow Jones & Company ranks 264th on the Fortune 500 list. In 1987 it posted sales of more than $1 billion, up 16% from 1986. Profits during that time, at $203 million, ran 11% ahead of 1986.

Dow Jones & Company is a major publisher of business news and information; among its well-known publications are *The Wall Street Journal* and *Barron's*. The company divides its business into five operating groups: The *Wall Street Journal*; the Information Services Group; Ottaway Newspapers, Inc.; Dow Jones Magazines; and Telerate, Inc.

The *Wall Street Journal* segment of Dow's business includes one of the nation's premier newspapers, concentrating on, but not limited to, the business and financial worlds. Because of its renowned business reporting and its high-quality, top-executive readership, the *Journal* brought in more than 6000 display advertisers in 1987. Its advertising base was further expanded by the *Journal's* geographic breakouts, which enable advertisers to reach readers within defined areas of the paper's four geographic regions. The paper maintained its ad lineage despite a steep falling off of its financial advertising due to the market crash in October 1987. For this and for their general excellence, Dow sales reps won *Sales & Marketing Management's* Sales Force of the Year award in their category. In bad times no less than in boom times, it seems that people look to the *Journal* for business news, a fact that is not lost on print advertisers looking for a dynamic, affluent market.

The Dow Jones Information Services Group provides instant world-wide business news and information through electronic publishing and the use of its extensive databases. News/Retrieval, the company's database publishing unit, had a 28% increase in revenue in 1987, reflecting its increasing acceptance as the preferred source of information among corporate executives.

Ottaway Newspapers, Inc., is Dow's community newspaper subsidiary, and it consists of some 22 newspapers published in 11 states. All told, the newspaper group garnered more than 90 state, regional, and wire service awards for journalism, photography, and marketing during 1987.

Dow Jones Magazines also increased its circulation and advertising lineage in 1987. For that year, single copy sales of *Barron's* rose 6%, exceeding the combined newsstand sales of competitors like *Business Week* and *Fortune*. The magazine is aimed at people who make their own investment decisions, and this market seems to be an expanding one. Dow's American Demographic, Inc., reports on demographic trends and consumer markets through a mix of magazines, books, and other media. It enjoyed a total sales gain of 41% in 1987.

Telerate, Inc., which is half-owned by Dow, is a leading supplier of a whole range of computerized financial information, including more than 60,000 video pages of quotations and other information on U.S. government securities, world money markets, foreign exchange, precious metals, energy markets, futures, and options, all offered to customers worldwide.

Selling at Dow Jones, especially at the *Journal*, the Dow segment featured here, involves selling advertising space primarily to major corporations and to ad agencies with clients interested in reaching Dow's high-level readership. Reps must know the demographics of the *Journal's* readership and be able to translate this into reasons why advertisers should spend their budgets on this publication. The business is now intensely competitive, particularly in view of the soft financial advertising market of recent years.

Dow looks for reps with at least a college degree and with some background in marketing, ad agency work, or media planning. The job calls for high energy, good analytical skills, social aplomb, and an ability to think on one's feet and make accurate decisions fast. New hires undergo a sort of apprenticeship rather than formal training. Trainees learn on the job in an almost tutorial situation with more experienced reps. There is a strong group interest in seeing newcomers succeed because incentives (commissions) are based on the sales group's meeting its quotas and goals. The existing sales force actually trains the new hires by showing them the ropes and guiding them through real-life situations. District managers are ultimately responsible for bringing the trainees along, and they accompany new reps on account calls until the reps feel comfortable in the job. Training is ongoing, but after about six months, the rep is generally ready to go out on his or her own. The *Journal* also offers some summer internship slots for get-acquainted purposes.

Territory size varies; it can be as large as West Texas or as compact as seven accounts in New York City. Reps spend all their time serving accounts, working alone but with good backup support from a well-organized, highly sophisticated corporation. Promotion and ad materials are slick and heavy, and the excellence of the publication itself keeps it well read and lavishly quoted by the movers and shakers in the business and government communities. Advancement opportunities are there, but reps not interested in management can find field work very rewarding.

Salaries for trainees average about $25,000; senior salespeople average about $60,000. Merit bonuses and group incentive payments add to this, making the job a highly desirable one. There is little turnover and few openings (only 60 reps in all). Long service with the company, especially in view of its stock purchase plan, can be extremely rewarding. Other benefits include: medical, dental, and life insurance; a disability plan; a profit sharing plan that acts as a retirement plan; a stock purchase plan (after three years); child care; partial health club payment; tuition assistance; paid relocation expenses; and a car allowance when necessary.

Dow Jones is a solid-gold company offering a fine career opportunity in selling. The atmosphere is warm, but a strict work ethic predominates. Reps with intelligence, drive, and strong egos will find the kind of challenge and excitement they're looking for at Dow.

THE
DUN & BRADSTREET
CORPORATION

VITAL STATISTICS

Entry Level Salary for Sales: **$22,000–$28,000**
Senior Level Salary for Sales: **$50,000–$100,000**

Benefits

medical/dental: **Yes**	child care: **No**
life insurance: **Yes**	retirement plan: **Yes**
disability: **Yes**	savings investment plan: **Yes**
travel allowance: **Yes**	tuition assistance: **Yes, 80%**
company car: **No**	relocation assistance: **Yes**
profit sharing plan: **Yes**	memberships: **On-site fitness**
stock purchase plan: **Yes**	**center**

Corporate Culture Index   (1 = lowest, 10 = highest)

training:	**9**	security:	**9**
support:	**8**	mobility:	**8**
benefits:	**9**	intangibles:	**9**

Address: 299 Park Avenue, New York, NY 10171
Contact: Human Resources; telephone 212/593-6800

The Dun & Bradstreet Corporation, a worldwide provider of information and services in financial areas, had sales of more than $3 billion in 1987, up 8% from 1986. Profits, at $392 million, were up 16% from 1986.

Dun & Bradstreet, through its various divisions, concentrates on providing products and services to meet the information needs of its customers and prospects worldwide. In today's fast-paced, global economy, knowledge—of markets, trends, preferences, credit ratings, demographics, and the like—is economic power, and the lack of it can be devastating. D&B's role is to research, collect, format, and disseminate the various kinds of information business executives must have to make crucial operating decisions. It also provides marketing services to different industries.

D&B increasingly relies on applying new technologies to make its products and services available to customers more rapidly, with higher levels of accuracy, and in easier-to-use formats. The customers themselves help shape new products and services through the suggestions they offer at such D&B-sponsored forums as its customer councils and user groups, research being the name of the game at D&B. The company divides its operations into three core segments: Business Information Services, Marketing Services, and Publishing.

The Business Information Services segment comprises eight operating divisions, of which Dun & Bradstreet Credit Services is the largest. It provides information on more than 9 million U.S. businesses through reports, reference works, and financial information services. The seven other divisions cover areas that include: international securities, economic and portfolio accounting, account marketing information, claims payment services, debt-management services, software systems, and others.

The Marketing Services segment comprises seven divisions, the largest being Donnelley Marketing. This company offers demographic and other direct marketing information services that help package-goods manufacturers, brokerage houses, insurance companies, magazine publishers, and banks to identify and reach their consumer markets. Other services provided by this segment include: marketing research to determine consumer response to products (TV shows included), information services for business-to-business marketers, administration of redeemable coupons, market information for high-tech industries, and circulation fulfillment for magazine publishers.

The Publishing segment comprises five operating divisions, the largest of which is the *Donnelley Directory*. This company compiles and publishes the Yellow Pages for more than 30 telephone companies. Other publications of this segment deal with such areas as: independent telephone directories (in western U.S.), an information-gathering group used by the Yellow Pages publications, transportation publications and services, and financial information and ratings of corporate and municipal obligations and issuers of commercial paper. In addition, D&B has a Corporate Resource Group whose units collect, maintain, and provide computerized information for all D&B operating divisions.

Hiring and training sales reps is a largely decentralized process at D&B. The sales field managers are the ones responsible for choosing new reps; they pick candidates whom they feel they need at a particular moment for a specific slot. Generally, D&B reps are college grads, preferably with a business background. Prior sales experience is not always necessary, but it is always helpful. Reps must have good social presence and excellent communications skills; after all, they will be dealing primarily with top company decision-makers (CEOs and the like).

D&B uses a more-or-less apprenticeship approach to train new reps. First, reps study an elaborate sales manual on their own, and then they receive several weeks of formal classroom training at Murray Hill, New Jersey. The bulk of their training, however, takes place in the field, where reps learn from other senior reps and their district managers. Training is continuous because of the many new products that D&B brings out every year; and as reps move into senior positions, they, in turn, help train new hires.

The sales territories vary in size, depending on density of accounts. Mostly, they cluster where large and medium-sized businesses have their headquarters, so there are few overnights. Reps call on decision-makers to show them how D&B's information and services can help them manage their companies more efficiently. Reps work alone, but they do have good backup support. D&B is not hung up on a strict hierarchical approach; reps with a problem can go to anybody in the company who may have the answer. Other support includes heavy ad and promotion materials, and, especially, constant development of new products and services.

Salaries vary from unit to unit. Average trainee salaries range from $22,000 to $28,000, while senior salespeople average from $50,000 to $100,000, again depending on division, location, and assignment. Compensation also includes a commission on sales, the amount of which depends on division, product, or service. Promotion opportunities are excellent; *all* managers come from the sales ranks. At D&B, promotion is based on sales ability. Such turnover as there is normally occurs in the first year or so of selling; after that D&B reps are generally doing so well they have little inclination to leave. Other benefits include: medical, dental, and life insurance; disability and retirement plans; a profit sharing plan (after one year); an investment plan; tuition assistance (80%); car and travel allowance; and paid relocation expenses.

D&B is an aggressive, sales-driven corporation that nevertheless is friendly (first-name basis) and very supportive. Because it deals with the top echelons of business managers and owners, it expects its reps to handle themselves with class and style and to show real expertise in their field. For this the company offers top compensation and excellent opportunities for a rewarding career.

McGRAW-HILL, INC.

VITAL STATISTICS

Entry Level Salary for Sales: **$20,000–$22,000**
Senior Level Salary for Sales: **$45,000**

Benefits

medical/dental: **Yes**	child care: **No**
life insurance: **Yes**	retirement plan: **Yes**
disability: **Yes**	savings investment plan: **N/A**
travel allowance: **Yes**	tuition assistance: **Yes, 80%**
company car: **Yes**	relocation assistance: **Yes**
profit sharing plan: **Yes**	memberships: **Weight Watchers**
stock purchase plan: **Yes**	**Smokenders**

Corporate Culture Index (1 = lowest, 10 = highest)

training:	**8**	security:	**9**
support:	**9**	mobility:	**9**
benefits:	**9**	intangibles:	**10**

Address: 1221 Avenue of the Americas, New York, NY 10020
Contact: Human Resources; telephone 212/512-4203

McGraw-Hill, Inc., ranks 211th on the Fortune 500 list. In 1987 it had sales of $1.7 billion, an increase of 11% from 1986. Profits at $165 million were up 7% from 1986.

McGraw-Hill, Inc., celebrated its 100th anniversary in 1988, while at the same time enjoying its sixteenth consecutive year of record highs in sales and earnings. It is a major publishing house that over the years has distinguished itself in every form of print media—trade books, texts, magazines, newsletters, trade reports, industry bulletins, and more. In addition, the company has moved along with the times into the world of computers, data processing systems, and global information systems. It defines its role as a provider of timely information to the business community, to professionals, to educators, and to the literate public. It is determined to meet the information needs of all these groups with state-of-the-art equipment managed by skilled analyzers.

In the mid 1980s, McGraw-Hill realized that its market, not the media it employs, should determine its organization. As a result, it undertook a reorganization that grouped all available media (print and electronic services, for instance) for a given market together. In this way, the company can bring a vast array of resources to bear on a single target or customer, for example, health care, transportation, business conditions, and the like. The idea is to manage the company as an immense gatherer and disseminator of information needed by many different groups and individuals.

As a book publisher, McGraw-Hill has maintained a reputation for excellence, innovation, and thoroughness. Its texts span the entire educational market from pre-school to post-doctorate, and the professional, reference, and home-study markets. McGraw-Hill recently dropped out of the trade book business, which was not large but did include some distinguished authors. In professional books, economics, politics, the sciences, business, and current events and trends, it remains a powerful and respected publisher.

The most stable segment of book publishing, however, is educational publishing. Most of the major successful book publishers in the U.S. are the ones with full educational lines, elhi (elementary–high school) to postgraduate. Reps in the educational market face a different set of problems from those of trade book reps. In educational publishing, the market is quite clearly defined; the numbers of students, subjects, curriculum requirements, and so on are known beforehand by all the players. It is the text that best meets all the required standards and still offers a little something more that is accepted and ordered by the schools for their students. Here McGraw-Hill offers tremendous support to its reps. It consistently turns out educational materials at all levels and in all media that are of top-notch quality, on target, and competitively priced. It is also very efficient in getting promotional materials and other support to reps promptly.

Reps in the college market (also called travelers) face still another situation. They call on the colleges and junior colleges in their territories, visiting faculty members and trying to persuade them to adopt McGraw-Hill texts for their classes. It's an indirect kind of selling because they do not sell to the end user, the student, but to the faculty. They, like their counterparts in elhi, must know their own products thoroughly, as well as those of the competition. They must also be well versed in their subject areas because they will be talking and selling to experts, and they must show that they are aware of the latest developments in the field. Part of their duties involves spotting potential new authors in their field and reporting back to McGraw-Hill on them and on any new developments in their disciplines. This can also lead to advancement up the corporate ladder, as travelers frequently move into the home office as sponsoring editors.

McGraw-Hill reps are generally college graduates, with just about all types of majors. Teaching experience is a real plus, particularly in the elhi areas, and prior sales experience is very helpful also. Reps should be interested in education and education problems in the elhi market and academically oriented in the college market. Training for new reps is relatively short. A ten-day program held in conjunction with the annual sales conference constitutes a rep's initial exposure to the company and the industry. On-the-job training figures most prominently in bringing new reps up to speed. There is a strong emphasis on product knowledge and on learning the concerns of the market the new rep will be servicing.

Salaries for sales trainees average from about $20,000 to $22,000, with senior salespeople averaging about $45,000. Bonuses are given depending on division and product line, and they can be quite substantial, matching or even going above base salary.

Other benefits include medical, dental, and life insurance; disability and retirement plans; stock purchase and profit sharing plans; tuition assistance up to 80%; and a travel allowance. McGraw-Hill is very sales conscious, and many of the top executive positions are filled by former sales reps. Reps may go into editorial, or they may stay in marketing as they move up the ladder.

McGraw-Hill's atmosphere is very corporate; there are procedures manuals and they are followed. It has a solid-gold reputation for quality and it listens to, supports, and promotes its reps.

TIME, INC.

VITAL STATISTICS

Entry Level Salary for Sales: **$24,000–$25,000**
Senior Level Salary for Sales: **$55,000**

Benefits

medical/dental: **Yes**
life insurance: **Yes**
disability: **Yes, short and long term**
travel allowance: **Yes**
company car: **Yes**
profit sharing plan: **Yes**
stock purchase plan: **Yes**

child care: **Yes**
retirement plan: **Yes**
savings investment plan: **Yes**
tuition assistance: **Yes, 75%**
relocation assistance: **Yes**
memberships: **Yes, 50% of fitness program is paid for Smokenders Weight Watchers**

Corporate Culture Index   (1 = lowest, 10 = highest)

training: **1**
support: **9**
benefits: **10**

security: **9**
mobility: **9**
intangibles: **10**

Address: Rockefeller Center, New York, NY 10020
Contact: Personnel; telephone 212/522-2507

Time, Inc., ranks 104th on the Fortune 500 list. In 1987 it had sales of over $4 billion, up 11% over 1986. Profits, at $250 million, were down 34%, but this reflects large nonrecurring gains in 1986, not poor performance in 1987.

Time, Inc., is a communications giant with four core businesses: the Magazine Group (the heart of the enterprise), the Book Group (the nation's third largest book publisher), Home Box Office, Inc. (HBO, the video programming unit), and American Television and Communications Corporations (ATC, the cable television unit).

The Magazine Group underwent a major restructuring and cost-reduction campaign in the mid 1980s, resulting in a much leaner and more efficiently run group. In 1987 its earnings jumped nearly 75%, despite a soft advertising market. It still claims some of the most prestigious and popular magazines in the country among its publications: *Time, Sports Illustrated, People, Fortune, Life, Adweek, McCall's, Working Woman, Parenting,* and many others. In addition, in the fall of 1987, the Magazine Group introduced the Maximum Advertising Exposure Plan (MAX Plan) to increase its market share and improve service to its customers. The plan is designed to reward advertisers who raise Time's share of their advertising spending by offering them credits toward additional ad pages. And the plan is working, generating new advertising business for the Magazine Group.

In 1986 the Book Group acquired Scott, Foresman and Company, a major educational publisher of elhi materials, and thus became the third-ranked publisher in the U.S. It now boasts a full educational line, having merged the college division of Little, Brown with Scott, Foresman. The group remains a significant trade book publisher in its own right (Time-Life Books; Little, Brown; Oxmoor House) and a major book distributor (Book-of-the-Month Club, History Book Club).

Home Box Office creates programming for its video subscribers and is the creative side of Time, Inc.'s, presence in the TV cable industry and in films. ATC is the management arm of the company's cable interests, and it and its managed affiliates count 3.7 million customers in 32 states —and ATC is growing. No one at Time, Inc., is ignoring the magazine or book units, but the bets are on the cable operations for future growth. Michael J. Fuchs, chairman and CEO of HBO, called his unit "the most exciting business Time has."

For those interested in a career in communications—in sales or any other aspect of the industry—Time, Inc., would seem to have it all: a top-flight line-up of magazines, a major book publisher of both trade and educational texts, movie and TV programming, and a cable TV network. There is every place in the world to go at Time, Inc., and with talent and a little luck, the sky's the limit. The downside, though, is that all the sharp people in communications think the same thing, too. Competition for jobs is tough, with 40 applications for every opening at *Sports Illustrated*, for instance.

Time, Inc., looks only for the top people. Candidates for sales jobs in the magazine group need to be college graduates *and* have a successful prior track record selling advertising space. Selling in the magazine unit means primarily selling space to potential advertisers, including some of the largest corporations in the most basic industries in the country—automobiles, tobacco, pharmaceuticals, distilleries, communications, hospitality and travel, and so on. Space reps must know the markets of their advertisers and the strategies of their advertising companies and how Time, Inc.'s, publications fit in.

Training in this unit is relatively informal at present. There is a corporate training program, but it was not being used at press time because it's being changed. In any case, much of the training is of the on-the-job variety, concentrating on the needs of the particular magazine the new hire is working for. This training is close, usually one-on-one, and intensive. New hires, perhaps because they are experienced and carefully selected, are not given a lot of time to get up to speed. Quick learners are the ones who make it at Time magazines. Being bright, articulate, and an achiever counts, too. Time wants reps who can be promoted within the company; it looks for publisher material in every sales rep it hires.

Sales reps in the Book Group face situations similar to the reps of any book publisher. At Scott, Foresman, they call on public and private schools from elementary levels through college, in direct competition with all the other educational publishers. At Time-Life Books, sales reps and marketing people hoe the same tough row that other trade publishers work. But Time, Inc., because of its size and diversity, can offer really extraordinary support to its sales reps in every group. For product promotions, there are elaborate media kits, A/V presentations, and the like. New products (new magazines), new ad rate plans, bonus plans like the MAX Plan, and special sections in current publications are all part of sales support at Time, Inc. So is client entertainment, with sports, meals, and special events—all available to help boost sales. Research, too, is sophisticated and elaborate, with a thorough analysis of primary and secondary demographics of the magazines' targeted populations.

Salaries at Time, Inc., average from about $24,000 to $25,000 for sales trainees to about $55,000 for senior salespeople. Sales reps also receive a commission and management receives a bonus. Other benefits are excellent: medical, dental, and life insurance; disability and pension plans; a credit union savings plan; tuition assistance; and a company car.

Time, Inc., is an aggressive, high-status, fast-paced company to work for. Turnovers result almost entirely from promotion, and the competition is fierce.

RECREATION, LEISURE, AND SPORTING GOODS

"The business of America," President Coolidge used to say, "is business." Increasingly, however, the business of America is fun. At least it seems that way to the recreation and leisure business, which today is enjoying a boom. Capitalizing on the notion that all work and no play makes Jack a dull boy, this industry sees to it that people enjoy their expanding leisure time to the fullest. The companies that we will be looking at deal primarily with sporting goods, both outdoor, like skiing and fishing, and indoor, like billiards and bowling.

Nationwide, the most significant shift in recreation in recent years has been away from less active, spectator activities and toward more active pursuits. Interestingly, older people are engaging in more recreation nowadays and young people in less. Whether this trend will continue into the future remains to be seen.

Another curious thing about this business is that, as one analyst has put it, "there are three markets for sports equipment: consumers who will use the equipment, those who might use it, and those who will never use it." At most, only half of the people who buy sports equipment actually make use of it.

The most popular sporting items in the country are fishing rods and bicycles, followed by jogging and tennis shoes, bowling balls, tennis balls, camping gear, hunting rifles, and golf equipment. Snow and ski equipment, weights, and racquetball equipment bring up the rear.

Sales of key sporting goods—equipment for fishing, golf, gymnastics, exercise, archery, bowling, billiards, tennis, winter sports, and team sports—totaled nearly $4 billion in 1987, an increase of nearly 2%. Imports, mostly from Taiwan and South Korea, have been flooding the market, and there has been a decrease in employment. At the same time, productivity has increased and manufacturers have worked to streamline and position themselves for the future.

Many companies have diversified and produce a wide range of sporting goods. For example, the Coleman Company manufactures and sells camping equipment, sailboats, scuba gear, airguns, bows and arrows, and trailers (not to mention lamps, air conditioners, and lawn mowers).

The industry is loosely organized, and sales reps will end up dealing with just about anybody who buys and sells significant quantities of sporting goods—wholesalers, department stores, sporting goods stores, hotels, camps, billiard halls, or bowling alleys. With more discretionary income around and greater health and fitness awareness in the air, a career in sporting goods will probably go the distance.

TRADE ASSOCIATIONS

American Recreational Equipment Association 614/363-9715
National Industrial Recreational Association 312/562-8130
National Sporting Goods Association 312/439-4000
Sporting Goods Manufacturers Association 305/842-4100

PERIODICALS

Recreation Management
Selling Sporting Goods
Sporting Goods Dealer

BRUNSWICK CORPORATION

VITAL STATISTICS

Entry Level Salary for Sales: **$22,000**
Senior Level Salary for Sales: **$50,000**

Benefits

medical/dental: **Yes**	child care: **No**
life insurance: **Yes**	retirement plan: **401K**
disability: **Yes**	savings investment plan: **Employee**
travel allowance: **Yes**	**Stock**
company car: **Yes**	**Ownership**
profit sharing plan: **Yes. Company**	**Plan**
gives stock to	tuition assistance: **Yes**
employees	relocation assistance: **Yes**
stock purchase plan: **Yes**	memberships: **No**

Corporate Culture Index   (1 = lowest, 10 = highest)

training:	**9**	security:	**9**
support:	**9**	mobility:	**7**
benefits:	**9**	intangibles:	**10**

Address: One Brunswick Plaza, Skokie, IL 60077
Contact: Corporate Headquarters; telephone 312/470-4700

Brunswick Corporation ranks 140th on the Fortune 500 list. In 1987 it enjoyed sales of more than $3 billion, up an enormous 80% from 1986. Profits, at $169 million, were up 53% from 1986.

Brunswick Corporation was founded in 1845 by John Brunswick as a manufacturer of billiard tables. Today, the corporation is a major recreation/ leisure company with important interests in defense/aerospace and industrial products. These lines of business are grouped into five segments: marine, recreation products, leisure services, defense, and industrial products. Nine operating divisions actually carry out the business of the corporation.

The marine segment comprises the Mercury Marine, U.S. Marine, and Sea Ray divisions. Mercury Marine is the largest and most profitable marine engine company in the world, producing both MerCruiser stern drive engines and Mercury and Mariner outboard motors. U.S. Marine is now the largest manufacturer of fiber glass pleasure boats in the world. Sea Ray has 30 years' experience in power boat making and long-established dealership organization.

The recreation products segment encompasses the Zebco and the Brunswick divisions. Zebco is the world's leading producer of fishing reels, reel/rod combinations, and electric trolling motors. The Brunswick Division is the leading manufacturer of bowling equipment for bowling centers and consumers, and also, as part of its heritage, of billiard tables. The leisure services segment comprises the Brunswick Recreation Centers division, which builds and operates bowling centers around the country. Defense comprises a division that supplies specialty items, such as fire and chemical agent detectors/alarms and tactical aircraft decoy systems, to the Army and Navy. The industrial products segment comprises the Technetics and Industrial Products divisions. Technetics manufactures products for aerospace and water filtration, as well as golf club shafts. The Industrial Products division serves two major markets: transportation (air conditioner components for railway and rapid transit manufacturers) and energy (control systems and components and tank storage equipment).

Brunswick's management style for these very disparate companies and divisions is quite sensibly one of decentralization. Decision-making is delegated to the lowest possible level, on the theory that this allows the corporation to respond more readily to changes in the marketplace and to better focus its resources on money-producing areas such as product design and development.

Although the recreation/leisure segments are sensitive to swings in the economy, Brunswick nevertheless believes that demographics are on its side and will remain so until the end of the century. This means that the marine and recreation areas—the core of Brunswick's business—have excellent growth potential. The company is also promoting these lines with a major television ad campaign. In all business areas, Brunswick is determined to increase productivity, lower operating costs, and focus even more sharply on its high-return markets.

Training for Brunswick reps in the recreation/leisure segments, by far the company's major breadwinners, is relatively short and intense. The initial program lasts a week and is given four times a year. It concentrates on selling skills, business management, and product knowledge. Brunswick reps are, particularly in the bowling-center area, business partners of their customers. For instance, the product a rep sells may be a bowling alley that costs $800,000. Reps in this segment of the business must know about real estate, law, and finance. They may have to help close a big real estate deal, so they also have to know about finance charges, payback, zoning, and so on. Likewise, in the marine segment, reps learn about pre-rigging U.S. Marine and Sea Ray boats with Mercury engines to deliver a complete, high-performance package to dealers.

Brunswick also runs meetings and management seminars for bowling alley owners and managers to help them make their businesses more profitable and to promote Brunswick products. The bulk of a rep's training, though, occurs in on-the-job experience. Brunswick looks for sales trainees with maturity and drive. Prior selling experience is helpful, but not necessary, nor is any technical knowledge. The company will teach whatever is required on the job. Reps may spend a maximum of 40% of their time on overnights on the road, and they also may have to relocate often. "How will your spouse like North Dakota?" is a stress question asked at the pre-employment interview.

Brunswick in turn offers much support to its reps. It is planning heavy media advertising of its products and companies, it helps with administrative/clerical chores, and it provides every kind of backup assistance a rep could need. For instance, it will fly a potential bowling alley operator to another location in order to see a Brunswick alley in operation.

Reps earn a salary plus commission, the total depending on the division and product line. Average starting salary for sales reps is around $22,000; senior sales executives' salaries average around $50,000. Other benefits include: medical and dental insurance plans, group life insurance, disability and retirement plans, a travel allowance, tuition assistance, a stock purchase plan, a profit sharing plan (Brunswick gives stock to employees, too), paid moving expenses, and a company car.

Brunswick does like to promote from within, but its sales staff tends to prefer selling. Turnover is low, only about 5%. The atmosphere at Brunswick is very friendly, but the market is very competitive and reps need to take a dynamic and aggressive posture to be successful. Brunswick is a stable company with a long history of quality products and services. It expects to stay that way.

THE COLEMAN COMPANY, INC.

VITAL STATISTICS

Entry Level Salary for Sales: **$22,800**
Senior Level Salary for Sales: **$35,000–$40,000 (with bonus, $55,000)**

Benefits

medical/dental: **Yes**
life insurance: **Yes**
disability: **Yes**
travel allowance: **Yes**
company car: **Yes**
profit sharing plan: **Yes**
stock purchase plan: **Yes**

child care: **No**
retirement plan: **Yes**
savings investment plan: **N/A**
tuition assistance: **Yes**
relocation assistance: **Yes**
memberships: **Contributes up to $400 toward YMCA dues**

Corporate Culture Index   (1 = lowest, 10 = highest)

training: **8**
support: **9**
benefits: **10**

security: **9**
mobility: **8**
intangibles: **10**

Address: 250 North St. Francis Avenue, Wichita, KS 67202
Contact: Group One Personnel; telephone 316/832-6145

The Coleman Company, Inc. ranks 428th on the Fortune 500 list. In 1987 it had sales of more than $598 million, an increase of 19% from 1986. Profits, at more than $19 million, were up 11% from 1986.

The Coleman Company began operations in 1900 as the distributor of a remarkable new lamp. Soon the Coleman lamp became world-famous and established the firm as a manufacturer of quality products, a position it holds to this day. At present, Coleman derives its sales from seven business units. Group One, the major revenue producer, offers a line of outdoor and camping equipment including: lanterns, camp stoves, catalytic heaters, tents, sleeping bags, Peak 1 brand back-packing equipment, canoes, fishing boats, inflatables, and more.

The next highest revenue producer is the Home and Heating and Air Conditioning Group, which sells furnaces, air conditioners, heat pumps, refrigerant coils, and components. The Recreational Vehicle Products Group offers fold-down camping trailers, awnings, and air conditioners. Water Recreation Operations produces water ski boats, fishing boats, water skis, sailboats, and scuba equipment. The Hunting & Shooting Sports Group sells airguns, hunting and optical accessories, archery equipment, and hunting knives. The Associated Group markets Coleman electric generators, riding lawn mowers, and high-intensity lighting. Finally, International Operations handles exports from North America and the manufacture of certain Coleman product lines abroad.

Coleman at present conducts two main lines of business. The recreational line, especially Group One, forms the core of the company's business. Coleman markets these products through both broad and selective distribution channels. The broad distribution channel uses mass merchandisers as the retail outlet, and the results have been excellent. The selective distribution channel utilizes individually owned and operated retail outlets. It is the channel that handles the widest range of the Coleman recreational line, including marine products, hunting products, light vehicles, and lawn mowers. This channel, too, has had good results and is expected to do well in the future.

Coleman sells its line of air conditioning and heating products through original equipment manufacturers, distributors, and dealers. This segment of the business fell slightly behind a few years ago, owing primarily to the slow pace of the manufactured housing industry, a segment of the industry in which Coleman has a 50% market share. This points up the only reason for caution in assessing Coleman's future performance. The recreational/ leisure time and housing industries for which Coleman produces are particularly vulnerable to swings in the business cycle. If the economy slows up or goes into a downturn, these industries are generally the first to be hit. So far, however, Coleman has felt no backlash from the October 1987 stock market crash and sees its prospects as very good, fueled by strong consumer spending.

Coleman looks for college graduates with a variety of majors, but it requires selling experience, too, on the retail or wholesale level. Coleman looks for new reps in their mid twenties who are attractive, bright, and articulate. Potential new hires must pass a series of tests that examine personality and mechanical aptitude. Successful candidates receive 12 weeks of training—two weeks in headquarters in Wichita, Kansas, and ten weeks in the field in on-the-job training. The two weeks at headquarters consist of one week in the repair center and one week in the office, rotating through all the departments. After that, the new hire is assigned to a territory.

Territories vary in size according to population density; they may be as large as four states or as small as Los Angeles. In any case, reps spend most of their time on the road, visiting their accounts, which include just about anyone in their territories who sells sporting goods and camping equipment. Reps do not normally demonstrate Coleman products, but they must be able to introduce their accounts to new products, showing how they perform and why they perform so well. Coleman supports its reps with good promotional materials, help with administrative/clerical chores, and continued product development research.

Salaries for sales trainees average around $23,000; senior sales executives average around $35,000 to $40,000. Reps earn bonuses in addition to their salaries, and the bonuses vary according to the sales of the Coleman group and according to the product line. They can, however, amount to from 30% to 50% of total salary. Other benefits include: a full medical and dental insurance plan; group life insurance; disability, retirement, and stock purchase plans; a company car and travel allowance; and a 100% tuition assistance plan. There is also an allowance for YMCA memberships for health purposes, and employees can purchase Coleman equipment at a discount.

Coleman had a reputation for paternalism, but, as a publicly owned company, it is losing some of that aspect. It still is a *caring* company, though, both for its employees and for its customers. For employees, the atmosphere is warm and friendly, and reps and their families are treated to employee clubs, a boys' club, and sports leagues. For the customer, Coleman offers a gold-plated product line that consumers can always rely on.

OUTBOARD MARINE CORPORATION

VITAL STATISTICS

Entry Level Salary for Sales: **$25,000**
Senior Level Salary for Sales: **$45,000**

Benefits

medical/dental: **Yes**	child care: **No**
life insurance: **Yes**	retirement plan: **Yes**
disability: **Yes**	savings investment plan: **N/A**
travel allowance: **Yes**	tuition assistance: **Yes**
company car: **Yes**	relocation assistance: **Yes**
profit sharing plan: **No**	memberships: **No**
stock purchase plan: **No**	

Corporate Culture Index   (1 = lowest, 10 = highest)

training:	**6**	security:	**8**
support:	**7**	mobility:	**8**
benefits:	**8**	intangibles:	**8**

Address: 100 Sea-Horse Drive, Waukegan, IL 60085
Contact: Industrial Relations; telephone 312/689-6100

Outboard Marine Corporation ranks 269th on the Fortune 500 list. In 1987 it enjoyed sales of $1.2 billion, up 33% from 1986; profits in 1987 were more than $61 million, an all-time high.

Outboard Marine Corporation (OMC), incorporated in 1936, is primarily engaged in the development, manufacturing, and marketing of powered equipment for leisure-time purposes. The bulk of the company's revenues comes from the marine sector, which includes OMC marine power products and OMC boat group. The marine power products group features a line of high-performance marine engines headed by the OMC Cobra stern-drive line (inboard-outboard), Evinrude and Johnson outboards, and OMC Sea Drive outboards. The boat group builds and markets a line of recreational power boats. It is made up of five boat manufacturers OMC acquired: Four Winns Boats, Lowe Boats, Seaswirl Boats, Stratos Boats, and Sunbird Boats. These specific boat builders were chosen to give the company a product line that would "encompass all of the most popular types of boats and offer models over a wide range of price points."

The power lawn products group features Lawn-Boy and Sensation brands rotary lawn mowers, Lawn-Boy lawn and garden tractors, and Lawn-Boy riding mowers. Also available are garden tillers and snow throwers. The turf care equipment group includes Brouwer turf equipment (sod harvesting equipment), and Ryan and Cushman turf care equipment. In addition, OMC's international group is pursuing sales of its products vigorously in international markets. The marine power products were the most successful in the international market in 1987, and the market penetration of outboards improved in nearly all major market areas.

Future plans involve aggressive marketing of OMC's boat, motor, and trailer packages, which were introduced in mid 1987. Also, the company plans to move strongly into the "packaged" segment of the boat market—pre-rigged boats, which are new boats with motors already rigged in them. Dealers like the packages because they relieve the dealership of most of the work of rigging a new boat. Consumers, especially the increasingly important first-time boat buyer, like them for their convenience. OMC, however, is also perfectly positioned to service experienced boat owners who want to select boat and engine themselves because the company offers a full line of recreational boats and marine engines suitable for every purpose and pocketbook.

With continued efforts to monitor product manufacturing costs and prospects for the incredible boom of potential first-time boat buyers as the baby boom generation matures into middle age, OMC feels confident about future profitability. The only problem may be that the recreational market that OMC serves is vulnerable to downturns in the economy which hit recreational sales first. Still, the company felt no adverse effects from the October 1987 stock market crash and economic forecasting holds that consumer spending will remain high. OMC needs only to get its products to its potential buyers.

This is the job of the 70 to 90 OMC sales reps. Because of the nature of the product and the selling situation, OMC sales reps are not exposed to a long or intensive training program. Prospective reps must pretty much have a feel for the products and the lifestyles of those who buy them. An affinity for sun and sea and wind in the face is more important than formal training programs. OMC uses an outside group to produce trade shows for dealers and reps alike, concentrating on product knowledge and the introduction of new products and on revving up motivation in both reps and dealers. The shows take place at dealerships around the country and last one to three days. These are complemented by some on-the-job training.

OMC looks for reps who are college graduates and who have some knowledge of outboard motors and boats. Sales experience is very helpful and technical knowledge is useful, too. Communication skills and selling ability, though, outweigh technical ability. Most of the customers OMC reps call on are authorized dealers of OMC equipment. They know the line and they know their customers. The rep's job is to introduce new products to the dealers and show them how these products will enhance their business. Reps cover a large territory (typically a state), so they spend a good deal of time on the road (about 30% overnights), working mostly on their own.

OMC supports reps with good promotional and advertising material, clerical/administrative help when possible, and a steady stream of new products, new lines, and new packaging and marketing ideas. For instance, the company has recently launched a new retail venture, Top of the Dock stores, located in specific high-volume shopping malls where the demographics match the population type for first-time boat buyers.

Salaries for sales trainees average around $25,000 plus bonus. Senior sales personnel average around $45,000 plus bonus. The bonus is based on meeting company or group goals, and it can be as high as 33% of total salary. Other benefits include: medical and dental insurance plans, group life insurance, disability and retirement plans, a travel allowance, a leased company car, paid moving expenses, and tuition assistance. The company does like to promote from within, and a rep could move into a district manager or marketing position at the Waukegan, Illinois, headquarters or even into top management. The turnover rate is low at OMC, indicating that reps who find a niche here like it, and tend to stay.

The company is "outdoorsy," as one would expect from its product line and customer base. It is very customer-conscious, and in recent years has acquired several companies that will enhance its ability to service its dealers and its end users. Still, it is a competitive industry, and OMC's reps need to be aggressive and innovative.

RUBBER PRODUCTS

Rubber is one of those things that don't seem very glamorous, but it's a product that our world just couldn't do without. Automobile tires, fire hoses, surgical gloves, running shoes—all would be unthinkable if it weren't for that strange bouncy substance.

Tires for cars, trucks, and buses account for 85% of the total value of the rubber industry, nearly $11 billion. They are bought by farmers, car manufacturers, aviation companies, makers of heavy machinery, and some smaller industries.

In the past 25 years, the United States' share of world tire production has declined by 20%. That still leaves the United States way out front, however, with nearly 30%, far ahead of its closest competitors in Western Europe, Africa, and Asia. The U.S. auto tire industry has been hurt by foreign competition as well as by the popularity of long-lasting radial tires. Several factors, however, are working in its favor. Increased gas mileage and lower fuel prices are encouraging people to drive more and go through tires more quickly. As suburbia spreads, people will be driving longer distances each day; and as demand for motor vehicles increases with population growth, so will demand for tires.

Rubber and plastic footwear is a half-billion-dollar-a-year industry. Demand for American products here has fallen in recent years, to be replaced by Far Eastern products, while prices have basically stayed the same. Effective salesmanship will play a key role in determining the futures of

American companies in this sector because success will depend on accurately and effectively targeting interested consumers.

American companies sell $2 billion worth of rubber hose and belting (for conveyor belts) annually. These products are used in agriculture, mining and manufacture, power transmissions, appliances, and garden, industrial, and fire hoses. The fortunes of this sector of the rubber industry are very closely tied to those of the manufacturers it services. Growth over the next few years should be steady but slow.

Nearly 1300 companies manufacture a wide array of rubber products: sponge and foam goods, floor and wall coverings, industrial compounds, and fabrics. The largest 25 plants account for one-third of the total output of these miscellaneous rubber products, some $3 billion.

The AIDS crisis has resulted in a skyrocketing demand for rubber surgical gloves. Hospital nurses will sometimes go through nearly a dozen pairs a day. Prices for the latex from which these gloves are made (most of which comes from the Far East) have risen astronomically, from $600 to $2200 a ton in the past year. This has generated widespread concern that some manufacturers may be taking advantage of the health hazard to gouge the hospitals who are the main consumers of gloves. In any case, it takes years for a latex-producing tree to grow, so the shortage, the high prices, and profits will probably be around for some time to come.

TRADE ASSOCIATIONS

National Tire Dealers and Retreaders Association 202/789-2300
Rubber Manufacturers Association 202/682-4800

PERIODICALS

Dealer News
Modern Tire Dealer
Rubber and Plastic News
Rubber World
Tire Review

COOPER TIRE & RUBBER COMPANY

VITAL STATISTICS

Entry Level Salary for Sales: **$23,000**
Senior Level Salary for Sales: **$50,000+**

Benefits

medical/dental: **Medical, but no dental**
life insurance: **Yes**
disability: **Yes, short and long term**
travel allowance: **No**
company car: **Yes**
profit sharing plan: **Yes**
stock purchase plan: **Yes**

child care: **No**
retirement plan: **Yes**
savings investment plan: **N/A**
tuition assistance: **Yes**
relocation assistance: **Yes**
memberships: **Pays half of YMCA dues**

Corporate Culture Index   (1 = lowest, 10 = highest)

training: **7**
support: **8**
benefits: **9**

security: **9**
mobility: **8**
intangibles: **9**

Address: Lima & Western Avenues, Findlay, OH 45839-0550
Contact: Salaried Personnel; telephone 419/423-1321

Cooper Tire & Rubber Company ranks 402nd on the Fortune 500 list. In 1987 it posted record sales of more than $600 million, up 15% from 1986. Record profits, at $31 million, were up 33% from 1986.

Cooper Tire & Rubber Company was founded in 1914 as a manufacturer of tire patches, tire cement, and tire repair kits. Today it is a major manufacturer and marketer of rubber products for consumer and industrial use. Its chief products are automobile and truck tires, inner tubes, reinforced hose, highly technical rubber-to-metal bonded parts, and complex molded and extruded rubber products. Since its formation, the company has specialized in the replacement market of the automotive business, but some of its customized rubber products are used by manufacturers of small appliances and business machines, and construction companies.

Cooper Tire markets its products directly to automobile manufacturers, independent tire distributors and dealers, large automobile parts retail chains, and industrial manufacturers. It services these accounts through its network of distribution centers, which are managed so efficiently that some of them are able to offer customers a 24-hour turnaround time on their orders. The success of Cooper Tire's operation depends to a large extent on two factors: the quality of its products and the quality of the service it provides.

Tires are not the most exciting things in the world to buy, and few people really think about them until they need them. Then car owners look for certain criteria. Price is important to them, but more so is quality. People use their cars constantly and they want to drive with confidence. Usually they want the same kind, style, and construction—if not necessarily the same brand—as their old tires. Cooper Tire supplies its dealers with just this kind of product. Its tires represent the highest level of quality control in the tire-making business. Cooper also offers its dealers—and the general public—a full line of tire products: passenger tires (radials, belted, mud and snow specialty tires, in all styles and prices), light and medium truck tires of all kinds, and a complete inner-tube line. This, combined with its excellent service, makes Cooper Tire a small but feisty competitor of the other giants in the tire and rubber field.

The service part of Cooper Tire's operations is crucial to its well-being. By providing its customers—manufacturers, distributors, and dealers—with quality products on time and at competitive prices, the company has been working hard to make itself part of its customers' profit picture. One of the primary goals of a Cooper Tire territory sales manager is to establish an excellent rapport with his or her accounts. The reps are constantly on the road, calling on accounts and helping them increase their sales of tires and tire products. The company supports their efforts with a full complement of customer service and customer relations experts to expedite orders and help dealers with any of their customer problems. In addition, several times a year, Cooper Tire holds intensive seminars at headquarters in Findlay, Ohio, for authorized Cooper Tire dealers and their employees. Topics include any new government regulations that affect the tire market, sales techniques to meet the growing sophistication of today's tire buyers, and methods for promoting the dealers' businesses. In line with this, Cooper Tire offers a wide range of display materials; designers who can give a dealership a whole new look; tire rack displays of all kinds; point-of-purchase materials and a host of advertising materials and concepts suitable for every medium. Cooper sales reps are backed up with the full force of the entire company.

Cooper Tire looks for college graduates who are interested in cars and who have demonstrated skills in selling. Prior sales experience is required, but no special technical training is necessary. Two internships per year are offered, in which recent college graduates are brought to the Findlay headquarters and trained for six months in the home office and in the plant, and then hired as reps.

Training for regular rep candidates also takes place at headquarters in Findlay. It lasts about three weeks and comprises two weeks of classroom training and one week of office orientation with plant tours and on-the-job training. The emphasis is on product and industry knowledge, as reps must know about tire sizes and features, different uses of tires, tread life, and the like. Most dealers already know about tires and what will sell, so Cooper reps do not spend their time demonstrating or installing tires, although they may have to acquaint dealers with new products. Cooper reps must learn the businesses and problems of the dealerships in their territory and find ways to introduce Cooper Tire products and its marketing expertise to help solve those problems.

Salaries for sales trainees are in the $23,000 range with senior salespeople earning $50,000 and up. Commissions are added to salary, and, as there is no ceiling on commissions, successful reps can earn a very substantial income. Other benefits include: medical, dental, and life insurance; disability and retirement plans; profit sharing and stock purchase plans; tuition assistance (100% of tuition and books); paid relocation expenses; and a company car.

The atmosphere at Cooper Tire is friendly and informal, and long-term employees abound. Although reps work mostly on their own, there is a real sense of across-the-board support and teamwork. Future prospects for Cooper Tire seem very bright. The demand for replacement tires should increase because people are driving more, more cars are on the road, people are keeping their cars longer, and new, high-performance cars are making more demands on tires. In such a market, productive reps can do very well for themselves.

THE GOODYEAR TIRE & RUBBER COMPANY

VITAL STATISTICS

Entry Level Salary for Sales: **$20,000–$25,000**
Senior Level Salary for Sales: **$35,000–$40,000**

Benefits

medical/dental: **Yes**	child care: **No**
life insurance: **Yes**	retirement plan: **401K**
disability: **Yes**	savings investment plan: **N/A**
travel allowance: **No**	tuition assistance: **Yes**
company car: **Yes**	relocation assistance: **Yes**
profit sharing plan: **No**	memberships: **No**
stock purchase plan: **Yes**	

Corporate Culture Index   (1 = lowest, 10 = highest)

training:	**8**	security:	**9**
support:	**8**	mobility:	**9**
benefits:	**8**	intangibles:	**8**

Address: 1144 East Market Street, Akron, OH 44316-0001
Contact: Personnel; telephone 216/796-7900

The Goodyear Tire and Rubber Company ranks 35th on the Fortune 500 list. In 1987 it realized $10 billion in sales, up 9.6% from 1986.

The Goodyear Tire & Rubber Company's principal business is the development, manufacture, distribution, and sale of tires throughout the world. Goodyear, the world's largest producer of tires, also manufactures and sells a wide range of products for the transportation industry and for various industrial and consumer markets. These include rubber, chemical, and plastic products, which the company produces in 44 plants in the United States and 44 plants in 26 foreign countries.

In addition, the company offers a variety of other products and services. Goodyear's Celeron subsidiaries are engaged in various crude oil transportation and trading activities. For example, in 1987 Celeron tested a 1225-mile mainline segment of its All American Pipe System, which will

320

be a 1750-mile heated crude oil pipeline extending from the Gulf Coast of Texas to the California coast.

Since Goodyear realized that its products were too limited in scope, that it was heavily dependent on the automotive industry, and that its markets were becoming increasingly global in nature, it has initiated a dual strategy of improving production and diversifying operations. It has upgraded its manufacturing system and invested heavily in research and development in order to create high-quality products at low cost, critical to competing successfully in the global marketplace.

The company's diversification was designed to lessen its dependence on the automotive industry. Cyclical swings in that industry can hurt sales very quickly, and Goodyear sought to protect itself from any possible sudden negative impacts. To this end, it invested in oil and gas and, ultimately, in pioneering construction of the first major east-to-west crude oil pipeline in the U.S. The dual strategy paid off in 1987 when both of the company's major business units—Tires and Related Transportation Products and Industrial Rubber, Chemical, and Plastic Products—showed record gains in sales and income.

The main job of Goodyear's reps is to staff its retail stores, which sell Goodyear tires and other products directly to consumers. Training for new hires takes place at the company Training Center in Akron, Ohio. The formal program lasts for three weeks, and is followed by on-the-job training in a retail store. The original training concentrates on developing selling skills, product knowledge, and terminology; it also covers store operation and management. To some extent, the training uses computer-assisted instruction materials. Classes are small, with a 10:1 trainee/trainer ratio most common. Because of the nature of retail store selling, initial training heavily stresses interpersonal skills and one-to-one customer relations.

Follow-up training consists of one-day-per-month seminars where new products are introduced and explained to sales reps, and store management and improved retail marketing strategies are discussed. The training program itself begins with a pre-test and ends with a post-test for purposes of evaluating how well the new hire has absorbed the material and for pinpointing areas that need strengthening during on-the-job training.

Goodyear looks for prospective salespeople who show intelligence, present a neat and professional bearing, and have a driver's license. Prior selling experience is usually required, and references on previous employment are checked. A college degree is preferred, but not necessary. No special technical training or knowledge is required; Goodyear will teach what is needed on the job. In addition, every summer Goodyear fills ten slots in its retail stores with college juniors in an intern program. This is a get-acquainted situation, where the interns and the company learn something about each other. Goodyear makes every effort to hire those promising interns when they graduate the following year.

Goodyear reps work in a store environment, but they are mostly on their own. They must be able to answer customers' questions about products, offer solutions to problems when asked, and demonstrate or install Goodyear products such as tires and batteries. There is a great deal of new product information to absorb—Goodyear R&D is always on the job—and there is also continuous training in how to improve retail store management and profitability as the rep moves up from selling items on the floor. The company believes strongly in promoting from within; it normally hires reps only at the entry level and then draws its management personnel from its own ranks. A rep's career path can run from salesperson to store manager to a more responsible position in a larger store (Goodyear has 900 stores to staff). Good marketing savvy and customer rapport are rewarded.

Salaries for sales trainees range from $20,000 to $25,000, depending on experience and education. Senior salespeople average $35,000 to $40,000. A commission of 20% is also paid on gross orders. There can also be a store bonus if the rep's individual store does well. Other benefits include: a full medical and dental plan, group life insurance, a disability plan, a 401K savings/retirement plan, a stock purchase plan, and tuition assistance.

Selling in a Goodyear retail store is a basic, no-frills type of job, but the company has an excellent record of finding and keeping top people. For instance, the current CEO, Robert Mercer, began by selling industrial hose for the company. For those who love cars and automotive equipment and like to work with people, it's a hard job to beat.

TEXTILES

The merger mania that has swept American businesses in the past few years has made itself felt very keenly in the textile industry. Of the top fifteen publicly owned U.S. textile companies that began the 1980s, only three—Springs Industries, West Point Pepperell, and Fieldcrest Cannon —remain. J. P. Stevens, 175 years old, was the most recent to bite the dust, as its new owners began to sell off its assets in May 1988.

Merger mania is a response to a critical development in the textile industry: In recent years, American markets have been flooded with imports. Companies have found that the best way to increase their share of the market and beat the competition is by uniting similar products under one management roof.

So far, these strategies have paid off. Textile sales increased by 4% in 1987; employment and prices were up, as imports went down. Industrial textile output rose by a huge 9% as factories worked to 95% of their capacity. All this added up to $57 billion in sales and one of the highest profit margins in American industry.

One development that will affect the industry for years to come is the introduction of sophisticated computer technologies into factories. These technologies cut down on labor costs, enhance quality, and generally make production much more flexible. Technology also has had a direct impact on sales. New "quick-response" databases and information systems link the entire production system to the wide network of salespeople and retailers in the field in an up-to-the-minute exchange of information, strategies, and ideas.

There are many facets to the textile industry and all of them are doing well. Sales of spun yarn grew by 12% in 1987, to more than $6 billion. Weaving and knitting yarns are doing extremely well as demand for sweaters grows. Sales of broadwoven and knit fabrics like denim, corduroy, and poplin have surged by 11%, to $5 billion, and synthetic fibers, like nylon and acrylic, by 6%. Carpet and rug sales have grown by 9% to a record $9 billion. Domestic production has also been helped by consumers' demand for natural fibers, especially cotton and cotton blends. Last year, as cotton prices climbed, America's cotton production rose by 10%.

With new international agreements that regulate competition firmly in place, the textile industry should gradually narrow its trade deficit (mainly in silk and wool) and continue to grow.

TRADE ASSOCIATIONS

American Association of Textile Chemists and Colorists 919/549-8141
American Textile Manufacturers Institute 202/862-0500
Industrial Fabrics Association International 612/222-2508
Textile Salesmen's Association 212/481-7792

PERIODICALS

Daily News Record
Textile Hi-Lites
Textile Organon
Textile World

BURLINGTON INDUSTRIES, INC.

VITAL STATISTICS

Entry Level Salary for Sales: **$24,000+**
Senior Level Salary for Sales: **$60,000+**

Benefits

medical/dental: **Yes**	child care: **No**
life insurance: **Yes**	retirement plan: **Yes**
disability: **Yes**	savings investment plan: **Yes**
travel allowance: **N/A**	tuition assistance: **Yes, 90%**
company car: **No**	relocation assistance: **N/A**
profit sharing plan: **Yes**	memberships: **Smokenders**
stock purchase plan: **No**	**Weight Watchers**
	Wellness program
	On-site fitness
	center
	Aerobics

Corporate Culture Index (1 = lowest, 10 = highest)

training:	**9**	security:	**9**
support:	**10**	mobility:	**9**
benefits:	**8**	intangibles:	**8**

Address: 1345 Avenue of the Americas, New York, NY 10105
Contact: Personnel; telephone 212/621-4191

Burlington Industries, Inc., ranks 130th on the Fortune 500 list. In 1987 it posted sales of more than $3 billion, up 18% from 1986. A leveraged buyout in September 1987 took the company private, so earnings figures for that and subsequent years are not available.

Burlington Industries came under siege in 1986 and 1987 as a prime takeover target. New York corporate raider Asher B. Edelman and the Canadian-based Dominion Textile, Inc., made a combined run on the company. Burlington seemed susceptible, despite the fact that it was the largest textile manufacturer in the U.S. Its main problem was that over the years, people had noticed that it had failed to respond to changing conditions in the textile industry. The company had doggedly upgraded its plants and machinery, but it stayed in the low-margin commodity fabric line, the market most severely affected by foreign imports. Its sales remained high, but its earnings trailed the rest of the industry. In 1986 Burlington's profits were just $56.5 million on total sales of $2.8 billion. As a result, takeover rumblings abounded.

Burlington settled the takeover question in 1987. Even as it was racking up record sales, management sold off nine divisions to raise the capital necessary to take the company private. The huge sell-off meant significantly lower sales in 1988, but stability doesn't come cheap, and the company gained the chance to restructure in relative peace. Burlington now has 15 divisions engaged in manufacturing fabrics for home furnishings, men's wear, textile woven fabrics, and yarns.

One segment of the company's operations that bodes well for the future is the sales staff. Rated at the top of their category in the June 1988 issue of *Sales and Marketing Management*, Burlington's sales force is a power in the industry. Part of its success is due to strong management support that gives the reps in the field an edge over their competitors. For instance, the home furnishings group, which was an ace performer in 1987, instituted a "Quick-Turn" program designed to lower delivery time for orders to only seven days, a move that drew high marks from customers. It also beefed up the customer complaint service, which pleased clients and helped increase sales.

Training is another reason for the success of Burlington's sales force. Because the company still comprises 15 divisions, training is necessarily decentralized, but the commitment to it is companywide. This mindset is likely to be strengthened if the company follows the lead of the home furnishings group. (Home furnishings includes products such as draperies, mattress ticking, and carpets.) There, sales training is ongoing, a continuous process of honing basic skills and reviewing the company's products and performance. Training in the company's menswear division is likewise ongoing, but there the tiny, 12-person sales force receives one-on-one tutorial-type training, learning on the job by observing senior salespeople for approximately three to six months.

Burlington reps, regardless of division, must spend a great deal of time learning about fabrics. Burlington's fabric is an "ingredient product," one used by other manufacturers (Hartmarx, J. C. Penney, Sears, Palm Beach, and a whole host of other private labels) in the creation of their garments. Burlington reps need to know the qualities of each type of fabric the company makes (polyesters, knits, denims, satins, wovens and unwovens, and all the rest) in order to help customers get the right materials for their needs. More than that, the reps must have a good sense of style and of fashion trends. In many cases, buyers for the major customers will place orders a year or more before their products hit the market. Reps must be able to anticipate what textures, colors, and styles will be in vogue when the items go on sale.

As Burlington moves into such specialized areas as customized fabrics for industrial use (in the automotive industry, for instance), it will need reps with even more expertise in fabric manufacturing and in the style trends of the industries they serve. Textile selling thus involves considerable teamwork, even if reps generally work alone. The rep often operates as a point person, coordinating all the company's departments (design, styling, manufacturing, customer service, delivery, and so on). Although previous sales experience and a college degree with some marketing courses may be helpful, the job calls for an entrepreneurial spirit. The individual who can identify and take advantage of opportunities, show innovation, and exercise judgment and independence possesses the basic qualities looked for in a new rep.

Salaries for Burlington reps vary from division to division. In the menswear division, trainees average about $24,000, while senior salespeople average $60,000 plus. The company awards "incentives," which act as bonuses or commissions in that they are designed to reward individual performance. In the home furnishings group, cash incentives are considered the backbone of sales force motivation. Burlington had instituted a cap on commission payments so that it would not have to pay heavy bonus dollars on a lucky sale or on an item that got hot and took off. However, the present management of the group has removed the cap, believing that the motivating power of letting reps keep everything they could make was more valuable to the company. Additional support includes improved customer relations and delivery services, excellent ad and promotion materials, administrative/clerical help, and the creation of new styles together with new and improved fabrics.

Other benefits include: medical, dental, and life insurance; an optional disability plan; a retirement/pension plan; a profit sharing plan; a savings plan; tuition assistance (90% up to $2000 maximum); and a credit union.

Although still in a state of flux from going private in 1987, Burlington believes it is on the way to maintaining and improving its position as the country's major textile manufacturer and marketer. With its fine sales staff and diverse product lines, it seems likely to do so.

FIELDCREST CANNON, INC.

VITAL STATISTICS

Entry Level Salary for Sales: **$22,000–$28,000**
Senior Level Salary for Sales: **$60,000–$70,000**

Benefits

medical/dental: **Yes**	child care: **No**
life insurance: **Yes**	retirement plan: **Yes**
disability: **Yes**	savings investment plan: **Yes**
travel allowance: **N/A**	tuition assistance: **Yes**
company car: **N/A**	relocation assistance: **N/A**
profit sharing plan: **Yes**	memberships: **No**
stock purchase plan: **No**	

Corporate Culture Index   (1 = lowest, 10 = highest)

training:	**8**	security:	**9**
support:	**9**	mobility:	**9**
benefits:	**8**	intangibles:	**9**

Address: 326 East Stadium Drive, Eden, NC 27288
Contact: Human Resources; telephone 919/627-3359

Fieldcrest Cannon, Inc., ranks 247th on the Fortune 500 list. In 1987 it posted sales of $1.4 billion, up 29% from 1986. Net earnings, however, were off because of increased manufacturing costs and costs incurred by restructuring.

Fieldcrest Cannon, Inc., is a leading manufacturer and marketer of a broad range of home furnishing textile products. The company also does commission finishing and manufacturing of yarn for other textile companies. Fieldcrest's two operating divisions are the Bed and Bath Division and the Carpet and Rug Division.

The Bed and Bath Division acquired the Cannon Mills Company in 1986, and throughout 1987 it was busy integrating the newly combined Fieldcrest Cannon facilities. This division manufactures and markets quality bed and bath products including: blankets, bedspreads, comforters, sheets, towels, bath rugs, and kitchen products. The company markets these products under several well-known brand names (Fieldcrest, St. Mary's, Cannon, Royal Family, Monticello) and also under private brand labels.

The Carpet and Rug Division, with the merger of Karastan and Bigelow, combines two of the market's strongest names into a major force in the industry. The division now has the largest capacity in the industry to produce woven goods. One problem area that increased manufacturing costs in 1987 was the production of stain-resistant carpet fibers. It seems that the chemistries for dyeing and stain-blocking the carpets were incompatible; the two processes had to be done separately, resulting in unacceptably high costs. A new plant is now available that can produce many more feet of stain-resistant carpet at a much lower cost, and the division anticipates good future sales growth in its operations.

Fieldcrest is a major force in an industry that has a number of built-in destabilizing factors. For instance, a sharp upsurge in the price of cotton in the first half of 1987 had a strong negative effect on the Bed and Bath Division's earnings. Expensive technology can be a problem, especially when it must be aligned with a world of changing styles and tastes, which is the case in the home furnishings market, the core of Fieldcrest's business. Moreover, the market for high-quality home furnishings is itself cycle prone. A downturn in the economy, an increase in interest rates, a plunge in the stock market—all can have a significant negative impact on Fieldcrest's sales and earnings.

However, the picture has an up side, too. The company manufactures high-quality products that command strong customer recognition and loyalty. In times of economic growth or even relative stability, Fieldcrest expects to perform well. With the bulk of its restructuring behind it, the company feels it now has in place the talent, the management, the manufacturing and design expertise, and the marketing and sales force to keep Fieldcrest at the forefront of the home furnishings industry.

To keep its competitive edge in a difficult marketplace, the company maintains an ongoing commitment to training and development programs for its employees at all levels. It takes particular care in the selection of its new sales reps, sending a recruiter to many colleges to interview numerous candidates.

Fieldcrest looks for college graduates with marketing or management majors who can demonstrate poise, achievement, and flexibility. The company prizes the work ethic and independence very highly. The recruiter also listens to suggestions from professors on whom to interview, so referrals can be valuable, too.

A rep's initial training is almost tutorial. It lasts for about ten weeks and takes place in the New York offices. It is made up mostly of class work, and the content is the usual mix of company procedures, product knowledge, and selling techniques. Because Fieldcrest's success depends on meeting the desires of fashion-conscious end users, its reps need to be sensitive to style and alert to developing trends Good taste, along with product savvy and marketing expertise, is what their customers, the buyers for the large retailers and department stores in their territories, demand. A flair for design and style will always stand a Fieldcrest rep in good stead.

Reps' territories vary in size; they are mostly concentrated where the major department and chain stores are, in key metropolitan areas (lightly populated areas are covered by a telemarketing program). Depending on the assigned accounts, reps may face little or much travel, but in no case do they spend more than 50% of their time on overnights. For the most part, the reps work alone, although they maintain close links with marketing people in the company. A lot of communication goes on back and forth between sales and marketing as they work to keep their fingers on the market's pulse.

Salaries for trainees average about $22,000 to $28,000; senior salespeople earn about $60,000 to $70,000. These figures include bonuses and incentives, which vary with the division and product line. Advancement opportunities are good; a career path runs from sales to marketing to management. Other benefits include: medical, dental, and life insurance; disability and retirement plans; a profit sharing plan; a 401K plan; and tuition assistance. Reps also get excellent support in the form of quality advertising and promotion materials and in the development of new and improved products.

The pace at Fieldcrest is hectic. The company is market driven, and the market in many instances is erratic. This means that the company reps must be fast on their feet, keeping tabs on the industry, serving their customers, and tracking consumer fashion trends in the home furnishings area—altogether a stimulating and rewarding job.

SPRINGS INDUSTRIES

VITAL STATISTICS

Entry Level Salary for Sales: **$30,000**
Senior Level Salary for Sales: **$100,000**

Benefits

medical/dental: **Yes**	child care: **No**
life insurance: **Yes**	retirement plan: **Yes**
disability: **Yes**	savings investment plan: **Yes**
travel allowance: **N/A**	tuition assistance: **Yes, 80 %**
company car: **Yes**	relocation assistance: **Yes**
profit sharing plan: **Yes**	memberships: **On-site blood**
stock purchase plan: **Yes**	**pressure and**
	cholesterol check

Corporate Culture Index   (1 = lowest, 10 = highest)

training:	*5*	security:	*9*
support:	*9*	mobility:	*5*
benefits:	*9*	intangibles:	*9*

Address: P.O. Box 70, Fort Mill, SC 29715
Contact: Consumer Division; telephone 803/547-3650

Springs Industries, the fourth largest textiles company in America, ranks 189th on the Fortune 500 list. In 1987 the company racked up $1.7 billion in sales, a 10% rise from 1986. 1987 profits were $56 million: a stunning 71% jump.

   If you haven't heard of Springs Industries, you may have heard of its brand names: Wamsutta, Springmaid, Ultrasuede, Custom Designs, and Pacific Silvercloth, to name just a few. From its earliest beginnings in Fort Mill, South Carolina, in 1887, the company has stuck to its fine-fabrics trade, producing finishing fabrics, home furnishings, and industrial fabrics.

   In Springs' Home Furnishings Division, Wamsutta sheets are the luxury leader, while the Consumer Fashion Division markets lower-priced Springmaid sheets and bed and bath fashions primarily to department stores and national chains. Springmaid has also now entered the luxury field with high-thread-count comforters, rugs, blankets, and pillows marketed under the Bill Blass name. In addition, the division sells Graber window treatments and a line of stuffed dinosaur animals called Video Vegetable Dolls.

The company's Finished Fabrics Division sells fabrics such as Nuage (polyester/cotton with a napped finish) and Ultrasuede as well as many fabrics with unusual finishes: flocked, napped, puffed, puckered.

The Diversified Products Division makes upholstery, luggage, and wall fabrics; the Clark-Schwebel Fiber Glass Corporation produces a wide range of industrial products, from printed electronic circuit boards to ballistic vests and helmets made out of bullet-proof Kevlar fabric.

Reps work for any of four regional divisions: East, West, South, and Sunbelt—reporting to regional managers, spending virtually all their time on the road, working alone. In the Consumer Fashion Division, reps call on department and variety stores to present a full line of Springmaid products. Reps install displays and demonstrate products, often in showroom settings.

College degrees are required for new reps, preferably with majors in business. Training takes place in New York or Dallas, with an employee/trainer ratio of a low 1:1. It's an informal apprenticeship with no formal classes; reps just learn the ropes from a veteran rep until, at some point after two to six months, management decides that "the rep is ready." Presumably, only an old sheet-and-pillow promoter knows for sure.

Then a new recruit is sent out to a territory, when one becomes available. Promotion involves graduating from smaller junior accounts to larger senior accounts. Further opportunities for promotion are few, whether to marketing or management posts. On the other hand, sales salaries are quite generous: $30,000 for a trainee, $100,000 for a senior executive, including bonus; there are no commissions.

This is a company proud to be "heavy" on both advertising and sales fronts, including full administrative aid, such as typing, filing, and computer support. The 5% turnover rate is exceptionally low, a reflection of the company's strong commitment to sales support at all levels. Benefits include: medical and dental insurance; tuition assistance (5 years; 80%); a company car; disability and retirement/pension plans; and profit sharing, stock purchase, and child care plans. Blood pressure and cholesterol checks are taken at the plant.

Springs Industries is a fine, old-line company committed to helping Americans achieve the best sleep money can buy. They also make fabrics we all can wear and wear out. If you thought sheets and towels were boring, take a look at wonderful products like Pillow People or Puppet Sheet Theatre (both Springs Industries products for the juvenile trade), and you'll probably change your mind quickly.

WEST POINT PEPPERELL

VITAL STATISTICS

Entry Level Salary for Sales: **$24,000–$27,000**
Senior Level Salary for Sales: **$40,000±**

Benefits

medical/dental: **Yes**	child care: **No**
life insurance: **Yes**	retirement plan: **Yes**
disability: **Yes, short and long term**	savings investment plan: **Yes**
travel allowance: **N/A**	tuition assistance: **Yes**
company car: **Yes**	relocation assistance: **N/A**
profit sharing plan: **No**	memberships: **On-site fitness**
stock purchase plan: **No**	**center**

Corporate Culture Index   (1 = lowest, 10 = highest)

training:	**9**	security:	**9**
support:	**9**	mobility:	**9**
benefits:	**8**	intangibles:	**9**

Address: 1221 Avenue of the Americas, New York, NY 10020
Contact: Corporate Recruiting; telephone 212/382-5194

West Point Pepperell, the third largest textiles firm in the country, ranked 189th on the 1987 Fortune 500 list of industrial corporations, with sales of more than $2 billion, up 14% from 1986. Profits for 1987 were $71.6 million, up 31.4%.

Newly merged with former rival J. P. Stevens, West Point Pepperell is now the number-one manufacturer of sheets in the nation, the third largest maker of towels, and one of the oldest textiles conglomerates in the U.S. Founded in 1844 by Lord and Lady Pepperell of Pepperell Mansion in Kittery Point, Maine, for more than 140 years the company has churned out miles of high-quality cloth, including acres of tents for the Union Army in the Civil War and parachute fabric during World War II.

Today, West Point Pepperell is best known for its brand names: Martex, Luxor, Lady Pepperell, Esprit bedding, Givenchy no-iron sheets, and Vellux synthetic blankets. A major supplier of industrial fabrics, Pepperell's core business still remains textiles for the consumer market. With 15 former J. P. Stevens mills now added to its portfolio, West Point Pepperell is far from throwing in the towel. In fact, it is well positioned to wipe up the market.

West Point Pepperell actively recruits on college campuses for BA degree holders with majors in business or marketing who have a clear, focused desire to sell. No prior sales experience or technical knowledge is necessary. The one-shot training program consists of three weeks of classes, and from two to six months of on-the-job training, rotating through merchandising, marketing, design, specialized product knowledge, and professional sales skills. The training is held in New York.

After training, the new rep is assigned to a junior territory (selling to Mom and Pop stores or small accounts). Territories tend to vary widely, from a small part of New York to all of Minnesota or Wisconsin. Department store density defines territorial size. A senior territory might be comprised of merchandise majors such as Macy's or Bullock's, which buy only premium brands (Martex, Luxor). Lower-priced brands (Lady Pepperell) are consigned to discounters and budget chains.

Reps can spend about two or three nights a week on the road, in rural territory, or none if the rep lives in his or her field. Reps travel solo, on expense account, and contact top management through their regional sales managers. At 10%–15%, turnover seems high for a company that earns such high marks for training, support, benefits, job security, and mobility, but it takes a certain kind of person to be happy selling sheets and towels.

For trainees, average income falls somewhere between $24,000 and $27,000, with senior sales executives pulling down $40,000, plus generous bonuses (up to 50% of sales). Benefits include: medical and dental insurance, tuition assistance (job-related only), a company car (no car allowance), and a retirement/pension and savings plans. There is no profit sharing, stock purchase, 401K, or child care plan.

Reps don't demonstrate products or teach customers what to do with them (there's not much to say when it comes to towels and sheets). The sales force of about 80 reps sells almost exclusively to department stores and large chains, with smaller accounts scattered in. The atmosphere is relaxed and corporate at the same time, providing a rep with real independence. As West Point Pepperell folds J. P. Stevens into its product niche, this company seems like a nice, cozy nest from which to sell.